MILTON STUDIES

IV

Edited by

James D. Simmonds

UNIVERSITY OF PITTSBURGH PRESS

MILTON STUDIES

is published annually by the University of Pittsburgh Press as a forum for Milton scholarship and criticism. Articles submitted for publication may be biographical; they may interpret some aspect of Milton's writings; or they may define literary, intellectual, or historical contexts—by studying the work of his contemporaries, the traditions which affected his thought and art, contemporary political and religious movements, his influence on other writers, or the history of critical response to his work.

Manuscripts should be upwards of 3,000 words in length and should conform to the *MLA Style Sheet.* They will be returned only if sufficient postage is enclosed (overseas contributors enclose international reply coupons). Manuscripts and editorial correspondence should be addressed to James D. Simmonds, Department of English, University of Pittsburgh, Pittsburgh, Pa. 15213.

Milton Studies does not review books.

Within the United States, *Milton Studies* may be ordered from the University of Pittsburgh Press, Pittsburgh, Pa. 15213.

Overseas orders should be addressed to Henry M. Snyder & Co., Inc., 440 Park Avenue South, New York, New York, 10016, U.S.A.

Library of Congress Catalog Card Number 69–12335

ISBN 0–8229–3174–5 (Volume I) (out of print)

ISBN 0–8229–3194–x (Volume II)

ISBN 0–8229–3218–0 (Volume III)

ISBN 0–8229–3244–x (Volume IV)

Henry M. Snyder & Co., Inc., London

Manufactured in the United States of America

CONTENTS

MARCIA LANDY — Kinship and the Role of Women in *Paradise Lost* — 3

ANTHONY LOW — Milton's God: Authority in *Paradise Lost* — 19

JACKIE DI SALVO — "The Lord's Battells": *Samson Agonistes* and the Puritan Revolution — 39

STELLA P. REVARD — Milton's Gunpowder Poems and Satan's Conspiracy — 63

MICHAEL LIEB — Milton and the Organicist Polemic — 79

JOSEPH ANTHONY WITTREICH, JR. — Milton's *Areopagitica*: Its Isocratic and Ironic Contexts — 101

EDWIN B. BENJAMIN — Milton and Tacitus — 117

MARILYN L. WILLIAMSON — A Reading of Milton's Twenty-Third Sonnet — 141

WILLIAM C. RIGGS — The Plant of Fame in *Lycidas* — 151

LAWRENCE W. KINGSLEY — Mythic Dialectic in the Nativity Ode — 163

JAMES R. MC ADAMS — The Pattern of Temptation in *Paradise Regained* — 177

SAMUEL S. STOLLMAN — Milton's Rabbinical Readings and Fletcher — 195

MILTON STUDIES

IV

KINSHIP AND THE ROLE
OF WOMEN IN *PARADISE LOST*

Marcia Landy

In *Paradise Lost*, Milton places marriage at the center of social institutions. It is from the point of view of marriage that all social
roles and attitudes are defined and judged valuable or destructive.
Sibling relationships and parental roles function to establish and
maintain male authority. Male-female relations in the human
sphere reflect the pattern of dominance and submission characteristic of the divine sphere, where it is seen particularly in the relationship of the Father to the Son. Adam's prelapsarian role is
analogous to that of God. He is defined as creator, author, disposer,
while Eve is confined to being a source of inspiration, and to the
roles of mother and wife, summed up in her title "Mother of
mankind." After the Fall, Eve must learn through pain, humiliation, and abasement that she should not have striven for equality
with Adam, that her duty is to be submissive to him as wife and
mother. In general, worldly activity belongs to the man: he is
artist, ruler, intellect. The woman's role is to be procreative,
skilled in domesticity, and obedient to her husband, upon whom
she depends for education and guidance. Her freedom is fully
expressed in her fulfillment of her family role as wife and mother.

O NE OF the major projects for women in this era is a revaluation of
their roles as critics and scholars.* While it is certainly true that
in Milton criticism excellent women have been writing—a few names
that come to mind are Rosemond Tuve, Marjorie Hope Nicolson,
Isabel MacCaffrey, Anne Davidson Ferry, Irene Samuel, Barbara K.
Lewalski—it is also true that the criticism has come largely from men
and that their views have basically determined the critical climate.[1]

* I am grateful to my colleagues Rae Lee Siporin and James D. Simmonds for
help in revising this study.

Until recently no one has been concerned with the question of critical perspective according to sex roles. It has been taken for granted that one does not differentiate male and female approaches to Milton's work. Rather, we have talked of the scholarly or critical attitude. Yet which of us is not aware that a reading of a poem is very much determined by the identity of the critic? Publically we maintain, nonetheless, that one can attain the necessary "objectivity," be "true" to the text, and continue to strive for a universally communicable reading; this has meant the ostensible submerging of the critic's identity and subjectivity and the presentation of a "fair" reading. The more verifiable the observations in terms of objectively developed evidence and measurements, the more acceptable the critical position. However, the critic is not a neutral voice, as many students have been trained to believe; a reading is that critic's reading and grows out of that individual consciousness. The critic's selection of a work, the selection of portions of that work to discuss, and the nature of the vocabulary used to discuss it are very much a part of the critic's own voice. The degree to which the critic's consciousness touches that of other readers and is validated by them determines the success or failure of, for example, a Tuve, a Nicolson, a Frye, or a Stein.

We have expected critical attitudes to be governed by particular categories of experience—sociological, political, psychological, and philosophical. Given these categories, critics continue to believe that the scholarly position is a neutral one with respect to male and female perspectives. However, with the recent focus on women's attitudes and on critical positions which account more fully for the experience of women, this neutrality also is questionable. Men set the standards, determine the approaches, create the styles, and are the predominant users of the printed word. This influences what they choose to write about and how they write about it.

This paper will regard *Paradise Lost* from a current feminist position and explore the complex network of familial relationships expressed in the poem. At the same time it will examine the attitudes associated with these familial relationships in order to see from this vantage point how Milton portrays feminine figures and their relationships to masculine figures. Many writers have attempted to establish Milton's misogyny on the basis of his portrayal of Eve and Dalila, the divorce tracts, and available biographical evidence. His use of myth and presentation of male and female roles indicate that rather than being a misogynist, Milton was a representative seventeenth-century Protestant poet who was committed to the centrality of marriage, to the designated roles of man as creator and provider and of woman as procreator, submissive to her husband's natural authority. An examination of the male and female attitudes corroborates the representative nature of Milton's treatment of male and female roles, and a close scrutiny of his presentation of the familial relationships in *Paradise Lost* should refine our observations of Milton's treatment of women.

My basic interest is in seeing what further light can be shed on the portrayal of women in art through examining how a great artist— whose mythopoeic powers have been acknowledged as incomparable— perceived and portrayed their role. Milton works with a most basic myth, that of the Fall; he confirms, elaborates, and alters the myth according to his own predispositions and those of his age. It will be very profitable to examine his language critically yet again, because, in his portrayal of Eve, Milton has captured central aspects of a myth which is being seriously questioned today.

The ingredients of the myth of the Fall are constant—God, Adam and Eve, the serpent, the forbidden tree, the garden, the woman eating the fruit first, then the fall of man; but character, situation, and motive vary, and the variations are as significant as the basic common elements. Milton's presentation of the myth, therefore, is not to be taken as a validation of the unchanging myth of feminine evil, but rather as a major writer's recreation of the myth from his own consciousness and from the consciousness of his time. Furthermore, an examination of the myth should lead to the understanding that myths are multilevelled and multifunctional; they cannot be reduced to a fixed meaning or even, perhaps, to a moral meaning. The myth of the Fall encompasses far more than the mere portrayal of the supremacy of God and man over woman. We are told that in myth "each matrix of meanings refers to another matrix, each myth to other myths. And if it is now asked to what final meaning these mutually significative meanings are referring —since in the last result and in their totality they must refer to something—the only reply . . . is that myths signify the mind that evolves them by making use of the world of which it is itself a part."[2] One element in Milton's use of myth, his presentation of male and female, should in no way be construed to represent the totality of his artistic vision. Milton's use of mythology, as so many critics have noted, is complex, resonant, and inexhaustible.[3] The purpose of this entry into the myth from the perspective of kinship is to illuminate another dimension of Milton's portrayal of human roles.

The understanding of Eve's role is dependent on understanding not only the various familial terminology applied to her but also the terminology applied to Sin, Death, Satan, God, the Son, and Adam. Lévi-Strauss tells us that "what is generally called a 'kinship system' comprises two quite different orders of reality. First, there are terms through which various kinds of family relationships are expressed. But kinship is not expressed solely through nomenclature. The individual or classes of individuals who employ terms feel (or do not feel, as the case may be) bound by prescribed behavior in their relations with one another, such as respect or familiarity, rights or obligations, and affection or hostility. Thus, along with what we propose to call the *system of terminology* (which, strictly speaking, constitutes the vocabulary system), there is another system, both psychological and social in nature, which we call the *system of attitudes*."[4] Thus, rather than looking merely for the names *father, mother, son,* etc., we will also look to see behavior which is correlative with the term.

In his book *Social Structure,* G. P. Murdock explains kinship terminology and attitudes in the following manner: "Terms of address form an integral part of the culturally patterned relationships between kinsmen . . . since any status is defined in terms of the culturally expected behavior in the relationship in which it is embedded, there are *a priori* reasons for assuming a close functional congruity between terms of reference and the relationships in which the denoted kinsmen interact."[5] Further, Murdock quotes Radcliffe-Brown: "We can expect to find, in the majority of human societies, a fairly close correlation between the terminological classification of kindred or relatives and the social classification. The former is revealed in kinship terminology, the latter . . . specifically in the attitudes and behavior of relatives to one another."[6]

There are many implications of the family relationship to be explored in *Paradise Lost.* In one sense, Adam and Eve—prior to being husband and wife—are brother and sister, siblings in their common descent. Their parentage is from nature and nature is God's handiwork, so like the rest of Creation they claim direct descent from God. If we accept the fact that as the first human creations, the children of God, Adam and Eve are brother and sister, then we can see that before he explores the marriage bond Milton works with their common humanity —an idea of brotherhood which later in eighteenth-century revolutionary rhetoric was to play a significant role, especially in the concept of *fraternité*.[7]

In noting the sibling role of Adam and Eve, we must also recognize the relationship of sibling to parent, since from this relationship grow the basic notions of masculinity and femininity which are to pervade *Paradise Lost*. For them God is the father, certainly the father of Adam, and nature is the mother. The identification of Adam with God the Father is a masculine one, whereas Eve is identified with the feminine Mother Nature: Eve is "the fairest of her Daughters" (IV, 324).[8] Those names and attitudes attributed to God the Father are "guide," "head," "instructor," "author," and "disposer." Significantly, the male is the creator, the actor, the active principle, the authority. Mother Nature is distinguished as creation, and is mainly acted upon. Her sole active attribute is procreation, her domain of creativity. The male principle is associated with "absolute rule," the feminine with "submission." The male is "instructor," the female is "pupil." The male "disposes" and "authors"; the female is identified with the "creation" and the "work." Milton identifies the epic poet with "Blind *Thamyris* and blind *Maeonides*, / And *Tiresias* and *Phineus* Prophets old" (III, 35–36). Thus for Milton the poet is male, "creator" and "author." Furthermore, past poets are exclusively masculine, as the quotation indicates, reinforcing the masculine creative principle. Significantly, Adam alone names the animals; thus Milton establishes again the masculine priority over language. However, "Inspiration" is female, as in Milton's reference to Urania, "my Celestial Patroness, who deigns / Her nightly visitation unimplor'd, / And dictates to me slumb'ring, or inspires / Easy my unpremeditated Verse" (IX, 21–24).

The sibling relatonship of Adam and Eve is only one of the sibling relationships developed in the work. Milton devotes more attention to the relationship of the Son to Satan, of both to the Father, and to the relationship of Satan and the other erring sons to God. (Significantly, Protestant and Puritan rhetoric united "wayfaring souls" through sibling terms.) In Books XI and XII, the reader is treated to the account of Adam's own sons—Cain and Abel—and their relationship to each other

and to Adam, the father of mankind. More could be said about the
brother-brother relationship, but we are focusing on the father-son-
brother relationship since it affects our understanding of the Adam-Eve
set of relationships. In this triad we have God the Father, Satan, and
the Son. Milton explores obedience-disobedience and dominance-
submission through his treatment of the Son and Satan as brothers in
relation to the authority of God the Father.

Satan refuses the role of obedient son, rejecting the father; that is,
he rejects what he interprets as subordination. He does not wish to
accept the submissive role which he finds humiliating, confining, and
restraining. The Son is exalted because of his humility, his submission
to the love of God. Satan will be satisfied with nothing short of the
role of the Father—the authority. But Milton awards "merit" to the
humble and submissive, whereas he ultimately debases and humiliates
Satan for his aspirations toward paternal power. In relation to each
other, too, the sons compete for the recognition of the Father and it is
Satan who alienates himself and is alienated from God because he
cannot adopt the necessary filial attitude. The Son is rewarded for
choosing to remain loyal, for choosing not to disobey the authority of
the Father. Satan is deprived of the shared paternal authority (as well
as other disobedient sons, one-third of those in Heaven), whereas
the Son is delegated some of His powers by the Father. As long as a son
chooses to remain in the sphere of paternal benevolence, he is rewarded
and elevated. If, however, he chooses to rebel, he is punished and diminished. Milton's Heaven is patriarchal; the roles are those of father,
brother, and son, with no talk of mother, sister, or wife. And the attitudes involve creativity, authority, power, or their reverse, destruction,
subversion of authority, misuse of power.

We have examined the sibling relationship of Adam and Eve as
children of God, the Father. We move from Adam, "first of men," and
Eve, "first of Women," to another phase of their roles. We find Adam
designated as the "father" of mankind and Eve identified as the "general
mother." In nature they are siblings, but in relation to God Adam takes
on the superior role of the father. The lines, "*Adam*, the goodliest man
of men since born / His Sons, the fairest of her Daughters *Eve*" (IV,
323–24), seem to give them equal roles in nature; yet the speeches of
Adam, mirroring the speeches of God, echo His firmness, His final word,
and His ultimate intelligence. They contrast to Eve's nonanalytic, remi-

niscent, nostalgic, curious, but submissive speeches. The larger equality of brother and sister is diminished in the inequality of the conjugal roles.

The first human kiss recorded is placed on Eve's "Matron lip," and this identification as mother seems to precede that as spouse. In the Bower, where they consecrate their marriage, emphasis—as in Spenser's *Epithalamion*—is on procreation: "Our Maker bids increase" (IV, 748). Milton emphasizes the necessity of chastity in the celebration of the Bower. Chastity, as in *Comus*, becomes his synecdoche for the observance of the network of familial relations which insures the appropriate preservation of roles and attitudes absolutely essential for the survival of human society. It means that no "adulterous lust," no violation of the sacred bonds of marriage between a man and a woman, will occur. The contrast between adultery and chastity determines the simultaneous recognition of nonacceptable and acceptable familial roles. It allows the poet to portray the sequence from mother to wife in that order. God's blessing to Eve when he gives her her significant name identifies her central role:

> And I will bring thee where no shadow stays
> Thy coming, and thy soft imbraces, hee
> Whose image thou art, him thou shalt enjoy
> Inseparably thine, to him shalt bear
> Multitudes like thyself, and thence be call'd
> Mother of human Race.   (IV, 470–75)

This identification, while inevitable since Milton is working with the myth of creation and the Fall, is, however, significant for where it is placed. The identification of Eve as "Mother of human Race" precedes the wedding night. The decree of God through the naming of Eve— that is, giving her identity—is legitimized in the wedding song, which reinforces the nature of marriage and the woman's role. Eve's roles seem to be those of sister of Adam in nature, daughter or child of both God and Adam, Mother of the human race, and finally spouse, a worthy title which now has taken on the implications of and is intertwined with that of Mother. It is significant that in the epithalamion an equation is established. The relations in "wedded love" mirror the relations between "the Charities / Of Father, Son, and Brother" (IV, 756–57). As a matter of fact, all relations, father-son-brother, mother-daughter-sister, and the rest, are made "known" through wedded love. Although the process looks as if marriage is not the origin but the conclusion of the recognition of familial roles, Milton concludes that no particular roles exist until the concept of marriage is identified.

Before describing Adam and Eve's roles and attitudes further, we must look at another marriage relationship in the epic—that of Satan and Sin. We see Satan as the husband of Sin, and, like Adam, as "Father, Son, and Brother." Although through God Adam and Eve are siblings in their common humanity, there is no conflict between the sibling role and the conjugal role because in the sibling relationship emphasis is not on consanguinity. However, in the case of Satan and Sin, Sin is simultaneously Satan's daughter and wife and their relationship is immediately perverse because it is incestuous, a fact that threatens the very sanctity of the nuclear family. On the subject of incest in relation to marriage, Murdock states: "Our first conclusion is that, with the exception of married parents, incest taboos apply universally to all persons of opposite sex within the nuclear family." He further finds, in extensive evidence compiled from 250 societies, "not a single instance in which sexual intercourse or marriage is generally permissible between mother and son, father and daughter, or brother and sister. Aside from a few rare and highly restricted exceptions, there is complete universality in this respect."[9]

Excluded from Heaven, woman is found on Earth and in Hell, and in both places her central role is that of mother-wife. She is deprived of authority and punished for attempting to usurp it. She is associated with lust and rape, and particularly with incest, which obliterates the appropriate separation of roles found in the heavenly hierarchy and in Eden before the Fall. This separation insures observance of the roles and perpetuation of the attitudes appropriate to them. In Hell, both son and father rape the mother who is also daughter and sister, confusing the roles of father, son, brother, and husband as Sin confuses her roles of mother, sister, daughter, and wife.

Satan, the father, does not recognize his daughter, Sin, who is also his wife, nor his son, Death, who is also his grandson, and the son and brother of Sin. All relations are confused and disrespected; no appropriate boundaries are established at all. In wedded love, on the other hand, the bonds of parent and child—based on obedience and piety, the loyalty of siblings, and submission—are perpetuated through the authority of the father and the submissive role of the mother, as we have seen in the garden scenes. Even in Hell, Satan is identified with father-hood and masculinity: "Thou art my Father, thou my author, thou / My being gav'st me; whom should I obey / But thee; whom follow?" (II, 864–66). Sin participates in the concept of motherhood and femi-ninity established above. She, like Eve, is mother of a multitude—Death and his progeny. Both she and Death acknowledge Satan as their "great Author" (X, 236), a term used frequently to describe Adam and God. Like Eve, Sin embarks on an independent task; like Eve she causes de-struction by the independent act. Sin encourages Death to build a bridge to that "new World," an act designed to bring about the destruction of humanity. Although the motives are different, the results of Sin's and Eve's actions are the same.

By examining these relations of Satan, Sin, and Death, one can see negative aspects of the kinship roles portrayed positively through the prelapsarian Adam and Eve. Certain relationships and attitudes are established and broken at the same time, revealing simultaneously values and disvalues, allowing the reader to experience both the ap-propriate observances and their breakdown. In these relationships, Milton's portrayal of woman reveals certain striking attitudes:

1. The principle of creativity, the highest principle of the cosmos, is denied to woman. The Father and the Son bound the cosmos. The male poet creates the epic, and the author and disposer of woman is her husband.

2. Woman's creativity is restricted to her progeny; she is dedicated to reproduction as the "Mother of a multitude."

3. The maternal image precedes that of spouse, and sex roles grow out of the sanctity of monogamous marriage ("Hail, wedded love" [IV, 750 ff.]). When the maternal image is not respected, as in the case of Sin, the female image is negative (the "foul" appearance of Sin).

4. Sexual pleasure apart from procreation is associated with sin.

5. Eve is less well equipped than Adam to understand the tempta-tions of the serpent. Although she is not fully responsible for the Fall, the fact that she succumbs, as Adam had implied she might, under-scores her need for guidance and protection. She is most vulnerable in those areas reserved to the male—desire to know and control. In aspiring to work alone and gain more knowledge, Eve forgets that "nothing lovelier can be found / In Woman, than to study household good, / And good works in her Husband to promote" (IX, 232–34).

6. Eve's desire to know is limited by Adam's censorship, much as Adam's desire to know is limited by Raphael. While Adam is being instructed, Eve is busy with the domestic chores, "on hospitable thoughts intent" (V, 332).

7. Eve's surrender to Satan's blandishments indicates her excessive curiosity, her vulnerability to flattery, her gullibility, and her capacity to forget her role as wife and future mother, with the attendant attitudes of obedience, submission to her husband, and mindfulness of her central responsibility as "Mother of Mankind." After the Fall, she is lustful and aggressive, like Adam, and like Sin. When sexuality overcomes chastity and procreation, a condition akin to chaos develops.

8. Eve's desire to know about herself is associated with Narcissus and potential vanity. Her gazing into the pool has negative potential as a reminder of the Fall, symbolically meaningful to the postlapsarian reader. "What there thou seest, fair Creature is thyself" (IV, 468), and the voice leads her to look at her mate and thus away from herself.[10]

This outline of the connections between roles and attitudes prior to the Fall could be greatly elaborated, but it affords an opening into the complexity of Milton's view of the female and male domains. Further elaboration of roles and attitudes can be traced through the Fall and after the Fall, in the recriminations between Adam and Eve, and in the account of the reconstitution of their world through their conversion to God.

Having enjoyed one another carnally after the Fall, Adam and Eve's interaction illuminates the way attitudes and role designations relate to each other and to the larger structure of the poem. In a series of stages, Eve's transformation can be charted to show the appropriate (and familiar to the woman reader) domain of the female, wife and mother. One must note, first of all, that it is the woman who is first seduced by the language of the serpent; it is she who eats first; it is she who is first disobedient; and it is she who becomes the agent, in place of the serpent, for Adam's fall (an act for which he, however, is solely responsible). It is she who first brings the thought of duplicity into the relationship by asking:

> But to Adam in what sort
> Shall I appear? shall I to him make known
> As yet my change, and give him to partake
> Full happiness with mee, or rather not,

> But keep the odds of Knowledge in my power
> Without Copartner? so to add what wants
> In Female Sex, the more to draw his Love,
> And render me more equal, and perhaps,
> A thing not undesirable, sometime
> Superior: for inferior who is free?   (IX, 816–25)

The conjunction of the Fall and the desire for equality, the connection between Satanic rebellion and the woman's desire to be equal (and perhaps, sometimes, superior), certainly the reaction against inferiority, are all counterattitudes to the ones outlined by the marriage celebration in Book IV. Insubordination, inappropriate observance of one's role, and the desire for equality are related to or confused with the desire for power, for to want equality if one is in a submissive role is really to want superiority in relation to the total system, because one is asking to rise above one's designated place. And, as countless critics have noted, these attitudes lead to chaos, to violation of civilized and sanctified codes, and ultimately to subversion of the cosmic and divine order. In this passage, Eve has violated the trust between herself and Adam, brought dishonesty and duplicity into the relationship, and articulated the battle of the sexes. Now ambiguity reigns—to submit and accept her role (too late, of course), or to strive for autonomy? The conflict is, of course, a mirror of Satan's ambivalence and refusal to accept limits, which proleptically reveals by association the humbling of Eve.

That the problem between Adam and Eve after the Fall should mirror the problem between God and Satan—the father and the disobedient son—intensifies the cosmic sanction for the acceptance of appropriate attitudes in the family. At the apex of this is the crucial role of the male authority figure, the definition of freedom as the acceptance of boundaries and limits (something Milton accentuates in Satan's bounding and leaping over fixed objects), and the rejection of the ambiguity or opposition which expresses itself in rebellion, anarchy, and insubordination. The boundaries for the woman grow out of her acknowledgment of the male authority figure, as articulated and sanctified in the epithalamion of Book IV.

The education of Eve, like the education of Adam, is a major project of the epic after the Fall, and is significantly in contrast to the containment of Satan. But even more significant are Milton's views of the transformation of attitude which Eve must undergo in order to restrain the antisocial, unnatural oppositions to her role. Eve reproves Adam for not keeping her by his side. She suggests that had he been with her he too would have been deceived by the serpent. Significantly she shifts to his role as male authority figure: "Why didst not thou the Head / Command me absolutely not to go, / Going into such danger as thou said'st?" (IX, 1155–57). The reader recalls Adam's arguments about freedom and his corroboration of Eve's need to go rather than violate her freedom, making her look ridiculous and illogical now when she forgets her earlier high-flown appeal to the nature and value of freedom. The possibility that Adam should perhaps have kept her by his side further intensifies the woman's inferiority. Later Eve, Adam, the poet, and the reader will agree, on the basis of the evidence given, that Eve should have remained by Adam's side.

The woman must also, in learning her place, accept that the man should not allow her to act without his superior judgment. She must know that it is demeaning for a man to obey her; to listen to a woman is to lose one's manhood, to become like a woman, thus abandoning the necessary superior role of guide:

> Was shee thy God, that her thou didst obey
> Before his voice, or was shee made thy guide,
> Superior, or but equal, that to her
> Thou didst resign thy Manhood, and the Place
> Wherein God set thee above her made of thee
> And for thee.   (X, 145–50)

She must also learn that she was made for man, ultimately to serve as wife and mother, not act in the male capacity as ruler (X, 155–56). Her appropriate demeanor is to attract—"lovely to attract / Thy Love, not thy Subjection" (X, 152–53). Later the second Eve, Mary, the Mother of Christ, will fulfill the perfection of Motherhood, betrayed by Eve. Mary is the embodiment, the fulfillment, of perfect obedience; her Son, too, is the embodiment of perfect obedience, faith, humility.

In the argument between Adam and Eve, before they acknowledge in speech and gesture the assumption of their rightful roles with the concomitant behavior, several significant transformations of attitude are developed. Adam in his anger with Eve sees her as "sinister," a "defect of nature," a "Rib / Crooked by nature, bent, as now appears" (X, 884–85). In his anger he globalizes his rage to include all women, attacking their very existence, an attack rampant with medieval anti-feminism.[11] He suggests that earth would be superior if—like heaven—it had only masculine spirits:

> O why did God,
> Creator wise, that peopl'd highest Heav'n
> With spirits Masculine, create at last
> This novelty on Earth, this fair defect
> Of Nature, and not fill the World at once
> With men as Angels without Feminine,
> Or find some other way to generate
> Mankind?   (X, 888–95)

The reader knows that Adam says this in anger and that Milton's view of woman as necessary partner, articulated in Books IV and IX, transcends the momentary rage, but the terms in which Adam identifies the masculine heaven and the emphasis on the generation of mankind as woman's domain nonetheless corroborate what we have heard before. Eve, witness to the intensity of Adam's rage, hearing that her transgression was due to the disregard of her role as generative force for mankind, responds to him in fear of rejection and isolation. When Adam has finished his vilification of the woman, Eve "at his feet / Fell humble, and imbracing them, besought / His peace" (X, 911–13), begging him not to reject her. She cannot function without him: "forlorn of thee, / Whither shall I betake me, where subsist?" (X, 921–22). Although Adam has committed a sin against God, she has sinned "against God and thee" (X, 931). She, finally, like the Son in relation to God, in a passage echoing the Son's offer to assume full guilt for mankind and Adam's subsequent offer to accept Eve's punishment as well as his own, articulates her guilt and willingness to accept total responsibility: "On me, sole cause to thee of all this woe, / Mee mee only just object of his ire" (X, 935–36). Adam, witnessing her "weeping, and her lowly plight," and seeing her "at his feet submissive in distress," loses his anger. Eve has returned to the submissive attitude which is part of her designated role as Adam's wife, also reflecting, as it echoes Adam's relationship to God the Father, the appropriate filial role which reinforces the nature of permissible submissiveness. Adam thus begins to return to the proper control which he executed before the Fall, only with much more awareness. Eve also has knowledge now of the consequences of straying from requisite behavior. Knowing alternatives more fully, both of them choose the ordained behavior. He has become submissive to God, but dominant over Eve, and she has accepted her submissiveness to Adam, the return to "Hee for God only, shee for God in Him" (IV, 299).

In Book X, as part of the return to their appropriate and necessary roles, Milton stresses the inferiority of Eve's intellect to Adam's by allowing Adam the opportunity to exercise his pedagogic, paternal role again. In verbalizing her own vileness, Eve suggests that she and Adam remain childless by practicing abstinence in order to end the race. By relinquishing her role as mother of the race, she is relinquishing the very purpose of her existence, an act of great "excellence," as Adam acknowledges. Adam in his wider knowledge recalls the "Sentence" that "thy Seed shall bruise / The Serpent's head" (X, 1031–32). He reminds her of the implications of this sentence, reminds her also of the "mild and gracious temper" with which they were heard and judged. Like a schoolmaster he tells her "Remember," he "instructs" her, and tells her "Hee will instruct us praying." Now that the two of them have in word and gesture resumed the divine model, they can turn to God to be further instructed. The end of Book X witnesses "our Father penitent" and Eve "watering the ground" in genuine sorrow and humiliation meek. As yet Eve has not been returned to the dignity of her role as Mother, but she has certainly, like Adam, become the penitent child of God the Father, and has also acted out the role of penitent child-daughter before Adam, signalling her adoption of one dimension of her role as wife. One should note that the childlike role is inseparable from Eve's role as wife and mother. No contradiction exists!

In Book XI, Eve is told by Michael that the consolation for her loneliness and for leaving Paradise will be that Adam goes with her: "Thy Husband, him to follow thou art bound; / Where he abides, think there thy native soil" (XI, 291–92). Prior to Michael's descent, Adam, anticipating that God has listened to their prayers, addresses Eve again as "Mother of all Mankind." Eve accepts the title modestly and humbly, "Ill worthy I such title should belong / To me transgressor" (XI, 163–64). She finds that "to mee reproach / Rather belongs," wishes she had never strayed from Adam's side, and is ready now to remain at his side in Eden (too late of course, the reader discerns, therefore all the more moving). In her "much humbl'd" state, she now has proper domestic cares for her garden; Adam appropriately worries about the cosmic questions, particularly about the fact that God's face from henceforth will be hidden. Their concerns are deemed appropriate to their proper roles, she adopting the domestic and he the cosmic.

Eve, of course, is put to sleep when Adam is taken by Michael to view the vision of history which contains both the suffering and salvation of humankind. In order to view this Adam must have his eyes purged, since the Fall has obscured his vision. (One assumes that Eve's intelligence, which was inferior to Adam's, has become correspondingly debased in its lower degree.) In the vision of history, Milton stresses the male figures of Cain, Abel, Enoch, and Noah, and the idea of the "one just man," sometimes referred to, like Noah, as "the only Son of light" (XI, 310). Adam sees "wicked Sons destroy'd," and rejoices "for one Man found so perfect and so just" (XI, 876). With the patriarchs and Moses we draw closer to fulfillment of the prophecy that one of the "Royal Stock / Of *David* (so I name this King) shall rise / A Son, the Woman's Seed to thee foretold" (XII, 326–28). The Son of God shall fulfill the Law of God "Both by obedience and by love," and salvation shall be preached not only to Abraham's own sons, but to all "the Sons / Of *Abraham's* Faith wherever through the world" (XII, 448–49). Milton has stressed the continuation of male authority in his retelling of Biblical history. There has been scant room for the wives of the patriarchs, the woman judges, the queens, although the first Mother of mankind and the Mother of Jesus, the second Eve, are included, because they produced the male destroyers and the great male leaders of mankind.

Historically, Milton reiterates the same model for men and women. Men who are virtuous, in the image of God the Father, are the "just sons" culminating in the most just redeemer; those who are disobedient are at times effeminate and always negligent in their filial responsibilities. Women are either obedient as "Matron Mother" or disobedient and wanton if they neglect their responsibilities as wife, which signifies motherhood and submissiveness. Milton is not a misogynist, but he conveys a very clear sense of how the family structure becomes the basis for models of authority, social order, and sanctioned behavior. Conversely, he conveys too how general disorganization threatens when marriage, which should solidify relationships and attitudes, contradicts the roles and attitudes he describes for man, woman, and child. His view of woman grows out of a widely ramifying sense of familial relationships which are sanctioned by an externalized divine model. The model in turn has been constructed out of the complex needs of the seventeenth-century world for authority and order. And the needs of the poet often coincide with the constructions of reality into which he was born and which he reinforced.

Milton develops this kinship system in *Paradise Lost* from the basic myth of the Fall, from his personal understanding of relationships, and from the heritage of Western culture transmitted in the art and mythology with which he was abundantly familiar. His view of women, which extends beyond the uniquely personal, is yet another presentation of woman's role as daughter, wife, and mother, of the subordination of woman to man, and of the taming of woman to accept what was concluded by Milton to be the necessary boundaries of the woman's world. Stage by stage, from Creation to Fall to regeneration, Milton traces the appropriate family role and the attitudes he and others of his time considered essential for the good woman, and these roles and attitudes are an outgrowth of a strong belief in marriage and in the family headed by the patriarchal husband.

University of Pittsburgh

NOTES

1. Rosemond Tuve, *Images and Themes in Five Poems by Milton* (Cambridge, Mass., 1957); Marjorie Hope Nicolson, *A World in the Moon*, Smith College Studies in Modern Languages, XVII (Northampton, Mass., 1936); Isabel Gamble MacCaffrey, *"Paradise Lost" as "Myth"* (Cambridge, Mass., 1959); Anne Davidson Ferry, *Milton's Epic Voice: The Narrator in "Paradise Lost"* (Cambridge, Mass., 1963); Irene Samuel, *Plato and Milton* (Ithaca, 1947); Barbara K. Lewalski, *Milton's Brief Epic* (London, 1966).

2. Claude Lévi-Strauss, *The Raw and the Cooked* (New York, 1969), p. 341.

3. For example, Northrop Frye, *The Return of Eden: Five Essays on Milton's Epics* (Toronto, 1965); MacCaffrey, *"Paradise Lost"*; Jackson I. Cope. *The Metaphoric Structure of "Paradise Lost"* (Baltimore, 1962); Stanley Fish, *Surprised by Sin* (New York, 1967).

4. Claude Lévi-Strauss, *Structural Anthropology* (Garden City, N.Y., 1967), p. 35.

5. George Peter Murdock, *Social Structure* (New York, 1949), pp. 106–07.

6. Ibid., p. 107.

7. Norman O. Brown, *Love's Body* (New York, 1966), pp. 4–5.

8. All quotations of *Paradise Lost* are from *John Milton: Complete Poems and Major Prose*, ed. Merritt Y. Hughes (New York, 1957).

9. Murdock, *Social Structure*, pp. 284–85.

10. Cf. Lee A. Jacobus, "Self-Knowledge in *Paradise Lost*: Conscience and Contemplation," in *Milton Studies*, III, ed. James D. Simmonds (Pittsburgh, 1971), p. 108.

11. See Francis Lee Utley, *The Crooked Rib* (Columbus, Ohio, 1944).

MILTON'S GOD:
AUTHORITY IN *PARADISE LOST*

Anthony Low

Milton's God consistently evokes an unfavorable reaction in the modern reader, the result not so much of our emotional response to Christianity as of our antipathy to absolute authority. This response is ironic because Milton too opposed authority, but only usurped human authority, since from the perspective of Adam all men are brothers. *Paradise Lost* presents, in contrast to the abuse of authority in the world, a vision of God's ideal justice, corresponding to the vision of bliss in Eden. The manner of Milton's God has offended, but he speaks as he must: with absolute certitude, with spareness and logic, without recourse to metaphor or sensuous appeal. Nevertheless, his speeches are transcendentally poetic. The Father has been accused of lacking love, but the love which the Son embodies originates with the Father, and is the necessary basis in *Paradise Lost* for just power. Although the Father reveals little directly of what he is, he is defined by his Son and by his creatures: man, the animals, the physical universe. The human love of Adam and Eve, apparently in contention with divine love, actually depends on it for its existence. So the Father is defined by everything he creates; and what he creates is beautiful and good.

G OD THE Father in *Paradise Lost* has been a continual problem both to critics and to common readers during the present century;[1] it is a rare Milton class in which at least a large proportion of the students—otherwise quite enthusiastic about the poem—do not react unfavorably to him.* At the same time, most Miltonists now agree that such a reaction was not intended, that it results either from a flaw

* Preparation of this paper was aided by a grant from the research fund of New York University. I wish to thank Dean Geo. Winchester Stone and the committee for this help.

19

in the poem or a bias in the modern reader. C. S. Lewis wrote in 1942
that in his view, "many of those who say they dislike Milton's God
only mean that they dislike God: infinite sovereignty *de jure*, combined
with infinite power *de facto*, and love which, by its very nature, includes
wrath also."[2] William Empson took up the challenge, agreeing that
indeed he did not like the God of Christianity, and suggesting that
Milton secretly did not like Him either, and subtly showed it in his
poem.[3] This line of argument, though ingeniously and sometimes
illuminatingly developed, is essentially perverse; it is clear to common
sense that it stands Milton on his head. To make Satan the hero of
Paradise Lost (or Dalila the heroine of *Samson Agonistes*), it is now
generally recognized, is to misread not only Milton's probable intention,
but what the poem actually says.

Some critics have suggested that the reason for the difficulty is
Milton's use of the Christian system. We are still too close to the Christian myth, too involved emotionally, one way or another, with its
implications. Therefore, we find it difficult to treat it as a fiction, to
suspend disbelief or wrong belief. We have no such problems, these
critics would argue, with poems based on Greek myth, or on archetypes
whose meaning is taken less seriously with our conscious minds. While
this extension of a critical truism—that the work of art no longer contemporary but not yet sufficiently classical is least easily received and
understood—partly explains the trouble Milton's readers have had with
his portrayal of God, it does not exhaust the matter by any means. If
one imagined a rewriting of *Paradise Lost* in which God the Father
were replaced by Jove, for example, it is evident that most readers
would still feel alienated from the deity in charge. If anything, they
would find tyranny in Jove more easily than in God.

The root of the difficulty is not that modern readers no longer like
the Christian God—in my experience students apparently representing
whole spectra of belief have difficulty with Milton's portrayal—but
simply and obviously that they are predisposed to dislike authority in
all forms. Even those readers who are over thirty are repelled by absolute
authority, authority unqualified and uncompromising—no matter if
it is absolutely "just" or "good" at the same time. As a result, they
are unable to look at Milton's God and to see him as he really is in
the poem; to read his speeches and to feel them as poetry; in short, to

make that adjustment of self which is necessary to the reception of any work of art.

The irony in this reaction is that Milton is perhaps more violently antipathetic to arbitrary authority than any of his readers. In *Paradise Lost*—and in his other mature works—Milton dismisses all human authority. Societies, states, organized churches at their worst are corrupt tyrannies which enslave and destroy; at their best, they are uneasy arrangements tainted by Adam's sin but necessary in order to prevent worse evils. Only the leaven of God's intervention in the world prevents the total corruption of all political institutions and social structures: "supernal Grace contending / With sinfulness of Men" (XI, 359–60).[4]

In his description of the postlapsarian world, Milton clearly differentiates natural hierarchy—such as God over man, man over beast, father over son, husband over wife—and arbitrary or sometimes unnatural hierarchy, such as king over people, conqueror over victim. Even the natural, divinely ordained hierarchy, such as husband over wife (an unpalatable idea for the modern reader), is corrupted in the fallen world and so is frequently unjust or arbitrary; that is why the Son pronounces obedience of wife to husband as a punishment on Eve and her daughters for her transgression. Before the fall, her obedience to Adam has been natural and easy—stemming as it does from her nature as God has created it—while Adam's rule has been natural, loving, and always just. After the fall, woman obeys with difficulty and against at least a part of her nature, while the rule of the husband necessarily includes elements of tyranny and injustice as well as love. Otherwise there would be no curse: Eve would be as well off as before. But the curse is brought about by man's actions, not by God's whim, for it reflects man's new nature in the fallen world.

Milton's predecessor Shakespeare wove his plays around a triple pattern of order and degree: in the universe, in the state, and in the individual. Although recent studies have suggested that Shakespeare may sometimes have viewed order in the state with an ironic eye, this order or its violation nevertheless pervades his histories and tragedies (and, in a different spirit, his comedies). The histories show what happens when the political hierarchy breaks down: civil war, bloodshed, injustice, waste. The tragedies begin when disorder enters the realm, and end with order reestablished. The axiom of the necessity for po-

litical degree, which underlies Shakespeare's plays as it does the works
of most Elizabethans, does not, however, underlie *Paradise Lost.* In
Milton's postlapsarian universe only one chain of order is unequivocally
to be relied on: the divine universal order. There is in Milton no mys-
tique of kingship as there is in Shakespeare. In *Paradise Lost,* though
Milton was never a democrat, all men are brothers, because they are
seen from the perspective of Adam, their universal father. There is a
hierarchy among men, but it is a hierarchy of natural excellence—a
segment of the universal hierarchy—and consists of God's choice rather
than of Man's social order: "Some I have chosen of peculiar grace /
Elect above the rest; so is my will" (III, 183–84). Men will persecute
and drive out those whom God has elected, however—whether Enoch
or the Messiah himself—substituting their own self-created societies, in
which the hierarchy is purely arbitrary and so has nothing to do with
the Great Chain of Being.

All men, from Adam's point of view, are his sons, brothers to each
other with no rights of precedence. Michael, with this fact in mind,
thus describes the rise of Nimrod, the first tyrant, the archetypal human
king, the founder of the earthly state:

> One shall rise
> Of proud ambitious heart, who not content
> With fair equality, fraternal state,
> Will arrogate Dominion undeserv'd
> Over his brethren, and quite dispossess
> Concord and law of Nature from the Earth.   (XII, 24–29)

Thus Milton recasts the social contract in terms not of agreement
between ruler and ruled, but of forced usurpation. Nimrod's rise to
power is criticized not only because he is an evil, warlike, ungodly
figure, but simply because he begins the practice of brother arrogating
rule over brother—unless one considers Cain to anticipate him. This
creation of the historical state, far from bringing order and degree,
drives out all true harmony and natural law from human society.

Adam, enraged by Nimrod's behavior, speaks from the vantage
of his own natural authority as father to condemn the tyrant's unnatural rule:

> O execrable Son so to aspire
> Above his Brethren, to himself assuming
> Authority usurpt, from God not giv'n:

> He gave us only over Beast, Fish, Fowl
> Dominion absolute; that right we hold
> By his donation; but Man over men
> He made not Lord, such title to himself
> Reserving, human left from human free.   (XII, 64–71)

Adam is correct in stating that man has no natural authority over man, as he has over the lower orders of creation. (No doubt this right will soon raise new difficulties among modern readers; let it suffice here to say that Milton would have assumed responsibility as a concomitant of authority over the lower orders.) But Adam has not grasped the full consequences of his sin, which will make it necessary for men to live in imperfect states and to obey their rulers as long as they are not too unjust or too insupportable. Milton accepted as an axiom of government Saint Paul's words from the Epistle to the Romans xiii, 1: "Let every soul be subject unto the higher powers. For there is no power but of God." The right to rebel was also given in Romans, according to Calvin and the English Puritans, but only in extreme and unusual cases.[5] The tyranny of Nimrod, as Michael points out, is a necessary consequence of the fall and of the resultant disorder in the human soul. Man, having rejected the just authority of God, must suffer the unjust authority of his fellows, exchanging, like Satan, a golden scepter for an iron rod (V, 886–87). Michael concludes: "Tyranny must be, / Though to the Tyrant thereby no excuse" (XII, 95–96). But he agrees with Adam on one point, the ground of his condemnation of Nimrod: "Justly thou abhorr'st / That *Son*" (79–80; my italics).

Thus there is no divine right of kings for Milton, no preoccupation with the beauty of an ordered society. On the face of it he is far less an authoritarian than Shakespeare and the Elizabethans, yet he suffers from a stigma which Shakespeare has generally escaped. For Shakespeare is protean, capable of being read differently in different times. He writes in the dramatic form, practices "negative capability," and puts his words in the mouths of his characters. Milton uses the relativism of dramatic technique only some of the time in *Paradise Lost*. He also makes absolute statements; and his first absolute, his underlying axiom, is the power, glory, goodness, and total authority of his God.

If Milton agrees with those readers who have reservations about the authority of the state, or of man, he parts company with them when he posits the absolute authority of God. One possible response to the abuse of authority in human experience is to revolt against all authority—against the very principle. Such, in general, is the Romantic response which still dominates much of Western thought. But another equally possible response is to turn from imperfect authority on earth to perfect authority in a higher realm. Such was the response of the Hebrews, who turned from present injustice to a promised future justice under their God; and of the Christians, who turned from earth to heaven. So Milton turns from human societies—which he had hoped before his disillusionment in the Commonwealth period to see re-formed—to God. It is a commonplace of Milton criticism that the outcome of the Civil War may have been at least partly responsible for his turning from an epic about his country to an epic about higher and remoter things.

Although not all readers are sympathetic to Milton's Paradise (nothing to do, static, boring), they are usually at least sympathetic to one of its functions. Paradise is among other things an ideal, an effort of the mind to escape its world, an unwillingness to accept things as they are: pain, sickness, failure, injustice, death. One wants at least to imagine an alternative where these evils do not exist, for—as Traherne's poems suggest—higher expectations are innate in us. Why is the same not true of justice, power, and authority? As Milton's Paradise portrays for the reader a perfect human existence, so his God represents perfect justice, authority without admixture of tyranny or illegitimacy, power not only infinite but absolutely beneficent. And as the imagination of a perfect or Utopian world is not simply a retreat from life, but enables the mind to return to this world enlightened, so the imagination of just authority does not excuse injustice or condone it: it offers a contrast and stimulates reform. It is plain enough that in *Paradise Lost* Milton means not to give his support to unjust power, but to contrast the rule of God and the Son with the rule of man—and with the rule of Satan, who, far from being a righteous rebel, better exemplifies authority and power absolutely corrupted, perverted to tyranny and force, craving idolatrous subservience (II, 477–79), demanding obedience but re-fusing it to lawful superiors.

The vision of perfect justice is as essential to *Paradise Lost* as the vision of perfect happiness in Eden before the fall. (And it is surely as easy to accept as the Romantic vision of endless rebellion: rebellion against what, and toward what?) Therefore, one essentially misreads the poem if God's justice seems merely vindictive, or punitive, or if it is opposed absolutely to mercy. The Son does not replace justice with mercy; he reconciles them. His sacrifice serves to "end the strife / Of Mercy and Justice" (III, 406–07); by sending the Son to judge man it is revealed that the Father intends "Mercy colleague with Justice" (X, 59); the Son, agreeing, will temper "Justice with Mercy" (X, 78). The two seemed to oppose one another, but through the divine plan they are reconciled—a familiar commonplace which Milton hardly needed to stress further.

That the Father represents just, beneficent, merciful authority is obvious enough in theory. It still may be questioned, however—indeed it has been questioned—how well Milton has demonstrated it in practice, through the blood of his poetry. One problem is the way the Father speaks. His tone is stern, powerful, absolutely without humility or any of the formulae of self-deprecation that normally accompany polite human speech. Behavioral scientists assure us that without these formulae, these constant reassurances that the listener is valued and respected, communication offends and repulses. Something of the kind probably happens in *Paradise Lost*, because readers unconsciously expect these human amenities, and are unconsciously offended when they do not receive them. But Milton's God could speak in no other way. Humility and self-doubt are virtues in men, but not in God. We would naturally bridle if a man spoke to us with absolute self-assurance, with a perpetual conviction that he was always right, with no trace of humility whatever. It would be a great deal more disturbing if Milton's God admitted he was wrong, changed his mind, or made mistakes. He would not then be God; and he certainly would not be someone to trust with absolute power and authority.

A second difficulty in God's speeches has been remarked recently by a number of critics: he speaks without metaphor or simile, without the aid of esthetic decoration or sensuous appeal. Some critics have flatly called this unpoetical—just as they have said that Comus is a poet but the Lady is not. Again, however, one could expect the Father to speak in no other way. The Father uses that part of rhetoric which includes logic—such verbal schemes and figures as division of a subject into heads, balance, equal phrase length, parallelism with inversion, and the like—but avoids metaphor and, in general, that part of rhetoric which is persuasive.[6] In this he is the opposite of Satan. The Father speaks to communicate as directly and simply as possible, while Satan speaks to obfuscate and persuade. The Father, who has given angels and men freedom, avoids enslaving them to persuasive rhetoric because, as he so often states, he wants to be loved and served freely. It is his intention to give information only, and to allow decisions to be made independently. Satan, on the other hand, conceals information, twists logic, and speaks not to inform but to seduce and enslave. The difference in the way God and Satan address themselves to Adam and Eve on the subject of the forbidden fruit illustrates their different approaches. God gives the command simply and in unforgettable terms; then he sends his messenger with a tremendous amount of information— all that is needed intellectually to make a wise choice. Satan disguises himself, tunes his voice like an Attic orator, and reveals no true information, but lies, confuses, and finally seduces the weaker Eve.[7]

Thus it is evident that God speaks in character when he avoids the sensuous and the metaphorical. His acts and not merely his assertions reveal respect for the freedom of his creatures. It might still be protested, however, that he is unpoetical. Long stretches of flat verse, though explicable on grounds of character, would not attract the reader to the speaker. Here the answer must be to some extent a value judgment. Modern tastes and critical views have inclined us to the sensuous and concrete. We abhor the abstract as something vague and bloodless. But the abstract or transcendent need not be vague or meaningless: there is good and bad abstract poetry just as there is good and bad concrete poetry. Dante's *Paradiso* is full of great poetry that is not based on material objects; the choruses of the Greek tragedies are as full of powerful abstractions as they are of solid images; Yeats' mature poems, though he thought he hated abstractions, are full of them. One must finally resort to Matthew Arnold's touchstone theory in a matter like this, and (with apologies) to his dogmatism. For abstract poetry can be great; and the Father's lines, which are usually abstract, are deeply poetic and often full of feeling, though they may seem on the surface emotionless.

Sternness is perhaps the tone most readers have been aware of:

> But yet all is not done; Man disobeying,
> Disloyal breaks his fealty, and sins
> Against the high Supremacy of Heav'n,
> Affecting God-head, and so losing all,

> To expiate his Treason hath nought left,
> But to destruction sacred and devote,
> He with his whole posterity must die,
> Die hee or Justice must; unless for him
> Some other able, and as willing, pay
> The rigid satisfaction, death for death.   (III, 203–12)

Several things are evident about this passage: the strong sense of logical sequence; the reinforcement of a sense of emotional culmination by the constant movement toward a significant final word; the heavy use of alliteration to underline the tone, to which some of those final words contribute: "done," "disobeying," "Disloyal," "destruction," "devote," "die," "Die," "death," "death." With "death for death," all the patterns come to their completion: logical sequence, alliteration, and emotional culmination. More effective than any of these devices, however, is the rhythm, including the rhythm of phrase length; if the Son usually speaks in the "rhythm of love,"[8] then the Father most often speaks in the rhythm of power, of absolute assurance and confidence.

While the poetry of this passage may be evident, its tone is not one to endear the speaker to the reader. The Father does not always use this tone, however. In a passage immediately preceding this one, quite a different note is struck:

> for I will clear thir senses dark,
> What may suffice, and soft'n stony hearts
> To pray, repent, and bring obedience due.
> To Prayer, repentance, and obedience due,
> Though but endeavor'd with sincere intent,
> Mine ear shall not be slow, mine eye not shut.
> And I will place within them as a guide
> My Umpire *Conscience*, whom if they will hear,
> Light after light well us'd they shall attain,
> And to the end persisting, safe arrive.   (III, 188–97)

Once more there is a sense of logical and emotional progression: from "senses dark" and "stony hearts," through "prayer, repentance, and obedience," to the safe arrival in heaven. The promise, first couched in negatives ("Mine ear shall not be slow, mine eye not shut"), gives way to the positive gift of conscience, and then to swift forward progress, "Light after light," which finally reaches journey's end. In this passage the most obvious sound effect is the alliteration of *s*, with subsidiary use of *r* and *l* and locally of other letters. The poetry still suggests power and surety—especially in the tutelary repetition of prayer, repentance, and obedience—but here the power promises rather than condemns. Infinite power appears in another light when it offers not condemnation but fatherly assistance in difficulties.

Still another tone is apparent when the Father speaks to a listener who has won through his trials successfully and arrived at the throne. Now the promise need not be counterbalanced by careful emphasis on what conditions must be met (or intended) for its fulfillment:

> On to the sacred hill
> They led him high applauded, and present
> Before the seat supreme; from whence a voice
> From midst a Golden Cloud thus mild was heard.
>   Servant of God, well done, well hast thou fought
> The better fight, who single hast maintain'd
> Against revolted multitudes the Cause
> Of Truth, in word mightier than they in Arms;
> And for the testimony of Truth hast borne
> Universal reproach, far worse to bear
> Than violence: for this was all thy care
> To stand approv'd in sight of God, though Worlds
> Judg'd thee perverse.   (VI, 25–37)

Although Abdiel is addressed here, he represents any just soul who has done his duty, persevered through difficulties, and finally arrived for his reward. And the Father's words are both fitted for the occasion and—as several of my students have spontaneously remarked—moving in the extreme.[9]

However, the emotion the reader feels in connection with this passage is the auditor's and the narrator's as well as the speaker's. Although—as Milton states in the *Christian Doctrine* (I, ii)—emotions such as love or hate can be attributed to God, they are in him without human frailty, so that he is at the same time impassive. It can be assumed that the Father's words express love, but that love is evident mainly by logical deduction from the meaning of the speech and by reflection in the feelings of his auditors. The emotion felt on hearing these words is first Abdiel's love and gratitude, supported by the approval of the angels who surround him; then the love and gratitude of the narrator, who by implication anticipates standing one day in Abdiel's place; then the warmth of the reader—and only indirectly the love of the Father who is speaking. For it is a peculiarity of Milton's technique that the reader never identifies directly with the Father, but always feels himself to be a listener, or at one with some person who is being addressed.

When Satan speaks in Hell, we both listen to him and identify with him, for whether or not we agree with him, he exemplifies forces most readers find in themselves.[10] When Adam and Eve talk together in Paradise we watch them with Satan from the underbrush, but we also feel with them what they are feeling. When the Father speaks, however, we are excluded from direct empathy. We are placed in a passive role and listen to what he says, for what he says is usually addressed directly to the reader as well as to the immediate auditors. There is in God's speeches a kind of verbal economy which Milton borrows from the Bible, where—as the interpreters have argued—all God's words have a double relevancy, to the specific actors involved in the specific event, and to all future readers of the Bible as well. The inability to identify with the Father, however, when the modern reader is used to identifying even with villains for whom he feels only a partial sympathy, naturally repels. So does the consciousness of being directly addressed, of being told, for example, in no uncertain terms, that prayer, repentance, and obedience are the necessary ingredients of spiritual progress. But identification is not the end-all of literature; and, more to the point, the gap between the reader and God is presumably deliberate on Milton's part, for it reminds the reader that he cannot expect more while he is in his fallen state. Abdiel looks on the golden cloud and is bathed in the Father's praise, but the reader must remain at several removes, and content himself with hearsay and reflected glory.

Perhaps the most serious charge against Milton's God, however, concerns not his manner but his essential character. Critics almost universally agree that while the Son represents love and mercy in *Paradise Lost*, the Father represents justice—without warmth or sympathy. It is a further commonplace that while Dante suffused the *Divine Comedy* with love, Milton's poem on the whole lacks this essential quality.[11] One might begin to answer this charge by pointing out, for what it is worth, that the index to the Columbia Milton lists thirteen passages in *Paradise Lost* that use the word *judgment* and forty that use *justice*, but ninety-one passages that use *love*. A more substantive reply, however, is that although Milton embodies divine love in the Son, he is careful not to speak of it without clearly indicating that the source of

the Son's love and mercy is the Father. It is inexplicable that critics
have not emphasized this point more.

When the Son first appears in *Paradise Lost*, he is presented as the
image of the Father:

> Beyond compare the Son of God was seen
> Most glorious, in him all his Father shone
> Substantially express'd, and in his face
> Divine compassion visibly appear'd,
> Love without end, and without measure Grace.   (III, 138–42)

The endless love and immeasurable grace which appear in the Son's
countenance are the substantial expression of the Father's nature. Here
the divine compassion visibly appears, implying that in the Father it is
present but invisible. The Son, having been introduced, pleads for man.
The Father notes in his reply that "All hast thou spok'n as my thoughts
are, all / As my Eternal purpose hath decreed: / Man shall not quite
be lost" (171–73). In other words, the Son is not arguing with the
Father, Mercy against Justice; he is expressing what has originated
from the Father—indeed, what the Father has decreed from all eternity.

The Father now asks for a volunteer who out of love will pay the
"rigid satisfaction" of "death for death" (212). He assumes that love as
well as rigid satisfaction will be necessary: "Where shall we find such
love?" (213). He knows who will volunteer, however, as the opening of
the Son's speech suggests: "Father, thy word is past, man shall find
grace" (227). The Son, when he concludes his offer, breathes "immortal
love / To mortal men, above which only shone / Filial obedience: as
a sacrifice / Glad to be offer'd, he attends the will / Of his great Father"
(267–71). In other words, the Son not only is satisfying a legal require-
ment, as so many critics have noted; he is, *in his love*, following the
will of the Father; and this, he says, is his primary motivation.

The Father immediately approves the Son's sacrifice. Although he
speaks of justice, he speaks also of love, and shows an equal understanding of both. His speech rises to heights of abstract poetry—or perhaps
transcendent is a better word. Once more, his words are characterized by
logical forward movement and emotional progression, from death to
life, from hatred to love:

> So Man, as is most just,
> Shall satisfy for Man, be judg'd and die,
> And dying rise, and rising with him raise

His Brethren, ransom'd with his own dear life.
So Heav'nly love shall outdo Hellish hate,
Giving to death, and dying to redeem.   (III, 294–99)

Out of death, life. In the play on "rise," "rising," "raise," one may well see the reversal of that grimmer permutation of "fall," "fail'd," "fell" (99–102). Rising, not falling, is the poem's last word. The Father's speeches never quite take on the rhythm of the Son's, for there is always an element of spareness and power about them. Nevertheless, the Father has his own "rhythm of love."

The Father concludes the heavenly consultation by exalting the Son, giving into his hand "all Power" (317), specifically because the Son has demonstrated, by his offer, the love and goodness which merit this authority. The Son has, in a sense, passed a test by demonstrating his love. He has proved himself worthy of wielding the kind of power which the Father justly wields, power which can be trusted only to utter selflessness and divine compassion:

                    because in thee
Love hath abounded more than Glory abounds,
Therefore thy Humiliation shall exalt
With thee thy Manhood also to this Throne;
Here shalt thou sit incarnate, here shalt Reign
Both God and Man, Son both of God and Man,
Anointed universal King; all Power
I give thee, reign for ever, and assume
Thy Merits.   (III, 311–19)

Satan, who covets power for its own sake, exalting himself only to be humbled, is the opposite of the Son, and also of the Father. He sees the Father as an arbitrary tyrant, ruling by virtue of his thunderbolts rather than by merit—but, of course, he is merely projecting his own desires. The Father is better characterized by the test which he gives to his Son. When the Son passes it, he proves himself like his Father: worthy of rule because he loves.

One more instance of the origin of the Son's love in the Father may be mentioned. When Adam and Eve send up their penitential prayer at the end of Book X, it is taken by the Son in his office as High Priest, and presented to the Father. The Son intercedes for man, and asks for divine mercy and forgiveness, once more offering himself as the sacrifice for man's reconciliation with the Father. The Father replies:

"All thy request for Man, accepted Son, / Obtain, all thy request was my Decree" (XI, 46–47). As the Father has sent down prevenient grace to enable Adam and Eve to repent (XI, 3–4, 22–23), so he has also initiated the Son's intervention on man's behalf: "all thy request was my Decree."

The Father's character, then, is defined to a large extent by his Son, who is his visible manifestation, and who acts not in opposition to the Father, but in obedience and (in a sense) in imitation. More details could be given to support this conclusion, but they seem unnecessary. Instead, we will turn to another (and, in this discussion, final) para- meter by which the Father's character is defined. This is the Father's reflection in creation, or the Book of Nature. It is again curious that, although the Book of Nature in *Paradise Lost* has occasionally been discussed, its full implications have been left nearly unexamined. Among the most familiar of Renaissance concepts, the Book of Nature underlies nearly the whole of the poem; and any criticism which fails to keep this in mind is bound to be distorted. Leland Ryken has taken up the matter in a recent study, enumerating the many passages in *Paradise Lost* that specifically refer to the concept of God's reflection in his creatures, and of approaching him through nature.[12] Adam prays to a God who "sit'st above these Heavens / To us invisible or dimly seen / In these thy lowest works, yet these declare / Thy goodness be- yond thought, and Power Divine" (V, 156–59). Indeed, the whole of Adam and Eve's hymn is a praise of God through the creatures. Raphael tells Adam that "Heav'n / Is as the Book of God before thee set, / Wherein to read his wond'rous Works" (VIII, 66–68), while Uriel praises Satan for his supposed desire "to know / The works of God, thereby to glorify / The great Work-Master" (III, 694–96).

These are only some of the references in the poem to the doctrine of the Book of Nature, and they demonstrate how conscious Milton was of it.[13] But far more important than these individual references is the application of the concept to the poem as a whole. For everything which is good, or loving, or beautiful in *Paradise Lost* is created by Milton's God, and is a reflection of his nature. Everything which is violent, or evil, or deadly, is the "creation" of Satan—but not really creation, rather perversion or destruction. Some of the critics inimical to Milton have demanded that his characters should be judged not by the narrator's comments on them, but by what they are and what they do.[14] However, they have not applied this criterion evenly. Satan boasts of eternal warfare against God, but instead he attacks an innocent woman by stealth and treachery. Though he is full of energy, it is purely destructive energy. His greatest boast is to have destroyed in a day what God took six days to create, "For only in destroying I find ease / To my relentless thoughts" (IX, 129–30). But creation is on another level entirely from destruction, as love is from hate and life from death. As the angels say in praising the Son on his return from making the universe: "thee that day / Thy Thunders magnifi'd; but to create / Is greater than created to destroy" (VII, 605–07). When the Son pauses earlier on his way to battle in order to replace the uprooted hills and to recreate the heavenly landscape with "fresh Flow'rets" (VI, 784), he reveals a power greater than what he then displays against Satan's army.

Milton's God, then, is defined by what he does: by the creation of the world in Book VII; by the beauty of heaven and the happy radiance of the angels; by the beauty and abundance of Eden and everything it contains. The elephant writhing his lithe proboscis says as much about Milton's God as God's pleasant conversation with Adam about his future mate. To go through all this material in detail would be impossible: everything in the description of Eden in Books IV, V, VIII, and IX; the whole of Book VII and its description of the creation; all the peripheral descriptions in the scenes in heaven; such relatively minor passages as the magnificent view of the universe when Satan peers down through the outer shell or of the sun when he talks to Uriel— all of these add to our understanding of Milton's God. As he is omnipresent in his creation, so, in a sense, he is omnipresent in the poem.

Of all the created universe, however, nothing in *Paradise Lost* more clearly reflects the creator than Adam and Eve. Just as critics have opposed the Father and the Son to each other, so they have opposed the Father and his human creatures. There is, however, no opposition until the fall. Adam and Eve, whom Satan finds the most impressive of all Eden's wonders, are described as the most beautiful because they are the most Godlike:

> Two of far nobler shape erect and tall,
> Godlike erect, with native Honor clad
> In naked Majesty seem'd Lords of all,
> And worthy seem'd, for in thir looks Divine
> The image of thir glorious Maker shone,

Truth, Wisdom, Sanctitude severe and pure,
Severe, but in true filial freedom plac't;
Whence true autority in men.   (IV, 288–95)

The language of this passage is abstract, as it so often is when Milton approaches transcendent matters. (Compare the similar words in the sonnet "Methought I Saw": "Love, sweetness, goodness in her person shin'd.") This is because the true beauty of Adam and Eve is more spiritual than physical—or rather, since the physical and the spiritual are not really separated or at war in this sinless world, their physical beauty and stance reveal their inward goodness. It is because they resemble the Father that they are permitted dominion over the earth, just as the Son's resemblance to the Father is the ground for his greater authority in heaven. No other ground for "true autority" exists; all else is the usurped power of Nimrod and Satan, or the "tedious pomp" of earthly princes (V, 354).

The beauty and attractiveness of Adam and Eve have often been contrasted with the unattractiveness of Milton's God. It is only after the fall, however, that beauty and pleasure can be opposed to goodness, or creation to creator. In Eden, Puritanism and humanism are not in tension with one another. This is why Adam, when Michael shows him his descendants, misjudges the daughters of Cain: because they are beautiful, he thinks they are good. Michael must teach him about the illusion of appearances and the Augustinian opposition of goods on various levels in the fallen world: "Judge not what is best / By pleasure, though to Nature seeming meet" (XI, 603–04).

In Paradise, the only lower good, the only pleasure which must be refused, is the forbidden fruit. After Eve has eaten it, however, various loves, pleasures, and goods begin to oppose each other. Adam must then make the most agonizing of all possible decisions: between love of God and love of Eve. Critics, perhaps encumbered by fear of committing the "intentional fallacy," often forget that Milton chose to put the opposition of the highest earthly love to heavenly love at this crux of the poem. It could not have been his intention to make the choice seem easy, for not easily does man go from a state of innocence to a state of sin. But Eve's beauty and Adam's love, though they may—along with the rest of the poem—owe something to Milton's unconscious mind, did not unconsciously run away with him. They are as much Milton's deliberate creation as the Father; and in the universe of the poem they are the Father's creation. The conflict between loves and between allegiances in Book IX arises because Satan intervenes and Eve freely if ignorantly succumbs to temptation. Satan thus succeeds in setting good against good, doing what he does best, corrupting and destroying what the Father has first created perfect. But he succeeds only in part and for a time.

The love of Adam and Eve has, until Book IX, been pure and innocent. It unashamedly and unselfconsciously includes both the physical and the spiritual, which are in perfect harmony. After the fall, however, their love—their best part—is corrupted. Eve, after sinning, first thinks of keeping the godhead she has gained to herself, but then worries that she may die after all, and Adam marry another Eve: "A death to think" (IX, 830). So, she resolves, "*Adam* shall share with me in bliss or woe: / So dear I love him, that with him all deaths / I could endure, without him live no life" (831–33). She speaks as if she were sacrificing her life for Adam, when, in fact, she is offering to sacrifice Adam with herself, in case the fruit of her transgression should be death and not godhead. She is not, however, deliberately lying or misrepresenting the situation. More likely she is speaking out of genuine love— but the confused, corrupted, selfish, romantic love of a fallen world. There is no reason to doubt her sincerity when she says that she has "agony of love till now / Not felt" (858–59), or when she praises Adam for his wrong decision: "O glorious trial of exceeding Love, / Illustrious evidence, example high!" (961–62). She sees herself as a kind of Iseult, and Adam as a Tristan (and their love is equally human, pitiful, disloyal, destructive, and suicidal). His love is at this point far less selfish than hers, but on the other hand, being yet unfallen, he is more conscious of what he is giving up—not merely his own happiness, but his love and allegiance to his creator.

After the double fall is completed, love turns to lust—from the House of Busirane, as it were, to the Bower of Bliss, further down the scale of values from heaven to earth. From lust, the progression is onward to shame, to recrimination, and to hatred, both of self and of each other. What begins as an attempted affirmation of union (IX, 906–16), ends in separation and disgust. The descent is thus completed. But the two do not remain long at this nadir. Through the power of love embodied in Eve, but ultimately because Milton's God has by means of prevenient grace "remov'd / The stony from thir hearts, and made new flesh / Regenerate grow instead" (XI, 3–5), they begin the upward journey that enables them to leave Paradise (and the poem) once more together, "hand in hand" (XII, 648). This regrowth of companionship and faithfulness between Adam and Eve, of a love less perfect and innocent than formerly, but deep, genuine, and self-sacrificing, is intimately connected with the healing of their love for God. In *Paradise Lost*, human love set against divine love withers and decays like Adam's garland, for all good things in the poem are dependent on God for their being, and lose their goodness and their beauty when—like Satan—they are cut off from their source. Reunited with the love of God, however, the love between Adam and Eve flourishes again.

Milton's God must be seen, then, not as an unpleasant figure at the periphery, who is occasionally glimpsed meting out justice, or grudgingly losing arguments with his Son, but rather as the source and end of everything good and beautiful in *Paradise Lost*. He makes use even of the evil and destruction which Satan introduces, but these perversions do not reflect his nature. The beginning of Raphael's great speech on the hierarchy is no empty formula, but a principle which deeply imbues the whole poem:

> O *Adam*, one Almighty is, from whom
> All things proceed, and up to him return,
> If not deprav'd from good, created all
> Such to perfection, one first matter all,
> Indu'd with various forms, various degrees
> Of substance, and in things that live, of life.   (V, 469–74)

The Father does not attempt to propagandize in his speeches, although he has often been accused of it. He does not attempt to sway his auditors to him by the power of rhetoric, although as the author of reason he uses as much rhetoric as is reasonable. He speaks in poetry, but not a poetry the modern reader is accustomed to. He veils himself from the fallen world and from readers who (in Milton's view) have partly cut themselves off from him in this life. The Father is sufficiently revealed, however, not only by what he says, but by what he does—and most especially by what he creates, and endows with life, or with free, separate intelligence. He is reflected in the Son, in man, in the beasts, birds, and plants, in the sun, moon, and stars, in the whole of his creation. God's words at the end of the sixth day, after he has finished making man,

sufficiently sum it up: "Here finish'd hee, and all that he had made /
View'd, and behold all was entirely good" (VII, 548–49).

New York University

NOTES

1. Even Milton's most sympathetic defenders have been somewhat uncomfortable about his characterization of the Father. See Douglas Bush, *"Paradise Lost"
in Our Time* (Ithaca, 1945), p. 43; C. S. Lewis, *A Preface to "Paradise Lost"* (London, 1942), pp. 130–31; Christopher Ricks, *Milton's Grand Style* (Oxford, 1963), pp.
18–20. See also C. A. Patrides, *Milton and the Christian Tradition* (Oxford, 1966),
pp. 156–58.

   I use the lower-case pronoun for Milton's God because I intend to treat him
as a character in the poem—although it is arguable whether Milton would have
allowed this simple distinction.

2. Lewis, *A Preface to "Paradise Lost,"* p. 130.

3. William Empson, *Milton's God*, 2d ed. (London, 1965). For two similar views,
see A. J. A. Waldock, *"Paradise Lost" and Its Critics* (Cambridge, 1947), and John
Peter, *A Critique of "Paradise Lost"* (New York, 1960). Earlier attacks by Walter
Bagehot, Walter Raleigh, F. R. Leavis, and T. S. Eliot are cited by Waldock and
Ricks.

4. The edition used throughout is *Paradise Lost*, ed. Merritt Y. Hughes (New
York, 1962).

5. See my " 'No Power but of God': Vengeance and Justice in *Samson Agonistes*,"
Huntington Library Quarterly, XXXIV (1971), 219–32.

6. On the Father's preference for schemes rather than tropes, see J. B. Broadbent, "Milton's Rhetoric," *MP*, LVI (1959), 224–42; Jackson I. Cope, *The Metaphoric
Structure of "Paradise Lost"* (Baltimore, 1962), pp. 164–76; Peter Berek, " 'Plain' and
'Ornate' Styles and the Structure of *Paradise Lost*," *PMLA*, LXXXV (1970), 241–42.

7. See Stanley Fish, *Surprised by Sin* (New York, 1967), pp. 57–91; Anne Ferry,
Milton and the Miltonic Dryden (Cambridge, Mass., 1968), pp. 21–121; John M.
Major, "Milton's View of Rhetoric," *Studies in Philology*, LXIV (1967), 685–711;
Arnold Stein, *Answerable Style* (Minneapolis, 1953), pp. 126–28; John M. Steadman,
Milton's Epic Characters (Chapel Hill, 1968), pp. 227–77; Irene Samuel, "The Dialogue
in Heaven: A Reconsideration of *Paradise Lost*, III.1–417," *PMLA*, LXXII (1957),
601–11, reprinted in Arthur Barker, ed., *Milton: Modern Essays in Criticism* (New
York, 1965), pp. 233–45. See also n. 6 and, for opposed comment, J. B. Broadbent,
Some Graver Subject (London, 1960), pp. 144–57.

8. See the note to X, 913, in *The Complete Poetical Works of John Milton*, ed.
Douglas Bush (Boston, 1965). I believe Bush originated the phrase, which I first heard
in a lecture in 1959. Cf. Joseph Summers, *The Muse's Method* (London, 1962), pp.
176–85, on "the voice of the Redeemer."

9. Besides these examples of "abstract" Miltonic poetry, perhaps the best
touchstone is the concluding chorus of *Samson Agonistes*.

10. As Lewis convincingly argues (*A Preface to "Paradise Lost,"* pp. 100–01).

11. See Patrides, *Milton and the Christian Tradition*, p. 156. Dante, of course,

portrays pain and hatred as well as love—though love, he says, founded hell as well as heaven.

12. Leland Ryken, *The Apocalyptic Vision in "Paradise Lost"* (Ithaca, 1970), pp. 155–58. For intellectual background, see Patrides, *Milton and the Christian Tradition*, pp. 54–90. Ryken also has a useful discussion of Milton's abstract poetry; since my interest in the topic developed independently, I have not cited him in detail.

13. See also IV, 412–17, V, 508–12, VIII, 100–02, VIII, 107–08, VIII, 276–79, and Ryken, *The Apocalyptic Vision*, pp. 155–58. In the discussion of creation which follows, I assume (with Patrides and Ryken) that in *PL* creation is the work not only of the Son, but also of the Father and the Spirit. The Father certainly joins in the creation of man (VII, 516–28), while the rest of creation is the work of a generalized "God." This interpretation is questioned by some Miltonists, but my argument does not absolutely depend on it, since in any case the Son acts through the gift and by the will of the Father. Two useful studies of creation and destruction in *PL* are Summers, *The Muse's Method*, and Michael Lieb, *The Dialectics of Creation* (Amherst, 1970).

14. The idea that Milton's poetry and feelings go one way and his theology another is something of a commonplace. It appears especially in speaking of the Fall, and of the degradation of Satan. See F. R. Leavis, *The Common Pursuit* (London, 1952), pp. 24–27; Waldock, *"Paradise Lost" and Its Critics*, pp. 78–83; Peter, *A Critique of "Paradise Lost,"* pp. 53–54; John Fraser, *"Paradise Lost*, Book IX: A Minority Opinion," *Melbourne Critical Review*, VII (1964), 23–24. See also the summary of critical views in Patrick Murray, *Milton: The Modern Phase* (London, 1967), pp. 99–115. Probably one of the origins of this critical interpretation is T. S. Eliot's theory of a historical "dissociation of sensibility," which he blames partly on Milton. An earlier influence is Blake's *Marriage of Heaven and Hell*.

"THE LORD'S BATTELLS":
SAMSON AGONISTES AND
THE PURITAN REVOLUTION

Jackie Di Salvo

Samson was a culture hero for the Puritan revolution, held up as a spiritual model by the preachers. *Samson Agonistes* expresses the central values of that revolution. Samson is an active hero with a divine vocation who eschews the idle life represented by Dalila, just as the Puritan middle class rejected the leisure values of the aristocracy. Samson's vocation, like those of many seventeenth-century Puritans, is military and revolutionary. He is fighting on God's side in a cosmic war against Satan, whose battlefield is not only in the soul but in the political terrain of England. His vocation is to free the Israelites from the oppression of the Philistines, just as the New Model Army believed it had a divine calling to free England from the demonic tyranny of Charles I. The contrast between Samson and Harapha reflects the development of a new kind of soldier armed with the advantages of internal discipline. On the spiritual level Samson battles against self-doubt to that same faith in providence which enabled men like Cromwell to lead a new class to power.

MILTON's *Samson Agonistes* has been read in the various contexts of Greek tragedy, Hebraic religion, Christian exegesis and allegory. Since Milton read almost everything available to a literate European in the seventeenth century, it is possible to find in his works the influence of writers from Xenophon and Aeschylus to Augustine and Aquinas. However, if we look closely at *Samson* and at Milton's other references to the biblical hero, we can also root the work in an immediate historical context. When, in *Areopagitica*, Milton expresses his hope that the Puritan revolution will establish a new society in England, he alludes to Samson: "Methinks I see in my mind a noble and puissant nation rousing herself like a strong man after sleep, and shaking her invincible locks" (*Works* IV, 344).[1] In the *First Defence*, when Milton turns to the Old Testament for a precedent to justify the fight against Charles I, his allusion is even more revealing: "We will now begin with the Jews whom we suppose to have known most the will of God . . . at the time when the Israelites, however they had been subjected to kings, cast the slavish yoke from their necks. . . . Samson, that renowned champion, though his countrymen blamed him (Judges xv, 11 "Knowest thou not that the Philistines are rulers over us?") yet made war single-handed against his rulers, and whether instigated by God or by his own valour only, slew not one but many at once of his country's tyrants. And as he had at first duly prayed to God to be his help, it follows that he counted it no wickedness but a duty to kill his masters, his country's tyrants even though the greater part of his country refused not tyranny" (*Works* VI, 219). Here Milton presents Samson as a military hero, a national champion, and, significantly, as a revolutionary opposing an unjust order.

Samson Agonistes may profitably be read in this light, for here Milton draws upon a tradition overlooked by Michael Krouse:[2] the sermons of the Puritan preachers in which Samson and other military heroes of the Old Testament became the moral models for men who, in a religious and political revolution, were not only to be saints but soldiers fighting "the Lord's Battells." Milton's Samson is a culture hero of the Puritan revolution; Milton's drama expresses the central interior drama of those Puritans who had to mold not only a new church and a new society, but a new ethos. An examination of the drama in that cultural context shows a central movement from passivity to activism, an activism that ultimately takes the form of a violent struggle against a political oppressor. This activism is seen in the context of the Puritan repudiation of sloth and reevaluation of "worldliness." The relevance of this ethos to the military situation can be shown in terms of the religious zeal of the New Model Army and the providential sense of its commander, Oliver Cromwell. I hope, in drawing this comparison, to avoid some of the pitfalls of historical criticism. I am not going to suggest that the poem is a political allegory or that *Samson* is about Cromwell. Nor do I wish to imply, although Cromwell was a powerful influence and fascination for Milton, a merely empirical connection between Milton's political role and his poetry. I am not interested in primarily occasional material or autobiographical content, such as Parker's suggestion that the drama reflects Milton's political hope in the late 1640s for a providential leader. Rather, I wish to explore the broader issue of Puritan consciousness during the Civil War. I focus on Cromwell only because biographical records give us greater access to his inner life than that of less famous fighters for the Puritan cause. Through its central themes of vocation, discipline, and providence, *Samson Agonistes* dramatizes, first, the inside story of the Puritan revolution—the struggle raging inside the men who opposed the old order—and, second, the relationship between religious faith and historical action which was the essence of that revolution.

The title *Agonistes* directs us to a major theme of the work and of Puritan thought. Paul R. Sellin has indicated the dual connotations of the Greek word, on the one hand related to *hypokrites*, and the idea of acting or dissembling, on the other hand connected to *certator*, the idea of a champion, an athlete and the contest in which he is engaged.[3] Michael Krouse shows that the latter meaning can include both the champion of games, as runners and wrestlers, and of wars, soldiers.[4] Milton's Samson has all these associations and is described in strong verbs as one who "stood," "ran," "duelled" in great feats against his enemies. His name recalls the sun which appears in Psalm xix "as a bridegroom coming out of his chamber and rejoiceth as a strong man to run a race." Repeated references to Samson's deeds emphasize that he was a man of action. In sharp contrast to this reputation, therefore, is the Samson of the opening scene, feebly seeking a comfortable bank where "I am wont to sit, when any chance / Relieves me from my task" (4–5). Samson is seeking "ease," a word that reverberates throughout the play in counterpoint to the "deeds" that are recalled three times in his first speech. The Chorus indicates that the main sign of his changed state is his passive posture as he "lies at random . . . / With languish't head unpropt" (118–19).

Samson's physical lassitude has moral connotations he himself recognizes in accusing the Danites of inaction against the Philistines, preferring "bondage with ease" to "strenuous liberty" (271). The confrontations with Manoa and Dalila, as critics have pointed out, are, on one level, temptations to sloth.[5] Samson rejects Manoa's advice that he forget his guilty ruminations and allow himself to be ransomed to a life of idle comfort, and insists instead on shouldering responsibility

for his condition. Dalila represents the connection of sloth, moral lazi-
ness, and lust. Neglecting his divine tasks Samson became "Soft'n'd
with pleasure and voluptuous life" (534). Dalila admits that she sought
to deter him from his "perilous enterprises" by keeping him in her bed
"day and night" (804, 807); now she offers him a nursing home only
more voluptuous than Manoa's. Samson rejects both temptations, re-
fusing "to sit idle on the household hearth / . . . till length of years /
And sedentary numbness craze my limbs" (566, 570–71), preferring
to "drudge and earn my bread" (573).

However, the contrast of this "servile toil" (5) to his former
"work from Heav'n impos'd" (565) drives Samson toward despair and
the longing for total passivity, the final sleep of death: "My race of
glory run, and race of shame, / And I shall shortly be with them that
rest" (597–98). Samson's earlier life had been not only energetic but
purposeful. His acts achieved their greatness in relation to their divine
purpose. Milton emphasizes the Bible's portrayal of Samson as a person
"separate to God" (31) and goes beyond the Bible in interpreting all
of his actions as part of a providential plan. In this Milton is typically
Puritan. The marginal notes to the Geneva Bible accommodate any
dubious details to a pious interpretation.[6] For example, when Samson
prays "to avenge the Philistines for his eyes" (Judges xvi, 28), the notes
add, "According to my vocation which is to execute God's judgment
on the wicked." Milton similarly seeks to erase any suggestion of a personal vengeance, or impulsive or brutal violence, from his hero. Just
as an "intimate impulse" from God (and no mere sexual attraction)
leads him to marry the woman from Timna so that he "might begin
Israel's Deliverance" (225), so all the other circumstances of his life,
from his divinely predicted birth to his captivity and blindness, are
finally related to a heavenly design. The Chorus speaks of Samson as
one "such as thou hast solemnly elected, / With gifts and graces emi-
nently adorn'd / To some great work, thy glory" (678–80).

This idea of a divine task was crucial to Puritan theology, in which
God did not call only a few heroes to miraculous tasks, but set for each
person a specific life's task. All Christians were to be "saints." Milton
himself was obsessed with this idea of vocation, the idea that one's gifts
were accountable to God, as evidenced in Sonnet XIX where he speaks
of "that one Talent which is death to hide." In Catholicism the word
vocation has always had a more specific reference, to those monks and

nuns who are called to leave the world for the contemplative life of the monastery and convent. Catholicism traditionally divided the ethical life into precepts (moral laws which are binding upon us all) and counsels (special commitments to the perfections of poverty, chastity, and obedience for which the zealous few give up the world of ordinary work and marriage). According to Max Weber, Protestantism, by abolishing this distinction, introduced "the valuation of the fulfillment of duty in worldly affairs as the highest form which the moral activity of the individual could assume."[7] By way of illustration, Weber contrasts the climax of the *Divine Comedy* with Dante in rapt contemplation to the active stance of Adam and Eve at the conclusion of *Paradise Lost*: "The World was all before them, where to choose / Thir place of rest, and Providence thir guide" (XII, 646–47).

Puritan preachers emphasized the virtues of the active life and spoke for what Slingsley Bethell called "the industrous sort of folk." Thus Richard Rogers is seen by William Haller as an example of a Puritan divine who urged that faith is a spur to activity: "The saint has no reason to fear the world or run away from it. Rather he must go forth in it and do the will of God there. Rogers scorns the suggestion that if men live according to the godly rule they will neglect their necessary affairs " 'and so poverty grow upon the land.' "[8] On the other hand, sermons abounded with attacks upon the idle, a category which, according to William Perkins, included beggars, vagabonds, monks, friars, and gentlemen "who spend their days eating and drinking."[9] Perhaps the spirit of these beliefs is best captured in Cromwell's appeal for recruits to the Parliamentary army in 1643; for him it is "as if God should say 'Up and be doing, and I will help you and stand by you.' There is nothing to be feared but sin and sloth."[10]

This aspect of Puritanism, which has been explored by Weber as the work ethic, can be found in all the controversies of the day—from the poor laws, to the theatre, to the organization of the army. Christopher Hill shows how the ethos was fought out in the conflict over sabbatarianism. In a half century of struggle, the Puritans attacked the liturgical system of holy days (very numerous with the inclusion of the feasts of local saints, the twelve days of Christmas, and so on). These holidays with their accompanying festivities were viewed by the Puritans as an excuse for idleness, and they fought to limit the holy day to Sunday and, further, to enforce a discipline then. One preacher complains, "the multitude call Sunday their revelling day which is spent in bull-baitings, bear-baitings, dancing, drunkenness and whoredom. . . ."[11] Both Charles I and James I entered the fray, issuing the Books of Sports of 1618 and 1633 which made Sunday recreations mandatory.

This controversy echoes in Milton's elaboration of the festivities of the Philistines on their pagan holiday. The contempt he pours on "th' Idolatrous rout amidst thir wine" (443), with their "Gymnic artists, Wrestlers, Riders, Runners / Jugglers and Dancers, Antics, Mummers, Mimics" (1324–25), reminds one of the preachers' invectives against the unreformed holy days of Anglican England. Ironically, the Philistines' festival allows Samson to spend his true Sabbath before his God. In the contrast lies the conflict of two cultures. Although the Puritans sought to prohibit work on the Sabbath, Christopher Hill notes that "the Sabbath was not a day of leisure, on which it was lawful to waste time; it was a day for a different kind of labour, for wrestling with God."[12] This is exactly how the Chorus describes Samson: "This Idol's day hath been to thee no day of rest, / Laboring thy mind / More than the working day thy hands" (1297–99).

Here one must return to the connotations of *agon*, a concept that came to mean a spiritual as much as a physical struggle. Thus Aristotle would use the word which meant "gymnastic exercise" to describe "anguish of mind."[13] In Puritanism there is an integral relationship between introspection and the advocacy of the active life. *Samson Agonistes* explores the interior struggle by which the hero becomes capable of action. The problem for the Puritan, and for Samson, was doubt in his vocation, in his election, and sometimes, ultimately, in his God. Richard Rogers could urge the saints to get out into the world and be fearless of success, but his own diary records an inner fight against doubts about his service to God: "and neither could I go about that his preaching with such unsetlednes of hart, and yet not to goe about it, my sorrow was the more to be idle."[14] Rogers saw the chief dangers before the saint as fear, weakness, self-deception, overconfidence, irresolution, and the slackening of attention. These are the precise attitudes Samson must repudiate in Milton's drama. Hanford quotes, in relation to Samson, Croce's description of the aesthetic process: "By elaborating his impressions man frees himself from them. By objectifying them he removes them from him and makes himself their superior. Activity is the deliverer."[15] This statement corresponds closely to Haller's analysis of the function of the Puritan diary: "the Puritan preacher kept a diary not as a diversion, but as a tactical manoeuvre against the enemy within. He could get the better of nervous depression and discouragement by thus driving black moods into the forefront of consciousness."[16] In his confrontations with the Chorus, Manoa, Dalila, and Harapha, Samson confronts objectifications of his inner state. By confronting their stances of self-deception, sloth, and passivity Samson rejects these qualities in himself. Numerous critics have noted that the movement of the poem is towards overcoming doubt and despair and regaining the capacity for action. Kenneth Fell describes it as "the purification by suffering of Samson's soul so that he may become a fit instrument for God's purposes."[17] In the final irony of the poem Samson performs his greatest act upon the pretense of taking a *rest* against the pillars of the Philistines' theatre. His spiritual posture has changed from the man in the opening scene, looking for someone to lean upon, to the man who finally acts out of individual faith and courage when all those supports prove futile.

In this process Samson acts out the spiritual *gestalt* of a culture. Christopher Hill, William Haller, and Michael Walzer all describe a new ethos by which men tried to cope with the chaotic process of transition to a new urban and commercial society. Thus Hill sees Puritan values as "the indictment of one system of ideas and social relationships by another. Popery is suited to a static agricultural society which offers the mass of the population no possibility of becoming richer than their fellows and in which poverty is a holy state. Protestantism is suited to a competitive society in which thrift and accumulation and industry are the cardinal values."[18] Haller writes of the social chaos and moral corruption of "many a swollen town and decaying country neighborhood. . . . The preachers . . . were endeavoring to adapt Christian morality to the needs of a population which was steadily being driven from its feudal status into the untried conditions of competition between man and man in an increasingly commercial and industrial society under a money economy."[19] Similarly Walzer states that "the Puritan demand for continuous, organized, methodical activity to banish idleness, was a reaction to the breakdown of country stability" visible in such phenomena as men without work in the cities, vagabonds on country roads, alongside great houses filled with idle, merry men.[20] Walzer argues further that the ideas of vocation and

spiritual discipline enabled men to withstand the anxiety of living
in a period of change, so that it became possible for a group of men to
define new roles for themselves, thereby shedding the confining demands
of tradition and pushing the kings and bishops off the stage as they
themselves now became the agents of history. The bourgeois revolution
is not cynically called the "revolution of the saints," but, rather, it was
the new concept of sainthood that freed the bourgeoisie, enabling
them to make a revolution. As Walzer writes, "the saints were indeed
activists, and activists in a far more intense and driven fashion than
the men who came later: English gentlemen after their conversions
attended to Parliamentary affairs with a new assiduousness; pious
mothers trained their sons to a constant concern with political life;
enthusiastic apprentices took notes at sermons and studied the latest
religious and political pamphlets. The outcome of Puritan activity
was godly watchfulness, magistracy, and revolution."[21]

One cannot overemphasize the transformation of consciousness
that must have been required for men to turn against the old authorities of church and king. To turn against them with military force required moral as well as physical preparedness. Milton spent the middle
years of his life creating a body of prose designed to give legitimacy to
a struggle which abandoned all the old sources of legitimacy. He, as
other Puritans, returned to the Bible in order to justify a new movement that broke with centuries of tradition. In such a task Samson
became an exemplary figure—a type of the military hero of the Old
Testament who warred against his rulers "even though the greater part
of his countrymen refused not tyranny" (*Works* VI, 219). In the period
between 1649 and 1654, Milton defended the Puritan cause against
men who saw Cromwell's army as an opponent, not only of king and
bishops, but of God and country. He wrote not only to silence European
critics and prevent counterrevolutionary aid from the Continent, but
also to encourage his hesitant and doubtful countrymen to continue
in the task they had begun. Whereas any military leader requires confidence, revolutionaries need also to be certain of the rightness of their
cause. Milton noted this as the crucial factor for military success in his
Commonplace Book: "The cause of valour is a good conscience, for an
evil conscience, as an English author noteth well, will otherwise gnaw
at the roots of valour like a worm and undermine all resolutions"
(*Works* XVIII, 135).

The presentation of Samson as a saint with a military and revolutionary vocation takes on enormous significance in this light. It is not necessary to dismiss all the criticism focused upon him as a hero of faith, but only to recognize the connection between that faith and military action. From the very first we are presented with Samson's military history. Manoa describes him as one "who single combatant / Duell'd thir Armies rank't in proud array / Himself an Army" (344–46). In fact, military imagery was a language in which the Puritans spoke about the spiritual life, and an important relationship exists between this symbolism, *Samson Agonistes,* and the actual civil war raging in England.

St. Paul, when he spoke of his own spiritual life, said he had fought the good fight of faith. For the Puritan imagination, the life of the spirit was often seen as a battle. Thus we find such sermons as William Gouge's "The Whole Armour of God," John Downame's "The Christian Warfare," Richard Bernard's "Bible Battells," and many others.[22] Bernard concludes from the Bible that "God is pleased to be called a man of war."[23] In general the sermons elaborate a metaphoric battle between God and Satan that is fought out continuously on the battlefield of the individual Christian soul, but also in the social world that "is a great field of God in which Michael and his angels fight the dragon and his angels."[24] On one level the battle, as in Samson, is against temptation: "For the time of our life being a time of war, a time wherein our spiritual enemies (who are many, mighty, sedulous, and subtile) put forth their strength and bestirre themselves to the utmost. . . . Seeking whom to devour, what can be more behoofull than to discover their cunning strategems and wyles, to declare wherein their strength lieth, to furnish Christ's soldiers with compleat armour and sufficient defence."[25] Samson uses the same kind of military imagery in describing his own submission to temptation: "Gave up my fort of silence to a Woman" (236). Such military metaphors add a sense of urgency to the themes we have already noted—the repudiation of ease and the emphasis on disciplined activity—since the satanic enemy was ready to take advantage of any slackness. Thus John Downame compares Christian souls to soldiers going forth to battle and warns against listening to the siren music of the world, lest they awake as Samson, strengthless out of the lap of Dalila.[26]

These advocates of spiritual warfare often went on to argue that since Satan had his troops in the world the Christian was obliged to engage in actual battle as well. Bernard's "Bible Battells," according to Michael Walzer, was one of many such sermons in the 1620s that created a kind of Christian jingoist movement to urge Englishmen to get involved in the religious wars on the Continent. Bernard, like Milton later, is aware that a religious justification of war will aid morale, and, thus, success, "for there is nothing more for encouragement in any action than to have conscience satisfied in the lawfulness thereof."[27] Bernard, like Milton, turns for precedents to the heroes of the Old Testament, such as Jeptha, Gideon, and Samson, whom he describes as soldiers fighting "the Lord's Battells."

This sermon literature not only legitimized a struggle against traditional, usually Catholic, authorities, but itself represented a break with the traditional view of war. The mainstream of medieval tradition revolved around the concept of the "just war." These churchmen saw war as one result of the fall whose effects had to be mitigated by Christian morality. They sought to limit the purposes of war and the means that might be employed, thereby hoping to civilize warfare with rules that prohibited such abuses as war for the purpose of conquest, the slaughter of populations. War could legitimately be fought only for defensive purposes, to preserve life, property, and legal order. There was, however, a tradition which preceded that of the scholastics. The Crusades were also rationalized as a defense of the Christians' right of access to the Holy Land, but were commonly viewed as an offensive battle against the pagans for the glory of God. The Puritans returned to the Old Testament tradition of such holy wars, and Samson is rooted firmly in this tradition. Samson never, for all his self-examination, doubts the divine nature of his battles on behalf of Israel. He is the one "Whom God hath of his special favor rais'd / As thir Deliverer" (273–74). Milton's version, like that of the Geneva Bible, eliminates any suggestion that Samson's violent acts reflect only a personal vengeance.

Milton underlines the providential nature of Samson's actions by constantly reminding the reader that his power to overcome the Philistines is always directly provided by God. The symbol of this dependence is the fact that Samson fought unarmed.

> Irresistible *Samson*, whom unarm'd
> No strength of man, or fiercest wild beast could withstand;
> Who tore the Lion, as the Lion tears the kid,

Ran on embattled Armies clad in Iron,
And weaponless himself,
Made arms ridiculous, useless the forgery
Of brazen shield and spear, the hammer'd cuirass
Chalybean temper'd steel, and frock of mail
Adamantean proof;
But safest he who stood aloof,
When insupportably his foot advanc't,
In scorn of their proud arms and warlike tools.   (126–37)

Milton repeats the denigration of arms five times in this passage, and then shows Samson defeating the Philistines "with what trivial weapon came to hand, / The Jaw of a dead Ass" (142–43). The fortuitousness of this weapon and its miraculous properties point to its divine provider. In the sermons the Christian preachers argued similarly that the Christian should be armed with virtue and grace. Thus, in "The Whole Armour of God," William Gouge quotes from Saint Paul, Ephesians vi: "Take unto you the whole armor of God that ye may be able to withstand in the evil day. . . . Stand therefore, having your loins girt about with truth and having on the breastplate of righteousness. . . . Above all, taking the shield of faith wherewith ye shall be able to quench all the fiery darts of the wicked. And take the helmet of salvation and the sword of the Spirit which is the word of God."

The function of this comparison of Christian spiritual with actual military armor is not a simple denunciation of war and its instruments, but rather a dialectical distinction between wars of pure force and wars of spiritual intent and inspiration. The condemnation of arms, ironically, becomes a defense of holy wars. This, I think, is what happens in Book VI of *Paradise Lost.* Direct scorn is poured upon Satan's reliance on artillery. After the first day's unsuccessful battle Satan's analysis is that his troops were defeated because "too unequal work we find / Against unequal arms to fight in pain" (VI, 453–54), and he prescribes "the remedy; perhaps more valid arms / Weapons more violent" (*PL* VI, 438–39). This reliance purely on physical force leads to the demonic cannon and the final absurdity of bodiless creatures hurling mountains at each other. I agree with Arnold Stein that this incongruity is intentional and satirizes Satan's attempt to "possess the power of spirit by means of matter."[28] However, Stella Revard's argument that the entire book is a repudiation of heroic warfare must be qualified by the assertion that it is simultaneously a defense of another kind of warfare, equally military, but spiritually motivated.[29]

Throughout the battle in Heaven Milton emphasizes that power ultimately resides in God, who can halt the fighting upon his will, which he does on the third day when "War wearied hath perform'd what War can do" (VI, 695). The faithful angels, however, have been as involved in the battle as the rebels and are described in military formation, armed with conscience: "th' inviolable Saints / In Cubic Phalanx firm advanc'd entire, / Invulnerable, impenetrably arm'd: / Such high advantages thir innocence / Gave them" (VI, 398–402). Indeed, the battle in Heaven was a primary metaphor in the sermons justifying holy war, and Milton's "armed saints" lead us not into an idealist pacifism but back into seventeenth-century England where Puritan preachers used the battle of God and Satan to urge the "saints" to arm themselves against the demonic royalist armies. The "Powers Militant" in Heaven mirrored the "Church Militant" on earth as they marched "Under thir God-like Leaders, in the Cause / Of God and His Messiah" (VI, 68–69).

This welding of military action and religious ideology took place concretely in England with the formation of the New Model Army. The army was itself a religious body, organized in many cases into congregations. Thus Richard Baxter records that Cromwell, "when he lay at Cambridge . . . with that famous troop which he began his army with, his officers proposed to make their troop a gathered Church and they all subscribed an invitation to me to be their Pastor."[30] Baxter refused, but became one of many chaplains traveling along with the troops, preaching the Gospel. In 1643 a *Souldier's Pocket Bible* was published to guide the fighting men in every vicissitude of warfare with examples of the saintly heroes of the Old Testament.

The influence of religion upon the New Model Army went far beyond incidental pieties and created a new kind of military recruitment and discipline. Under the Tudors and Stuarts the troops were more an armed mob than an army—untrained, ill-armed, and unwilling to fight.[31] The army was organized locally by nobles who could press their dependents into personal service. "In England," wrote Barnaby Rich in 1587, "when service happeneth we disburthen the prison of thieves, we rob the taverns and alehouses of tosspots and ruffians, we scour both town and country of rogues and vagabonds."[32] Since men of substance could buy their way out of service, John Falstaff's band was not really an inaccurate representation of the state of the English army.

Military leadership in this army was based entirely on social rank, deriving from those times when each noble had his own troops and the lords battled chiefly among themselves. As the nation replaced the feudal barony as the unit of government, the military role of the nobility became more customary than real, and military training became a mere aristocratic sport. Cromwell abolished these aristocratic forms when he had Parliament pass the Self-Denying Ordinance, which deprived all lords, himself excepted, of their military offices. Cromwell then reorganized his army around a new kind of soldier. "You must get me men of a spirit," he told an officer, "or else I am sure you will be beaten still. . . . I raised such men as had the fear of God before them and made some conscience of what they did."[33] Cromwell defends his replacement of "men of honour and birth" with "men patient of wants, faithful and conscientious in their employment. . . ."[34] Such men were likely to be imbued with the Puritan sense of vocation and disciplined in their style of life. Commitment to the cause replaced status as Cromwell's criterion: "I had rather have a plain russet-coated captain that knows what he fights for and loves what he knows, than that which you call a gentleman and is nothing else. . . ."[35] Cromwell's officers were, therefore, drawn from men who had voluntarily served in the religious wars on the Continent and who, as the Civil War approached, trained in the Voluntary Artilleries that formed in London. They included many Fifth Monarchy men, like Major Thomas Harrison, who believed they were fighting, not merely for Parliament, but to establish the reign of King Jesus. They were men recruited by the sermons on Christian warfare. Thus Simeon Ashe told the London commanders in 1642, "If the Lord please to beat up the drum; if the Lord bid them arm and come aboard, his call is sufficient."[36] Soldiers recruited by ministers to military life as a religious calling created a different army than that of affluent local nobles commandeering their servants and renters. The religious zeal of these troops went so far as to frighten Parliament, as they marched across the countryside taking over pulpits, and practiced in their military congregations a democracy far more radical than that espoused by the good Presbyterians in the assembly. A ban against preaching by soldiers was issued, then rescinded under pressure from the army. Presumably, the organization of religious and political life in the army

The Anthony Wayne Library
The Defiance College

could become a model for all England. Milton himself came to the defense of the army in his *Second Defence of the People of England*:

Those who do not calumniate our army, acknowledge it to be not only the bravest of armies but the most modest and religious. Other camps are usually distinguished for drunkenness, . . . for rapine, gaming, swearing, and perjury: in ours, the leisure which is allowed is spent in the pursuit of truth, in diligent attention to the holy scripture; nor is there anyone who thinks it more honorable to smite the foe, than to instruct himself in the knowledge of heavenly things—more honorable to engage in warfare of arms, than in the warfare of the Spirit. (*Works* VIII, 179)

Honor, in a word, summed up the military code of the old nobility who fought because it was their customary role to preserve and justify their otherwise dubious social function. Thus, when we hear Harapha telling Samson about Harapha's "honor" (1166), we can expect a confrontation of two different kinds of soldiers from two opposing cultures. The Harapha incident is Milton's addition to the biblical story. In contrasting Samson to such a soldier, Milton underscores the values of spiritual warfare in the play. Harapha identifies himself as a feudal soldier in several ways. He immediately refers to his birth "of stock renown'd" (1079) and continually refers to his "honor" won by mortal duel. He expresses his preference for courtly combat as a mere athletic test of strength "in camp or listed field" (1087). Finally, he repeatedly asserts his rank which, he claims, makes him disdain combat with Samson "no worthy match / For valor to assail, nor by the sword / Of noble Warrior so to stain his honor" (1164–66). Harapha regards combat as a feudal duel in which men fight for completely private ends in personal quarrels over prestige. In his study of Harapha in relation to Renaissance comedy, Daniel Boughner summarizes this code: "The distinguishing mark of the gentleman was honor. The purpose of the duel was to prove that someone had lost his honor. Society fell into two classes, those incapable and capable of honor; in the latter class were men of noble rank, gentlemen and soldiers."[37]

Michael Walzer shows how, under this code, Renaissance warfare degenerated into a farce with soldiers less involved "in actual fighting than in soldierly pageants and the rich ornamentation of weaponry."[38] The aim of courtly warfare became the gracious evasion of contact, an art that Harapha practices rather clumsily. Since the Cavalier is distinguished by courtly ornament, Samson's contempt for Harapha's chivalric equipment expresses his contempt for that way of life.

> Then put on all thy gorgeous arms, thy Helmet
> And Brigandine of brass, thy broad Habergeon,
> Vant brace and Greaves, and Gauntlet and thy Spear
> A Weaver's beam, and seven-times-folded shield,
> I only with an Oak'n staff will meet thee.   (1119–23)

During this confrontation Samson recovers faith in his own ability to fight and dares Harapha three times. He affirms that this renewal of strength is a spiritual effect: "My trust is in the living God" (1140). Samson is completely serious while Harapha is bragging and hypocritical; the Hebrew soldier's fight involves no mere proving of his own reputation, but the realization of the vocation that is his life's meaning, service to Israel's God. Thus he interprets the conflict "By combat to decide whose god is God" (1176). If we read this as the confrontation of a Puritan and a royalist soldier, there is some truth in Milton's insinuation that the combat is decided, not by force, but by conviction. Firth argues that Charles was able to put as large an army into the field as Parliament, but it was a different kind of army. The advantage of the Puritans was that they were "fairly drilled, fairly disciplined and eager to fight."[39]

The eagerness Samson shows here refers back to the relationship of faith and action, a relationship central to the poem. This appears not only in the military significance of the idea of vocation, but also in the related value of discipline that is explored in Samson's encounter with Dalila. The Chorus tells him early in the play that it was self-discipline that saved him from the typical soldier's downfall: "Desire of wine and delicious drinks, / Which many a famous Warrior overturns, / Thou couldst repress" (541–543). The military sagacity of the Chorus is confirmed by a Colonel Ward who wrote in Milton's day that the chief thing the traditional troops were trained to do was to drink.[40] Yet, Samson's own catastrophe comes finally through a breach of discipline as he remonstrates "what avail'd this temperance, not complete?" (558). His repudiation of Dalila is a rejection of a life "soft'n'd with pleasure" for manly valor.

Such discipline was the quality of military life praised by the Puritans as most conducive to the life of the spirit. Richard Sibbes wrote,

"The people of God are beautiful, for order is beautiful. . . . An army is a beautiful thing because of the order and well disposed ranks that are within it."[41] One quality distinguishing the good angels in *Paradise Lost* is their discipline.

> At which command the Powers Militant,
> That stood for Heav'n, in mighty Quadrate join'd
> Of Union irresistible, mov'd on
> In silence thir bright Legions.
>
>   .   .   .   .
>
>   On they move
> Indissolubly firm; nor obvious Hill,
> Nor straitening Vale, nor Wood, nor Stream divides
> Thir perfect ranks.   (VI, 61–71)

Milton had also drawn the analogy between military and moral discipline in *The Reason of Church-Government*, where he attributes to discipline "those perfect armies of Cyrus in Xenophon" and proceeds to praise discipline as "the very shape and image of virtue" (*Works*, III, 185). John Davenport in *A Royal Edict For Military Exercises* recommends military drill as a religious exercise and a substitute for idle pleasures.[42] Military discipline, the preachers argued, would enhance spiritual preparedness, and to be unprepared for war was to tempt God.[43] Here we find the same dialectic between ideas and practical necessities that emerged in the sabbatarian issue and in the ironic repudiation of armor in the process of creating a defense for war. Military discipline is not only evoked as an image of the spiritual life, but advocated as a practice of virtue ultimately serving the practical purpose of uniting and rendering effective the New Model Army. Thus, Thomas Palmer, a minister, could admit pragmatically that it was no longer numbers or weaponry, but "experimented order" that won battles.[44]

Few Puritans made so mundane a connection between the piety and the victories of the troops. Usually the successes of the New Model Army were seen as the direct intervention of Providence to reward the just and punish the unrighteous. This idea of a divinely inspired military vocation, which pervades Milton's treatment of Samson, emerges clearly in the career of Oliver Cromwell. Cromwell and many others in the New Model Army saw themselves as men directly chosen by God to fight His battles; and their victories were continuously attributed to the direct intervention of God. Thus, Cromwell writes of Naseby:

"I can say this of Naseby, that when I saw the enemy draw up and march in gallant order towards us, and we a company of poor ignorant men, to seek how to order our battle . . . I could not (riding alone about my business) but smile out to God in praises, in assurance of victory, because God would, by things that are not, bring to naught things that are. Of which I had great assurance and God did it."[45] Robert Paul, in his biography of Cromwell, regards this statement as an indication that Cromwell is beginning to see his military successes as a sign of divine approval for his Independent political policies. A myth grew up around Cromwell's victories, sanctifying his political actions, a myth of which Milton was a prime creator. In the *Second Defence* Milton presents Cromwell as a direct agent of the Almighty: "For while you O Cromwell are left among us, he hardly shows a proper confidence in the Supreme who distrusts the security of England, when he sees that you are in so special a manner the favored object of divine regard" *(Works* VIII, 219). The resemblance between this and Milton's portrayal of Samson as "a person separate to God, / Design'd for great exploits" (1331–32) is obvious and significant.

If we view Samson, not only as a universal Christian hero, but also and more immediately as the hero of the Puritan revolution that conjoined religious values with a military goal, we must show that the substance of the play, and not just incidentals, are related to the essential problems of the revolution. The theme of *Samson*, as many critics agree, is his inner struggle to recover the ability to serve as a divine instrument. Now we must note that not only the idea of Providence, but just such a struggle is crucial to the lives of the Puritan revolutionaries. We have already examined the relationship between introspection and action. This becomes crucial when the idea of Providence is applied in political affairs, for the doctrine creates a dilemma. If military successes are signs of the justice of one's cause, failures threaten one with paralyzing doubt.

The problem of making and justifying decisions in relation to Providence can be seen in a quality of Cromwell's noted by various biographers. Robert Paul remarks that "one of the most striking things about his career . . . is that in times of tension and crisis there were curious periods of inactivity preceding every big decision that he made."[46] Christopher Hill states that "Oliver curiously combines hesitation . . . with sudden violent action."[47] Such examples are given as the time of Pride's Purge when Cromwell inexplicably remained un-involved, delaying his stay at Pontrefact and claiming afterwards to have been unaware of the plan but glad that it was done. Or his delay-ing, to the exasperation of his officers in the winter of 1652–1653, then suddenly dissolving the Long Parliament in a fit of anger. And again in 1657, hesitating to reject the kingship, then again exploding and dissolving the House of Commons.

Hill agrees with Paul that "there is no apparent explanation for such lacunae in his affairs but the one he himself gave, that he was waiting on God, i.e., waiting for God's hand to show itself in events, to guide him into his next step."[48] Thus, in 1648, faced with the task of bringing the king to trial, Cromwell could write, "We in this north-ern army were in a waiting posture, desiring to see what the Lord would lead us to."[49] This waiting was, however, an active posture, as shown in a dispatch of 1645. Attributing a recent victory to "the prayers of the people of God with you and all England over who have waited on God for a blessing," he took up his pen, crossed out "waited on" and wrote "wrestled with."[50] In this active interior struggle Crom-well "agonistes" stands in sharp contrast to Charles I, who, as his end neared, also turned to Providence, but with resigned passivity: "We know not, but this may be the last time we speak to you . . . publicly: we are sensible into what hands we are fallen; and yet, we bless God, we have those inward refreshments the malice of our enemies cannot per-turb. We have learned to busy ourself in retiring into ourself . . . ; not doubting but that God's providence will restrain our enemies power."[51] Here, as these two men approach their confrontation, the contrast is striking. Charles sees his role as part of an unchangeable order created and maintained by God; Cromwell sees himself volun-tarily responding to a calling to act aggressively in the world, to trans-form history that it might become holy. Charles had only to accept his role and be king; Cromwell had to prove his leadership by forging victories. And, he had asserted, "there is nothing to be feared but our own sin and sloth."

The contrast between these attitudes provides the sharpest irony in *Samson Agonistes*, the interplay between Samson's and the Chorus' view of Providence. The Chorus says, "Just are the ways of God / And justifiable to men" (294), but proceeds to treat Providence as the arbi-trary will of God, completely independent of human action: "For with his own Laws he can best dispense" (314). The Chorus and Manoa suggest that God had ordained Samson's fall; Samson insists that the responsibility lies in his own sin: "Appoint not heavenly disposition, Father, / Nothing of all these evils hath befall'n me / But justly; I myself have brought them on" (373–75). And Samson's sin, he discovers, was his failure to be true to his divine task. By the end of the play Samson has demonstrated his religious faith by a courageous act; he has conquered the leaders of the Philistines. Now is the time for the Danites to rise up and follow him to their liberation. Earlier Samson accused *"Israel's* Governors, and Heads of Tribes" of failure to act (242), preferring "Bondage with ease" to "strenuous liberty" (271). If they were awaiting a sign, what could be clearer than the event at the Philistine theatre, but the Chorus, rather than responding to Providence, stands around praising it: "All is best, though we oft doubt" vies in its complacency and acquiescence in the status quo with Pope's "Whatever is, is Right" and Browning's "God's in His heaven; all's right with the world."

Samson's political action comes only after an active interior strug-gle with doubts about his role as an instrument of Providence. We return to the dilemma inherent in the idea of Providence and under-lying both Cromwell's hesitation and Samson's inner drama. For if victories vindicate one's divine role, failures undermine faith in one's activity. Cromwell, despite his military victories, faced political setbacks that threw him into the same doubt and paralysis that Samson exhibits at the opening of the drama. If their common faith could at one time unite the New Model Army in "a Cubic Phalanx" behind Cromwell as divine standard-bearer, later he faced a dispute among the godly sol-diers themselves about which side God was on. In 1647 there were de-bates in the army over what form the government of the Commonwealth should take. Cromwell was attacked by the Levellers for restricting democracy, collaborating with the Presbyterians, and hesitating to deal with Charles. The attack came from some of the most religious officers, who questioned whether their commander was still listening correctly to the voice of God. Thus Edward Sexby argued, "We have been by Providence put upon strange things. . . . The Army acting to these ends, Providence hath been with us, and yet we have found little fruit for our endeavors. You are convinced that God will have you act on," he continued, challenging Cromwell to reconcile his sense of divine support with his failures in handling the conservative Parliament which threatened to rescind the gains of the revolution.[52] One Lieutenant Goffe went so far as to suggest that Cromwell had fallen out of divine favor and should resign: "I hope our strayings from God are not so great but that conversion and true humiliation might recover us again; and I desire that we may be serious in this and not despise any other instruments that God will use."[53] The problem with basing politics on Providence is that there is no preventing "other instruments" from asserting themselves. In the army's disputes both sides claimed divine support for their political goals. As Cromwell moved further away from the early democracy of the army towards dictatorship he was accused by such Fifth Monarchy men as Major Thomas Harrison of having abandoned God's cause for Satan's. And his theology demanded that Cromwell take such accusations seriously. Thus, after the army debates, he alternately imprisoned his opponents and sought their forgiveness. In 1649 he sided with the radicals to execute the king and approached them in a repentant mood, acknowledging "that the Glories of the World had so dazzled his eyes that he could not discern clearly the great works the Lord was doing."[54]

Just as the idea of Providence gave men the courage to succeed, the discipline of repentance enabled them to recover, after failure, their ability to act again. The spiritual agon of hesitation and doubt in a man so apparently confident as Cromwell was repeated in the lives of his contemporaries as they fashioned totally unprecedented careers. A leading genre of popular literature at the time was the spiritual biography of some pious man's lifelong fight to retain faith in his vocation, written both to edify others and to render praise to God for worldly success.[55] *Samson Agonistes* is a great literary transformation of this genre. The close parallel between its themes and those common to the preachers, the radical soldiers and Cromwell himself is neither circumstantial nor intentional, but historically somewhat inevitable.

In summary, the Puritan emphases on the active life, the idea of vocation, the virtue of discipline, the idea of Providence—accents preserved in *Samson*—are not just religious ideas; they are ideological and psychological weapons in the hands of men who are transforming English society. Specifically, they become, in the metaphor and vocation of holy war, a justification of the use of violence to create the new social order. These ideas inspired a new breed of men, who were stepping onto the stage of history and who needed a justification of conscience in pushing off the kings, lords, and bishops. *Samson Agonistes* cannot be viewed only as religious drama, because religion itself had become part of a battle for power over the direction of history: "This was the effect of Puritanism: it made revolution available to the minds of seventeenth century Englishmen. . . . It trained them to think of the struggle with Satan and his allies as an extension and duplicate of their internal spiritual conflicts, and also as a difficult and continuous war, requiring methodical, organized activity, military exercise and discipline. These ideas were underlying themes of the new politics; permanent warfare was the central myth of Puritan radicalism. . . . Here moral confusion and social strain were turned into systematic enmity and this, in a sense, was the 'secret history' of the English revolution."[56]

Literature reveals to us the interior of history. In it we see the changes in ideas, feelings, and modes of consciousness that accompany alterations in social forms. All so-called objective historians to the contrary, history is made by men who in the process must remake themselves. Milton is the most engaged of English writers, and we should expect to find his poetry, as well as his prose, reflecting the cause to which he had committed himself. *Samson* is not just a drama that reflects the spiritual and military struggle going on in England; it is part of that war. To understand how Milton saw himself participating in the battle, we can turn to his use of military imagery throughout his prose. Critics, like Theodore Banks in *Milton's Imagery* (New York, 1950), have noted that Milton's knowledge of the art of war supplies him with a whole language of discourse. In fact, the extent of his military knowledge leads James Holly Hanford to debate whether Milton was ever actually a soldier.[57] An entire battle can be reconstructed from his scattered metaphors, from the clarion call to the negotiation of peace. What emerges from his use of these metaphors is that Milton saw himself as a soldier, but a different kind of soldier, fighting battles in the "wars of truth" he spoke of in *Areopagitica*. Thus he describes his task in the *First Defence* as one of "defending [the army's] deeds from envy and calumny against which steel and furniture of war avail not—of defending I say, with far other arms and other weapons the works which under God's guidance they had gloriously wrought" (*Works* VII, 7). In the *Second Defence* Milton defends his choice of an intellectual rather than a military vocation: "For though I did not participate in the toils or dangers of the war, yet I was at the same time engaged in a service not less hazardous to myself and more beneficial to my fellow citizens. . . . For since from my youth I was devoted to the pursuits of literature and my mind had always been stronger than my body, I did not court the labors of the camp . . . that the truth which had been defended by arms, should also be defended by reason" (*Works* VIII, 11).

Milton was most thoroughly engaged in this intellectual battle in the late forties and early fifties, the period of *The Tenure of Kings and Magistrates, Eikonoclastes,* the first and second defence of the English people. In his revised dating of *Samson Agonistes,* William Riley Parker argues that it was written in this period.[58] If he is correct, this would give added force to the parallels I have drawn between the themes of the poem and the ideology of the New Model Army. The poet and political writer would become one and the poem would take on a polemical significance. Milton could be seen as writing to give to those already engaged the good conscience he thought so necessary to a successful revolution, and to those faltering the stirring example of *Samson,* fighter for God and liberty—an example which, though the people of Israel did not follow, the people of England might.

Livingston College, Rutgers: The State University

NOTES

1. Quotations from Milton's prose are from *The Works of John Milton,* ed. Frank Allen Patterson et al. (New York, 1931–1940); references are to volume and page number. Quotations from Milton's poetry are from *John Milton: Complete Poetry and Major Prose,* ed. Merritt Y. Hughes (New York, 1957); references are to line numbers.

2. Michael Krouse, *Milton's Samson and the Christian Tradition* (Princeton, 1949), p. 108.

3. Paul Sellin, "Milton's Epithet Agonistes," *SEL,* IV (1964), 137–62.

4. Krouse, *Milton's Samson.*

5. Don Cameron Allen, "The Idea as Pattern: Despair and *Samson Agonistes,*" *The Harmonious Vision: Studies in Milton's Poetry* (Baltimore, 1954).

6. Arnold Stein, "Dalila," *Heroic Knowledge: An Interpretation of "Paradise Regained" and "Samson Agonistes"* (Minneapolis, 1957).

7. Max Weber, *The Protestant Ethic and the Spirit of Capitalism* (New York, 1958), p. 80.

8. Slingsley Bethell is quoted by Christopher Hill, *Society and Puritanism in Pre-Revolutionary England* (New York, 1964), p. 133. Richard Rogers, *Seven*

Treatises (London, 1603), p. 577, is quoted in William Haller, *The Rise of Puritanism* (New York, 1938), p. 123.

9. William Perkins, *Works* (London, 1616), I, 755–56.

10. *The Writings and Speeches of Oliver Cromwell*, ed. W. C. Abbott (Cambridge, Mass., 1937–1947), I, 245, hereafter cited as *Cromwell*.

11. *The Lancashire Lieutenancy Under the Tudors and Stuarts*, ed. John Harland (Manchester, 1859), II, 218.

12. Christopher Hill, *Society and Puritanism*, p. 184.

13. Krouse, *Milton's Samson*, p. 11.

14. *Two Elizabethan Puritan Diaries*, ed. M. M. Knappen (Chicago, 1933), pp. 78–80.

15. James Holly Hanford, *John Milton, Poet and Humanist* (Cleveland, 1967), p. 277.

16. Haller, *The Rise of Puritanism*, p. 41.

17. Kenneth Fell, "From Myth to Martyrdom: Toward a Vision of *Samson Agonistes*," *English Studies*, XXXLV (1953), 145–55.

18. Hill, *Society and Puritanism*, p. 132.

19. Haller, *The Rise of Puritanism*, pp. 116–17.

20. Michael Walzer, *The Revolution of the Saints: A Study in the Origin of Radical Politics* (New York, 1968), p. 209.

21. Ibid., p. 308.

22. For example, William Perkins, "The Combate Between Christ and the Devil"; Thomas Adams, "The Soldier's Honor"; Thomas Sutton, "The Good Fight of Faith"; Andrew Leighton, "Looking Glass of the Holy War." A remnant of this consciousness remains, of course, in the most common Protestant hymn, "Onward, Christian Soldiers."

23. Richard Bernard, *The Bible Battells or the Sacred Art Military for the Rightly Waging of War According to the Holy Writ* (London, 1629), p. 25.

24. Thomas Taylor, *Christe's Combate and Conquest* (London, 1618), p. 8.

25. William Gouge, *The Whole Armour of God* (London, 1622).

26. John Downame, *Christian Warfare* (London, 1609), pp. 34–35.

27. Bernard, *Bible Battells*, p. 25.

28. Arnold Stein, *Answerable Style: Essays on "Paradise Lost"* (Minneapolis, 1953), p. 36.

29. Stella Revard, "Milton's Critique of Heroic Warfare in *Paradise Lost* V and VI," *Studies in English Literature*, IX (1967), 119–39.

30. Richard Baxter, *Reliquiae Baxterianae* (London, 1969), p. 51.

31. Charles Firth, *Cromwell's Army* (London, 1902), p. 14.

32. Ibid., p. 3.

33. *Cromwell*, IV, 471.

34. *Cromwell*, I, 261.

35. *Cromwell*, I, 256.

36. Simeon Ashe, *Good Courage Discovered and Encouraged* (London, 1642), pp. 6–7.

37. Daniel Boughner, "Milton's Harapha and Renaissance Comedy," *ELH*, XI (1944), 298.

38. Walzer, *The Revolution of the Saints*, p. 272.

39. Firth, *Cromwell's Army*, p. 14.

40. Quoted in ibid., p. 9, from Col. Ward, *Animadversions of War* (London, 1639), p. 30.

41. Richard Sibbes, *Complete Works*, ed. Alexander B. Grosart (Edinburgh, 1863), II, 232.

42. Davenport is quoted by Walzer, *The Revolution of the Saints*, p. 288.

43. Sibbes, *Complete Works*, II, 282.

44. Thomas Palmer, *Bristol's Military Garden* (London, 1639), pp. 26–27.

45. *Cromwell*, I, 364–66.

46. Robert Paul, *The Lord Protector; Religion and Politics in the Life of Oliver Cromwell* (London, 1955), p. 177.

47. Christopher Hill, *Oliver Cromwell* (London, 1958), p. 25.

48. Paul, *The Lord Protector*, p. 177.

49. *Cromwell*, I, 669–70.

50. *Cromwell*, I, 377.

51. Quoted in Paul, *The Lord Protector*, p. 179, from Earl of Clarendon, *History of the Rebellion and Civil Wars in England* (Oxford, 1849), XI, 191.

52. A. S. P. Woodhouse, ed., *Puritanism and Liberty: Being the Army Debates from the Clarke Manuscripts* (Chicago, 1958), pp. 1–2.

53. Putney Debates in Woodhouse, *Puritanism and Liberty*, pp. 19–21.

54. Quoted in Paul, *The Lord Protector*, p. 180, from Sir John Berkeley, *Memoirs* (London, 1699), p. 70.

55. Haller, *The Rise of Puritanism*, pp. 94 ff.

56. Walzer, *The Revolution of the Saints*, p. 290.

57. Hanford, *John Milton, Poet and Humanist*.

58. William Riley Parker, "The Date of *Samson Agonistes*," *PQ*, XXVIII (1949), 145–66.

MILTON'S GUNPOWDER POEMS
AND SATAN'S CONSPIRACY

Stella P. Revard

The gunpowder sermons, preached in annual celebration of the discovery of Guy Fawkes's plot (1605), were powerful influences on the young Milton's treatment of this conspiracy in his Latin epigrams and *In Quintum Novembris*. The sermons also influenced the mature Milton's depiction of Satan's conspiracy in *Paradise Lost*. The influence of the gunpowder sermons is apparent in the many striking resemblances between them and Milton's work, early and late. The preachers and Milton alike regard Satan as the archetypal conspirator, who invented gunpower as a weapon to rival God's thunderbolt. They are alike in dramatically characterizing God as the unmoved deity, who easily defeats the most subtle of intrigues. For example, both the preachers and Milton are indebted to Psalm ii, the spectacle of God laughing at his enemies. Finally, the particular ironic contempt which Milton affects toward the rebel angels in *Paradise Lost* may be traced to the irony employed by the sermonists to mock the pretentious futility of the gunpowder plotters. The gunpowder sermons, then, bring into sharp relief some political contours of *Paradise Lost*.

MILTON'S GUNPOWDER epigrams and his brief epic on the gunpowder conspiracy, written in Latin while he was a student at Cambridge, are usually dismissed as juvenile poems on a then popular subject.[1] The irony of the epigrams is considered heavy-handed, and the figure of Satan in *In Quintum Novembris* is hardly more than an exercise in the traditional portrayal of the devil. Yet, Milton's poems on the gunpowder conspiracy ought to be examined more carefully, for they reveal how the young poet viewed contemporary attitudes toward political intrigue and presage more mature views in his later work. The conspiracy itself continued to be a live issue throughout the seventeenth

century, celebrated not only by preachers and laymen alike yearly on
November fifth, but also called to mind whenever any crisis in politics
and religion warranted comparison. The Popish plot of Dryden's time,
for example, was almost immediately linked with the plot of 1605 as
another instance when the devil was at work, and the documents concerning the trial and arraignment of the conspirators were reprinted
and recirculated at that time.[2] Milton as a seventeenth-century English-
man must have shared in November fifth as a religious and secular
festival and have known the considerable body of sermon literature on
the subject. Moreover, it is likely that he shared as well the opinion of
his countrymen that the gunpowder conspiracy was the most shocking
and nefarious attempt that the devil had advanced in their time. Readers of *Paradise Lost* will do well to remember that Satan's schemes in
Book V begin in conspiratorial secret and that in Book VI his most
potent weapon is to be gunpowder, invented to surprise and overwhelm
the Almighty and his angels by its unexpected introduction. It is useful
then to examine *Paradise Lost* and its conspiracy in the light of the
November fifth sermons and Milton's own early poems.

The gunpowder sermons were in their way sensational tracts; the
preachers dramatized the shocking elements of the plot itself to move
their hearers and readers. They were concerned to show that it was
Satan who was the first conspirator, he who inspired the others with
his ugly plot. There is much allusion to hell-fire and darkness: William
Barlow mentions in his sermon on 10 November 1605 that the planting
of the gunpowder beneath Parliament was Satan's attempt to create a
miniature hell. Bishop Andrewes calls the conspirators the *"primogeniti
Satanae,"* and Bishop Ussher names them "incendiaries of the world."[3]

The gunpowder sermons stress Satan's brutality in provoking the
conspirators to a crime which, as Bishop Ussher notes, "exceeded all
measure of cruelty; as involving not the king alone, but also his children
and the states of the kingdom, and many thousands of innocent people."[4]
Satan's conspiracy, in fact, was seen by many as a repetition of his original offence. As the Earl of Northampton, one of the prosecutors in the
trial of the conspirators, had remarked, Satan in his latest affair had
become more bold than he was in Heaven: "The Dragons ambition
extended no further, than the sweeping away with his tail of the third
part of the Stars in the Firmament: But now the plot of him and his
Disciples was, to sweep away the Sun, the Moon, and the Stars, both

out of the Star-Chamber and Parliament, that no light be given in this Kingdom to the best Labourers."[5]

The Satan portrayed by the gunpowder sermonists delights in the extravagance of his plans and gloats over their secrecy, reflecting upon his revenge when the godly will be taken by surprise and destroyed.[6] Yet, as the sermonists remind their audience, Satan in his gloating and machinations is shortsighted; he is forgetful that God is aware of his activities and has only permitted him and his conspirators to achieve their full-scale preparations. God has watched, unperturbed and serene, even though, as Stephen Marshall comments, "there wanted nothing, but to put the match to the powder, and the blow had been given."[7] The conspirators assume that their plot is directed against a temporally appointed king. But, as Lancelot Andrewes tells them, their plot is truly directed against the omnipotent God, who sees their folly and knows how vain their undertaking is. The true king cannot be separated from God, who appoints his reign; the conspirators "cannot deal with Kings, but they must begin with God first."[8] The affairs of men and God are inextricably involved.

Repeatedly, the preachers cite the discovery of the gunpowder conspiracy as the highest example of God's providence. As Isaac Barrow argues, God could have prevented, if he had so wished, the beginnings of Satan's design. Instead, "he rather winketh for a time, and suffereth the designers to go on, till they are mounted to the top of confidence, and the good people are cast on the brink of ruin; then . . . surprisingly, unexpectedly he striketh in with effectual succor." In so delaying his action, God has demonstrated both "how vain the presumption is of impious undertakers" and "how needful and sure his protection is over innocent people."[9] In a similar vein, Lancelot Andrewes pictures the providential God sitting in Heaven and looking down upon "all this doing of the devil and his limbs." God, declares Andrewes, has allowed Satan's evil to flourish only that he might show to his people that he retains a sure control over it: "If ever God shewed that He had a hook in Leviathan's nose, that the devil can go no farther than his chain, if ever that there is in Him more power to help than in Satan to hurt, in this He did it."[10]

Thus, with the discovery of the plot, God's grace is revealed. The preachers celebrate the discovery as though it were a military victory in which God has triumphed over Satan. In a sermon on 5 November

1641, Cornelius Burges portrays God as an invincible warrior arriving
in a chariot to assure victory and salvation to England: "This is that day
wherein our God came riding to us in his Chariot of Triumph, and
made himself *fearfull in prayses,* by *doing wonders* and leaving us no
more to doe but praise his Name." In this extended military metaphor,
God is seen to break *"the arrows of the bow, the shield, the sword, and
batell,* whereby he is become *more glorious and excellent than moun-
taines of prey."* [11] The sermonist has here affirmed both the providence
and the omnipotence of God. God has turned the devil's weapons
against him, has forced him to acknowledge, in the defeat of the conspirators, his own defeat. At the same time, this stirring demonstration
of divine power has reassured God's people of his unfailing grace toward
them. The gunpowder sermon invariably concludes with an anthem of
rejoicing: November fifth is proclaimed the day of the Lord.

The young Milton in his gunpowder poems could hardly have
failed to react to the vehemence and passion of the sermons. Milton
probably did not have Phineas Fletcher's *Locustae* or *Apollyonists*
(1627) as a literary model, if the traditional date of 1626 is to be accepted for the gunpowder poems. The impact of the sermons is, I think,
unquestionable, not only because Milton must have heard such preachers as Lancelot Andrewes, but also because the prime concerns of the
gunpowder poems are the same as those of the sermons. In both epigrams
and narrative, Milton makes the devil the principal agent in the plot,
and he shows us the darkness and fire of Hell as the conceptual influences in the conspiracy. Gunpowder is repeatedly identified as the
infernal or Tartarean fire, the hellish perversion of God's heavenly
thunderbolt. Like the gunpowder sermonists, Milton is strongly anti-
papal; in the epigrams he makes the pope appear as a Tartarean monster, the beast of the seven hills, who wears the triple crown and menaces
all with his ten horns: "Frenduit hoc trina monstrum Latiale corona /
Movit et horrificum cornua dena minax." [12] In the narrative poem, the
references to Hell are explicit, for not only is Hell alluded to, it is visu-
ally evoked: the fiery streams of Acheron, the wild tempests, the lurid
sulphur, the unspeakable and joyless kingdom. The conspiracy is born
in a type of antechamber of Hell, the cave of Murder and Treason, a
place forever dark, where unburied bodies and bones lie scattered.

The Satan of the narrative poem has come from Hell to stir up
trouble and is contrasted with James, who has come from the north to

establish peace and prosperity among the English. Envying the blessings of wealth and peace which the English enjoy and angered at their service of the true God, Satan determines to unsettle matters and win England to his domination. His means, Milton tells us, are to be treachery and guile, for Satan is a master of silent plot and unseen nets, unparalleled in instigating hatred among loyal friends. Satan is called a cruel tyrant, a Caspian tiger who pursues his prey by night, a monster like Typhoeus, who emits sulphurous sighs and grinds an adamantine array of teeth. Clearly, Milton is equipping his Satan in this poem with a conventional Plutonian personality; he is a pagan god to whom the pope does service. Milton has pictured the pope as an idolater, and the rites of the Roman church, their processions in the streets, and their chants in the temples as analogous to the rites of Bacchus and his followers. But the pope in this poem, in sharp contrast to the epigrams, is no monster; he is merely profane and worldly, the ruler of kings, the heir of Hell, the secret adulterer. Satan inspires the pope with a detailed suggestion for the plot: to explode nitrous powder under the halls where the king and nobles will assemble. The pope, from then on, becomes principal actor, summoning, when he awakens, Murder and Treason from their dark cave to urge his agents in England to become tools of the plot. Like the gunpowder sermonists, Milton makes much of the swift action of God, who, discerning the conspiracy, determines to undo it speedily. Fame is dispatched to make the plot known. God has saved the innocent: youths and maidens and old men are amazed at the abominable plot and joyous at their salvation. Milton concludes that the wicked have been swiftly punished and the people spared from their outrages.

After examining these early poems, however, we must ask what Milton as the poet of *Paradise Lost* owes to the gunpowder tradition and to these youthful exercises of his own, besides, of course, general assent to the seventeenth-century notion that Satan as a conspirator was acting in the meanest of his roles, the corrupter of individuals and society. Assuredly, neither the Satan of the sermons or even of Milton's own poems is the Satan of *Paradise Lost*; assuredly, also, a localized conspiracy against an earthly king cannot pretend to vie in significance with a conspiracy against God which threatens the fate of Heaven and earth. But, whereas the situations of the conspiracies are different, the attitudes evoked by the word *conspiracy* are not. How Milton and the sermonists react to Satan's architecture of evil in the gunpowder conspiracy is analogous to the way the angels react to the discovery of Satan's fully constructed but secret war.

One should not be greatly swayed by the physical differences between Milton's early and later Satan.[13] Satan as conspirator in *Paradise Lost* is not a deformed monster or the leviathan; in Book V, as he begins his conspiracy, he is still angelic in demeanor. But, even as he is introduced by Raphael, he already is characterized by one indispensable mannerism of the conspirator: he moves quietly, unseen by all but God. He is dangerous and undiscoverable, as Andrewes had called his plot. As the master of fraud, he tempts even the heart that might appear sealed against sin; he sets his plots so silently that the nets laid to entangle remain unseen. So Satan appears as he moves Beelzebub to set his plot to action. Interestingly enough, the manner of the conspirator which Milton outlined in the small epic, *In Quintum Novembris*, has remained largely unchanged, even if his outward demeanor has changed. Milton's later Satan is only inwardly enraged, whereas his earlier Satan had breathed sighs of Tartarean flame and had flashed fire from his eyes. Hell is literally—not as one might say of the later Satan, metaphorically—present in his person.

Thus in act, if not in person, the early and the later Satan are strongly parallel. Each chooses to approach the person whom he will persuade to undertake his conspiracy while that person sleeps, disarmed and susceptible. If the early Satan transfers his influence by means of a dream, the later one is yet more subtle. Waking Beelzebub in Book V, he infuses "Bad influence into th' unwary breast / Of his Associate" (V, 695–96). Outwardly, his rebuke seems one of a friend who is hurt that his confidant dissents by sleep instead of waking to share thoughts and counsel. Satan in the gunpowder poem, if he does not appear as a friend, appears as a confessor, a grey-haired Franciscan friar, girt in a hood and trailing robe; he speaks, moreover, to the pope as a father. As in *Paradise Lost*, the rebuke occurs, first gently, restrained, but Milton's early Satan quickly becomes imperious. He exhorts that the pride and prestige of the pope have been irreparably damaged by the upstart English who challenge him. He urges the pope to remember the devastation of the Armada, the executions of Catholics under Elizabeth, and to avenge these injuries to the name of Rome. But at the same time that he presses for revenge against the English, he maintains that it should not come by open and declared war, but by deception and surprise. The military forces should be dispatched only after the king and his nobles have been conquered, their limbs scattered through the air by the explosion of nitrous powder. And the whole conspiracy should be executed quietly by use of the faithful followers in England, who shall first disarm the land. In *Paradise Lost* the plans for Satan's war in Heaven follow a similar order and principle. Satan, in appealing to Beelzebub, insists that secrecy and quiet be maintained. The legions are to be dislodged at night, the faithful led to obey without being told the reason for their obedience. Motives are to be whispered, the cause suggested, but "ambiguous words and jealousies" cast between "to sound / Or taint integrity" (V, 702–04). As in the gunpowder poem, Satan remains aloof, using his second as a tool, and luring his followers on. One significant difference exists. In *In Quintum Novembris* Satan employs the terror of his fallen nature to command respect; in *Paradise Lost* he uses the beauty of his unfallen nature to draw allegiance: "His count'nance, as the Morning Star that guides / The starry flock, allur'd them, and with lies / Drew after him the third part of Heav'n's Host" (V, 708–10).

When Satan in *Paradise Lost* does address his angels, it is with the sense of arrogant irony that the earlier Satan used in his address to the pope. As Milton's early Satan suggested that the pope's title and authority were being undermined by the English, the later Satan suggests that the "magnific titles" which the angels once possessed are now merely titular, since Messiah has undermined them and engrossed all power to himself. Milton's early Satan cited evidence that Elizabeth's reign had caused the Catholics to be abused and undone; his later Satan warns that the reign of the Messiah will exact "knee-tribute" and "prostration vile." As the early Satan asserts that the prestige of Rome must be restored by force, the later Satan pledges that the angels must reassume their native right, become, as their "imperial titles" promised, the governors once more and not the servants.

The manner in which Milton describes God in *Paradise Lost* also owes something to the gunpowder tradition. When the gunpowder sermonists portrayed a God who, sitting in his Heaven, looked down and saw the futile rage of the devil his enemy, it is clear that they had in mind the God of Psalm ii, who oversees the tumult of his adversaries and laughs at the presumption of their plottings. Milton in his November fifth epic echoes Psalm ii as he presents God in triumph: "Interea longo flectens curvamine caelos / Despicit aetherea dominus qui fulgurat arce, / Vanaque perversae ridet conamina turbae, / Atque sui causam populi volet ipse tueri" (ll. 166–69). Milton's God here is imperious, exalted, and amused. For his people, he offers an immediate and sure salvation; for his enemies he offers immediate and utter destruction, rendered with impassive laughter. Thus, the ironic attitude, for which Milton's God in *Paradise Lost* has been known, may be traced back to one of the earliest depictions of the deity, a depiction which may well have been influenced by the gunpowder sermonists, who stressed God's serene, detached scorn for the conspirators. For the gunpowder sermonists, for the young Milton, and for the later poet of *Paradise Lost*, Psalm ii is central for this characterization of God.

Thus, it may be valuable to look at Milton's own translation of Psalm ii, worked out probably in 1653 when he was producing metrical versions of the psalms.[14] The psalm is framed by Milton as a denunciation not only of rebellion, but of rebellious conspiracy. His translation of the first part of the psalm almost reads like a resumé of Raphael's account of the war in Book V of *Paradise Lost*: "Princes in their Congregations / Lay deep their plots together through each Land, / Against the Lord and his Messiah dear." Chafing against authority, they plan to "break off . . . by strength of hand / Their bonds." The central point in Milton's translation becomes the defense by God of the Messiah's place as king.

> he who in Heaven doth dwell
> Shall laugh, the Lord shall scoff them, then severe
> Speak to them in his wrath, and in his fell
> And fierce ire trouble them; but I, saith hee,
> Anointed have my King (though ye rebel)
> On Sion my holy hill. A firm decree
> I will declare; the Lord to me hath said,
> Thou art my Son, I have begotten thee
> This day. (8–16)

In *Paradise Lost* Milton is to echo this passage in two ways: the latter part becomes the council edict by which God announces the Messiah's kingship and the former becomes part of the Son's speech in which he reacts to the Father's announcement of the imminent uprising.

> Mighty Father, thou thy foes
> Justly hast in derision, and secure
> Laugh'st at thir vain designs and tumults vain. (V, 735–37)

The change here is significant. In the psalm, as Milton translates it, we are merely told directly that God laughs at his enemies. This is also, in effect, how Milton presents the scene of God's laughter in *In Quintum Novembris*. But in *Paradise Lost* it is the Son who tells us that God laughs. The Father has been commenting ironically on the aim of those who suppose they are able to erect a throne equal to God's and engage God's power in battle. He has implied that the conspirators actually expect that God must defend himself and "this our high place, our Sanctuary, our Hill" against their attack. The Son thus is reacting both to the situation that the Father has described and to the ironic tone that the Father has adopted in face of the conspirators' presumption. The Father's tone has conveyed to the Son the utter folly of the conspirators. The Son responds by saying that no other response but laughter would be truly appropriate to a God who is impervious to attack, but who is being plotted against by would-be attackers with the pomp and solemnity of secret ceremony. It is not only just for God to laugh, as the Son comments; it is unavoidable. Milton has expanded the laughter of God as it occurs in the psalm into a dramatic situation in which the Son responds to and interprets divine laughter.

The conclusion of Psalm ii, as it appears in Milton's 1653 translation, is also relevant to *Paradise Lost*, for it serves as a prediction of the conquering wrath of the Son.

> them shalt thou bring full low
> With Iron Scepter bruis'd, and them disperse
>
> .   .   .   .
>
> ye Kings averse
> Be taught, ye Judges of the earth; with fear
> Jehovah serve, and let your joy converse
> With trembling; kiss the Son lest he appear
> In anger and ye perish in the way.   (19–26)

This part of the psalm was not echoed directly in Milton's 1626 narrative. It does suggest, however, a characteristic of God even in this early poem: his speed in action. As the gunpowder sermonists repeatedly portrayed him, he is swift to dispatch his enemies. He has sent Christ, not only to save the innocent, but to judge and destroy the wicked, as the closing lines of the brief epic reveal. In *Paradise Lost*, divine wrath will be manifest with lightning suddenness when the Son appears in the chariot to drive the rebels out of Heaven. However, these lines of Psalm ii are not used by Milton to portray the scene of the Son's victory but to predict it. At the end of Book V Abdiel reminds Satan of the danger of tempting "the incensed Father, and th' incensed Son" (V, 847). "That Golden Sceptre" which the rebels have rejected will become "an Iron Rod to bruise and break / [Their] disobedience" (V, 887–88). Again Milton in echoing the psalm has altered the speaker and situation. It is through the eyes of the humble angel that we see the awesome power of God's anger awakened at insult to the Messiah.

Thus *Paradise Lost* marks a genuine advance of technique over the earlier *In Quintum Novembris* in the employment of biblical material. Whereas in the short epic the psalm was echoed, only, as it were, to announce biblical authority for God's laughter at his enemies, in *Paradise Lost* the words of the psalm are woven into the dramatic fabric of the situation. Not only do we hear God's voice from the throne denouncing his enemies, but also we hear the Son responding and Abdiel reinforcing the defense of God in the very face of the rebellious. One factor has remained constant, and that is that Milton still characterizes God as a deity who holds his enemies in ironic derision.

Irony of a different sort is an ingredient in Milton's early gunpowder epigrams and in the gunpowder sequences of his later epic. If in *In Quintum Novembris* and Book V of *Paradise Lost* Milton has shown us a God who can laugh at his enemies, he has in the gunpowder epigrams and in Book VI shown us conspirators who think they can safely laugh at God. The conspirators in both cases assume that their possession of a powerful secret weapon accords them a kind of divine control over the fates of others. With gunpowder in their hands, they can play God. Arrogating God's power, they also arrogate his ironic manner; secure, they laugh at their enemies. In both the epigrams and *Paradise Lost* Milton tells us that the conspirators think their gunpowder equal to God's thunderbolt. In an epigram on the inventor of gunpowder, Milton says that the inventor seems in effect to have stolen three-forked lightning from Jove. In *Paradise Lost* Satan's rebels boast that they have "disarm'd / The thunderer of his only created bolt" (VI, 490–91). With elaborate ceremony they compound the powder from the dark and crude elements of Heaven, but unlike God they cannot temper their creation with light; thus it can only produce a sulphurous blast which darkens, not a cleansing flash which will illuminate and control.

I believe that Milton owes something to the sermon tradition for his depiction of both the gunpowder conspirators and Satan's rebels. The sermonists had stressed that the original gunpowder conspirators were haughty, presumptuous, but petty men. They possessed an almost insane confidence in their plot, hoping through the device of their secretly laid powder to win all power to themselves. The young Milton dramatizes the conspirators' presumptuous blasphemy. They profess with worldly irony that they act piously in laying gunpowder against the king; with its very blast they will lift James to Heaven. Likening their exploit to God's own translation of the saintly Elijah in the chariot of flame, they proclaim that they are sending James to the high courts above. Milton denounces the conspirators indirectly in the first four epigrams by dramatizing their ironic statements and questioning with his own irony their purposes. He thus uncovers their true nature and the nature of their conspiracy. First, he attacks the basic hypocrisy of those involved; the perfidious Fawkes, addressed in the first epigram, he upbraids for his attempt to cover up his evil deed with evil piety. The Church of Rome, named in the fourth epigram, he denounces as having first threatened James with passage *below* to Hell, and then attempted with hellish fire to blast him *above* to Heaven. Hypocrisy, Milton shows, is the cloak of those who would play God. But even while he exposes the high pretensions of the conspirators and their Roman authority, he reveals that they with their Tartarean powder have only hellish impotence rather than heavenly power. Like the purgatorial fire they have threatened James with, their power is delusive, a fable. They do not control heavenly fates, and in fact, as Milton scoffs in the second epigram, the only way they and the falsely profane gods of Rome may reach Heaven is to be blasted there physically by their own explosive powder. It is God alone who truly lifts above, says Milton, and judges below, and who has sent James to Heaven in his own good time, and who by implication has judged and doomed the conspirators.

These dramatic epigrams are interesting exercises in the use of double irony and prefigure its use in the gunpowder sequences of *Paradise Lost*. Their verbal irony is overlaid with dramatic irony. The gunpowder conspirators jest ironically that they control the situation; they laugh at lifting James to Heaven when they intend to blast him to Hell. But irony for the conspirators only proves to be a verbal subterfuge. Dramatic irony proves that God, not the conspirators, has control. In a similar way, the rebel angels in *Paradise Lost* think themselves masters of the situation: they have constructed the cannon and loaded it with gunpowder, and then concealed it in their midst, so that only at the last moment will the spark be applied when the cannon is revealed to deliver its destructive blow. Finally, sure of themselves, they approach the loyal angels, and veiling their words in verbal irony, promise to seek peace and composure, propose to receive their enemies with open breast, and hope that they like the overture and "turn not back perverse." Maliciously, the rebel angels pretend peace, while with devious intent they promise to "freely" discharge their part, appointing those "in charge" to touch what they "propound" so that "all may hear" loudly and clearly (VI, 564–67). Of course, the opening they propose is not of a conference, but of the flanks of the army to disclose the cannon; and the discharge is not of free will and amity, but of the gunpowder.

As was true of the gunpowder conspirators, Satan and his angels propose one thing, while they intend another. Their ironic speech is meant to confuse issues, to veil the truth of the situation. There is no doubt, however, that the angels think they are imitating the manner of God, who also speaks ironically, as they have imitated his thunderbolt in constructing the cannon. By ironic words, Satan and his angels would assume a type of divine omniscience; that is, they would be omniscient in knowing their true meaning (that the cannon was about to be unveiled) while the loyal angels would remain ignorant and lowly. By ironic control, their superiority would be proved; like God, they could laugh at their enemies. But as the cannon was created in parody of God's manner of creation, so Satanic irony is a parody of divine irony. God, in speaking ironically of his enemies, reveals the truth of their situation: that they are creatures rebelling against the source of their being and thus engaged in a process that is basically foolish and vain. Satan, in contrast, in addressing his enemies ironically, is bent on deception; his ironic words lure the loyal angels into what proves a trap.

The guileful irony, used before the discharge of the cannon, degenerates into the mocking irony of the aftermath: Belial, "in like gamesome mood" puns that the "terms" offered were too "hard" for the angels to receive and understand. For Satan the overthrow of the loyal angels is opportunity to ridicule the posture of their surprise. Secure, he questions what strange vagary moved them, for they "flew off . . . / As they would dance, yet for a dance they seem'd / Somewhat extravagant and wild, perhaps / For joy of offer'd peace" (VI, 614–17). As the angels scoff at their enemies, the entire situation turns into a monstrous joke. The destruction of Heaven, which the cannon has wrought, is not a light matter. The folly and presumption of one's enemies might be a proper target of laughter, but is it appropriate to hold in derision their "foul dissipation" and "forc't rout"? Nor should the devastation of Heaven provoke laughter.

> Immediate in a flame,
> But soon obscur'd with smoke, all Heav'n appear'd,
> From those deep-throated Engines belcht, whose roar
> Embowell'd with outrageous noise the Air
> And all her entrails tore, disgorging foul
> Their devilish glut, chain'd Thunderbolts and Hail
> Of Iron Globes.   (VI, 584–90)

Milton has clearly shown his readers that gunpowder is not God's second thunderbolt, but a foul and pestilential explosive which dirties the atmosphere of Heaven, destroys its concord. How far from scoffing, from gamesome mood and pleasant vein, is God's reaction to this disorder. To Him war has let loose "disorder'd rage"; it has wrought "wild work in Heav'n, and dangerous to the main" (VI, 698). The joke which the rebels enjoy is as transitory as it is inappropriate. As was true of the gunpowder conspirators, their end will come swiftly and suddenly. So the loyal angels cover the cannons with the weight of mountains and render them useless; so the blasphemous glee of the conspirators is checked as they must now seek new weapons, deprived instantaneously of the gunpowder which they vaunted equal to the lightning of Heaven. That the divine lightning in the hands of the Son will come to amaze and destroy them is only ironically fit, for dramatic irony belongs to the Lord God.

The gunpowder sermons, as well as Milton's own gunpowder poems, all end with the assurance that the power of God is infinitely superior to any of the vain plots which the devil might hatch. As the Son readies himself to appear in the power and eminence of his Father, the reader of *Paradise Lost*, if he keeps in mind what the seventeenth-century preacher has said of Satanic conspiracy, knows God has dispatched the Son to save, "that there is in Him more power to help than in Satan to hurt," when "surprisingly, unexpectedly he striketh in with effectual succor." He may see the Son's victory as analogous to the salvation of England: "this is that day wherein our God came riding to us in his Chariot of Triumph, and made himselfe *fearfull in prayses, by doing wonders* and leaving us no more to doe, but praise his name."[15] If the gunpowder conspiracy differs in kind and degree from the primal conspiracy of Satan in the courts of Heaven, the emotions which it inspires in the hearts of seventeenth-century Englishmen, who rejected Guy Fawkes and his crew as foul underminers of royal authority, are relevant to those basic emotions a Christian feels in rejecting Satan and his first and archetypal band of conspirators. Milton in depicting Satan as a conspirator and in giving him gunpowder as the first weapon against the Almighty clearly wishes his readers to be mindful of how Satan has remained alive and threatening in the political affairs of their own time.

Southern Illinois University, Edwardsville

NOTES

1. See Merritt Y. Hughes' introduction to *In Quintum Novembris*, in *John Milton: Complete Poems and Major Prose* (New York, 1957), p. 15, and Douglas Bush, *The Latin and Greek Poems, A Variorum Commentary on the Poems of John Milton* (New York, 1970), I, 142–43, 167–72.

2. *The Gunpowder Treason: With a discourse of the Manner of Its Discovery; And a Perfect Relation of the Proceedings against those horrid Conspirators; Wherein is Contained their Examinations, Tryals, and Condemnations: Likewise King James' Speech to Both Houses of Parliament on that Occasion* (London, 1679).

3. William Barlow, *The Sermon Preached at Paules Crosse, the tenth day of November, being the next Sunday after the Discoverie of this late Horrible Treason* (London, 1606); Lancelot Andrewes, *Ninety-Six Sermons* (Oxford, 1841), IV, 293; James Ussher, "A Sermon Preached Before the Commons House of Parliament, in St. Margaret's Church, at Westminster, the 18th of February, 1620, First Printed in 1621," *The Whole Works of the Most Rev. James Ussher, D.D.* (Dublin, 1847), II, 454.

4. Ussher, *Whole Works*, II, 455.

5. Earl of Northampton in *The Gunpowder Treason*, p. 213.

6. Andrewes ironically comments upon the conspirators' love of darkness and secrecy: "In darkness they delighted, dark vaults, dark cellars, and darkness fell upon them for it" (*Ninety-Six Sermons*, IV, 311).

7. Stephen Marshall, *Emmanuel: A Thanksgiving-Sermon Preached to the Honourable House of Commons Upon their Solemn day of praising God for the victory obtained by the Parliament Forces in South-wales, May 17, 1648* (London, 1648), p. 21.

8. Andrewes, *Ninety-Six Sermons*, IV, 293.

9. Isaac Barrow, "Sermon XI—On The Gunpowder-Treason," *The Works Of Dr. Isaac Barrow* (New York, 1830), I, 268.

10. Andrewes, *Ninety-Six Sermons*, IV, 213.

11. Cornelius Burges, *Another Sermon Preached to the Honorable House of Commons now assembled in Parliament, November the fifth, 1641* (London, 1641), pp. 1–2.

12. The text of the epigrams, *In Quintum Novembris*, and *Paradise Lost* cited is *Complete Poems and Major Prose*, ed. Merritt Y. Hughes.

13. Macon Cheek, "Milton's 'In Quintum Novembris': An Epic Foreshadowing," *SP*, LIV (1957), 172–84, considers the figure of Satan an early study of Milton's later epic character.

14. Charles Dahlberg, "*Paradise Lost* V, 603, and Milton's Psalm II," *MLN*, LXVII (1952), 23–24, has remarked that the parenthesis, "though ye rebell," in Milton's translation of Psalm ii, "shows that as early as 1653 Milton associated the idea of rebellion with the idea of elevation to kingship."

15. Quotations from Andrewes, Barrow, and Burges; see notes 10, 9, and 11.

MILTON AND THE
ORGANICIST POLEMIC

Michael Lieb

The pervasive influence of organicism in the Renaissance is especially discernible in religious controversies that distinguished
between the visible and invisible church. In Milton's antiprelatical
tracts, the body is seen from the points of view of liturgy, as reflected in the communion, and investiture, as reflected in the
controversies regarding ministerial dress. Those controversies express symbolically the Puritan desire to "divest" and "tear" the
body, on the one hand, and the Anglican desire to "invest" and
keep it whole, on the other. Integral to the Puritan and Anglican
responses to the church are their responses to the state. Whereas
the Anglican impulse is to unite the political body and the ecclesiastical body under one head, the Puritan impulse is to sever the
two bodies. Thus Milton associates the body politic with outward
concerns, the body ecclesiastical with inward ones. When the two
bodies are unnaturally joined, a monster results, and the body
can only be re-formed and returned to health through proper am-
putation of the corrupt limbs. Milton's organicist views, therefore,
reflect not a desire to destroy, as might be charged, but a desire
to make whole.

W E ARE already quite familiar with the Renaissance predisposition
to view the world in bodily terms.* Referred to by the sociologists
as *organicism*, that tendency in thought is one which "constructs its
picture of the world on an organic model."[1] If the universality of the
organicist tendency is attested by the fact that it may be found in "ancient Hindu, Chinese, Greek, and Roman writers,"[2] its presence in the
Renaissance is no less pervasive. Basing his entire treatise upon the

* I would like to thank the Folger Shakespeare Library for the grant that
aided me in the completion of this study.

organicist idea, Edward Forsett, in *A Comparative Discourse of the Bodies Natural and Politique* (1606), devotes a full introductory section to the matter. First, he traces organicism to none other than "that thrice renowned Philosopher *Trismegistus*," who "imagined an huge and mightie Gyant, whose head was aboue the firmament, his necke, shoulders, and upper parts in the heauens, his armes and hands reaching to East and West, his belly in the whole spaciousnesse under the Moone, his legges and feet within the earth."[3] Then, he justifies his use of the organicist analogy by invoking the commonplace Renaissance association of the body of the world (macrocosm) and the body of man (microcosm). For Forsett, this was no arbitrary correspondence: he insisted, as Michael Walzer states, "that the whole system of analogies was the creation of God" and that "they had a real existence prior to their recognition by men."[4] Thus, Forsett concludes, "Wherefore seeing that the uttermost extent of mans understanding, can shape no better forme of ordering the affayres of a State, than by marking and matching of the workes of the finger of God, eyther in the larger volume of the uniuersall [that is, the body of the world], or in the abridgement thereof, the body of man: I account these two to be the two great lights for enquiry and meditation concerning this businesse" (p. 2).

That Renaissance writers would have concurred with Forsett's views may be seen by the proliferation of works (predominantly allegorical) based solely upon the organicist analogy. One thinks of works so diverse as Phineas Fletcher's *The Purple Island, or The Isle of Man* (1633); Richard Bernard's *The Isle of Man: or, The Legal Proceeding in Man-shire against SINNE* (1626); and *Lingua: or The Combat of the 'Tongue,' and the fiue Senses for 'Superiority,' A pleasant Comoedie* (1607), attributed to Thomas Tomkis. But perhaps the most apt illustration of the willingness with which the Renaissance looked upon the world in bodily terms is discernible in Francis Gray's *The Judge's Scripture or, God's Charge to Charge-givers* (1637). In that work, Gray envisions at least five bodily categories: "body celestial," "body astronomical," "body natural," "body economical," and "body politic."[5]

With so great a stress upon the organicist analogy in the Renaissance, then, it is little wonder that organicism should be brought to bear upon polemic. Indeed, so pervasive was the polemical tendency in the Renaissance to formulate one's position through a bodily correspondence that controversies in general tended to resolve themselves into arguments about bodies. Hooker's *Of the Laws of Ecclesiastical Polity* provides a case in point. In Book 8, chapter 4, he quotes Thomas Cartwright as saying: "If the Church be the body of Christ, and of the civil magistrate, it shall have two heads, which being monstrous, is to the great dishonour of Christ and his Church." Hooker responds: "It is neither monstrous nor as much as uncomely for a Church to have different heads," since God has made Christ "the supreme head of the whole Church; the head not only of that mystical body which the eye of man is not able to discern, but even of every politic society, of every visible Church in the world."[6] Implicit in Cartwright's statement and Hooker's response are those elements that formed the cornerstone of the organicist polemic in the Renaissance. Their importance to Milton's use of the body as polemical device will become apparent only after we have explored, within the context of his times, his view of the church, both invisible and visible, and the relationship of the church to the state. An understanding of these matters will provide the necessary background for an appreciation not only of Milton's polemical practices but of the organicist polemic in general.

As invisible entity, the church for Milton had its source in the concept of the mystical body of Christ (*corpus mysticum*). Thus, Milton states in *Christian Doctrine* (Bk. I, ch. 24): "from [the] union and fellowship of the regenerate with the Father and Christ, and of the members of Christ's body among themselves, results the mystical body called *The Invisible Church*, whereof Christ is the head."[7] Milton's statement derives, of course, from 1 Corinthians xxi, 12–31: "For as the body is one, and hath many members, and all the members of that one body, being many, are one body: so also is Christ. . . . Now ye are the body of Christ, and members in particular."[8] Despite the New Testament source, however, the concept of the invisible church as *corpus mysticum* is of medieval origin. As Ernst H. Kantorowicz makes clear, although the idea of the church as *corpus Christi* goes back to Saint Paul, it was the medieval world that ascribed to the church those sacramental and sociological characteristics underlying the concept of the *corpus mysticum*.[9] This is precisely the view that emerges in John of Salisbury's *Policraticus*, which compares "the commonweal with the organism of the human body, a simile popular among the jurists." "Similar comparisons of the Church with a human body, stimulated by St. Paul . . . are found sporadically throughout the Middle Ages, and it was only an adaptation to the new terminology that Isaac of Stella, a contemporary of John of Salisbury, applied the metaphor of the human body with great precision to the *corpus mysticum* the head of which was Christ and whose limbs were the archbishops, bishops, and other functionaries of the Church. That is to say, the anthropomorphic imagery was transferred as a matter of course to both the Church as the 'mystical body of Christ' in a spiritual sense and the Church as an administrative organism styled likewise *corpus mysticum*."[10] For the Renaissance understanding of the idea, we might invoke Richard Hooker's eloquent exposition in his *Laws* (Bk. III, ch. 1): "That Church of Christ, which we properly term his body mystical, can be but one; neither can that one be sensibly discerned by any man, inasmuch as the parts thereof are some in heaven already with Christ, and the rest that are on earth (albeit their natural persons be visible) we do not discern under this property, whereby they are truly and infallibly of that body. Only our minds by intellectual conceit are able to apprehend, that such a real body there is, a body collective, because it containeth an huge multitude; a body mystical, because the mystery of their conjunction is removed altogether from sense" (*Works* I, 220).

In contradistinction to the mystical body of the invisible church, Hooker refers in the same place to the corporeal body (those who are "incorporated into . . . *one body*") of the visible church. Comprised, as Milton says, of "those indiscriminately who have received the call, whether actually regenerate or otherwise," the visible church functions temporally in various congregations throughout the world (CM, XVI, 219). As such, its importance is decidedly inferior to that of the invisible church. This may be seen particularly in the fact that Milton associated the visible church with the Old Dispensation, the invisible church with the New. For Milton, the Old Dispensation emphasized the ceremonial law (the "materiall Temple," as he calls it), which prefigured but was superseded by "the new alliance of God to man."[11] According to that new alliance, "the spirituall eye may discerne more goodly and gracefully erected then all the magnificence of Temple or Tabernacle, such a heavenly structure of evangelick discipline . . . that it cannot be wondered if that elegant and artfull symmetry of the promised new temple in *Ezechiel*, and all those sumptuous things under the Law were made to signifie the inward beauty and splendor of the Christian church thus govern'd" (YP, I, 758). The ceremonial law, therefore, becomes important in its prefigurative capacity but must not be subscribed to literally, "unlesse," Milton says, "we mean to annihilat the Gospel" (YP, I, 757), for the gospel expresses the word of the Holy Spirit, which, enlightening us "inwardly," impresses itself upon our hearts, "according to the promise of God" (CM, XVI, 273). Such an idea bears directly upon the place of the visible church in Milton's beliefs: "For with regard to the visible church, which is also proposed as a criterion of faith, it is evident that, since the ascension of Christ, the *pillar and ground of the truth* has not uniformly been the church, but the hearts of believers, which are properly 'the house and church of the living God' " (CM, XVI, 279). This movement in Milton from the corporeal to the mystical, the external to the internal, the visible to the invisible, has prompted Malcolm Ross to observe that for Milton the church became "*utterly* invisible, as is the fellowship it is said to contain." [12]

If this is so, then we can more nearly appreciate the thrust of Milton's criticism of the prelates in his antiprelatical tracts. There, he exploits the bodily associations of the invisible and visible churches for polemical purposes. *Of Reformation* is a case in point. At the outset we encounter "the mysticall body" (*corpus mysticum*) of the invisible church, whose "every joynt, and sinew" is inspired by "the Spirit of unity and meeknesse" (YP, I, 547). In that form, Milton reveals to us "our Saviour *Christ*, suffering to the lowest bent of weaknesse, in the *Flesh*, and presently triumphing to the highest pitch of glory in the *Spirit*, which drew up his body also, till we in both be united to him in the revelation of his Kingdome" (YP, I, 519). The pure body, then, is represented through a spiritualizing movement, whereby "that Doctrine of the *Gospel*" is "winnow'd, and sifted, from the chaffe of overdated Ceremonies, and refin'd to such a Spirituall height, and temper of purity" that the body is "purifi'd by the affections of the regenerat Soule, and nothing left impure, but sinne" (YP, I, 519). In connection with that idea, one might recall the Elder Brother's statement in *Comus* that the effect of chastity is "to cast a beam on th' outward shape, / The unpolluted temple of the mind" and to turn it "by degrees to the souls essence / Till all be made immortal," while the effect of lust ("By unchast looks, loose gestures, and foul talk, / But most by lewd and lavish act of sin") is to let in "defilement to the inward parts" so that "the soul grows clotted by contagion, / Imbodies and imbrutes, till she quite loose / The divine property of her first being" (ll. 459–469). [13]

The uniquely ecclesiastical bearing this idea assumes in *Of Reformation* may be seen in the organicist vision of that "Corporation of Impostors," "mis-shapen and enormous *Prelatisme*" (YP, I, 537), a fitting contrast with the elect members of the mystical body of Christ. Through the prelates, "the inward acts of *worship* issuing from the native strength of the SOULE, run out lavishly to the upper skin, and there harden into a crust of Formallitie" (YP, I, 522). Having caused the purity of doctrine "to backslide one way into the Jewish beggery, of old cast rudiments, and stumble forward another way into the new-vomited Paganisme of sensuall Idolatry," the prelates have brought "the inward acts of the *Spirit* to the outward, and customary ey-Service of the body, as if they could make *God* earthly, and fleshly, because they could not make themselves *heavenly*, and *Spirituall*":

they began to draw downe all the Divine intercours, betwixt *God*, and the Soule, yea, the very shape of *God* himselfe, into an exterior, and bodily forme, urgently pretending a necessity, and obligement of joyning the body in a formall reverence, and *Worship* circumscrib'd, they hallow'd it, they fum'd it, they sprincl'd it, they be deck't it, not in robes of pure innocency, but of pure Linnen, with other deformed, and fantastick dresses in Palls, and Miters, gold, and guegaw's fetcht from *Arons* old wardrope, or the *Flamins vestry*: then was the *Priest* set to *con his motions*, and his *Postures* his *Liturgies*, and his *Lurries*, till the Soule by this meanes of over-bodying her selfe, given up justly to fleshly delights, bated her wing apace downeward: and finding the ease she had from her visible, and sensuous collegue the body in performance of *Religious* duties, her pineons now broken, and flagging, shifted off from her selfe, the labour of high soaring any more, forgot her heavenly flight, and left the dull, and droyling carcas to plod on in the old rode, and drudging Trade of outward conformity. (YP, I, 520–22)

Characteristically inveighing against what he considers to be the results of prelatical corruption, Milton causes the many aspects of that corruption to express themselves in a vision of a deformed body. The fraud of traditions, idolatry, formal worship, vestments, set liturgy—all these are resolved into an image of God being re-embodied, reincarnated in human form. Once "triumphing to the highest pitch of *glory*, in the *Spirit*," the *corpus mysticum* now becomes a "dull, and droyling carcas," a debased version of what the corporeal body of the visible church is supposed to signify. Ideally, as Milton states in *Christian Doctrine* (Bk. II, ch. 3–4), the visible church should serve, especially in matters of worship, as an outward manifestation of the invisible (CM, XVI, 221).

After all, as Hooker says (*Laws*, Bk. III, ch. 1), the members of the corporeal body of the visible church are "one in outward profession of those things, which supernaturally appertain to the very essence of Christianity" (*Works* I, 220). This view is certainly in agreement with Milton's attitude, as indicated in *Christian Doctrine* (Bk. I, ch. 29), that the visible church should express itself in "the proper external worship of God" (CM, XVI, 221). When it does not, however, an embodying occurs. In matters of worship, Milton articulates this idea in a number of ways.

For example, implicit in the *corpus mysticum* image we are discussing is a liturgical dimension. The debased "joyning" of the body "in a formall reverence and *Worship*" (characterized by the hallowing, the fuming, the sprinkling, and the bedecking) suggests a perversion of the rite of communion. That suggestion is perfectly in accord with the *corpus mysticum* concept, since, traditionally, there was "a close connexion . . . between the Eucharist as the body of Christ and the Church as His mystical body."[14] Indeed, *corpus verum* and *corpus mysticum* traditionally bore an integral relationship: "Holy bread," states *The Rationale of Ceremonial* (circa 1540), reminds us "that all Christian *men* be one mystical body of Christ as the bread is made of many grains and yet but one loaf."[15] What results from the implicit association of the Eucharist and the mystical body in Milton's tract is a criticism of the prelatical overemphasis upon the ritual trappings of the communion. To Milton, such ostentation, with its stress upon externals rather than what they symbolized, represented a return to popery. The implications of that return he treated graphically in *Christian Doctrine* (Bk. I, ch. 28). There, he criticizes the doctrine of the Real Presence by contrasting Christ's true presence in the incarnate flesh with his symbolic presence in the Lord's Supper. Attributing to "the outward sign the power of bestowing salvation or grace by virtue of the mere *opus operatum*," the Papists in their Mass have "converted the Supper of the Lord into a banquet of cannibals" (CM, XVI, 197). Similarly, with their acceptance of outward signs to the exclusion of all else, the prelates have caused the *corpus mysticum*, in its association with the rite of communion, to become perverted.

From an organicist point of view, that idea represents only one aspect of Milton's antiprelatical criticism. Likewise important is his castigation of the prelates through the imagery of investiture. Thus, we recall that the prelates are accused not only of "joyning" the body "in a formall reverence and *Worship*" but of investing it as well: "they be deck't it, not in robes of pure innocency, but of pure Linnen, with other deformed, and fantastick dresses in Palls, and Miters, gold, and guegaw's fetcht from *Arons* old wardrope, or the *Flamins vestry*" (YP, I, 521). The use of the imagery of investing as a characteristic of the embodying process is not arbitrary: ecclesiastically, it has its roots in existing controversies over ministerial vesture. First becoming an issue in 1549, the idea of proper ministerial attire made itself felt when by 1552 "albs, copes, and vestments were forbidden throughout England." Such strictures were reflected in the 1552 Edwardine Book of Common Prayer, in which "all references to vestments were deleted" from "the directions for the ordering of deacons, priests, and bishops."[16] That atmosphere was, of course, altered when Mary (and, even after her, Elizabeth) came to the throne. As a result, in 1565, three hundred of the fellows of Saint John's College, Cambridge, appeared in church without their surplices. "When Sir William Cecil, Chancellor of the University, commanded the students to wear their vestments or be expelled, the heads of the Colleges, along with John Whitgift . . . petitioned for dispensation because of the threatened loss of students."[17] Shortly thereafter disputes were waged like the Vestiarian controversy, comprised of such tracts as *A briefe discourse against the outwarde apparell and Ministring garments of the popishe church* (1566). The issues implicit in tracts like these became part of the Admonition controversy between Whitgift and Cartwright, were treated at length by Richard Hooker in his *Laws*, and were taken up again with renewed virulence in the seventeenth century.

From the Puritan point of view, ministerial vesture recalled popery and was therefore a defilement. John Wyclif had earlier admonished the clergy in "De Papa" (circa 1380) by saying that God's "men shulden not be cloþid" in rich garments.[18] His admonition was, in turn, elaborated upon by such later writers as William Prynne, who complained, in *A Looking-Glasse for all Lordly Prelates* (1636), that although Christ's clothing was very poor, "one poore thread-bare Coate without a seame," the prelates "have many silken, sattin, scarlet, Gownes, cassockes, robes, coapes . . . patterned up with many seames and piebalde colours," which "poore Christ never wore" (pp. 67–68). This clothing led the Puritans to refer to prelatical attire as "abominable rags, polluted garments, marks and sacraments of idolatry," indeed, downright "filth."[19] That criticism found ample expression in *The Letany of John Bastwick* (1637), where we discover the following castigation: "One would think that hell were broke loose and that the devils, in surplices, in hoods, in copes, in rochets, and in foursquare cowturds upon their heads, were come among us and beshit us all—foo, how they stink!"[20]

In contrast to the extreme Puritan view, the Anglican attitude toward ministerial vesture reflected their via media outlook. Whitgift, Hooker, and Hall should provide a firm foundation for understanding this outlook. Countenancing the use of ministerial vesture, Whitgift says, in his *Defense of the Aunswere* (1574): "Wherefore that which I say is true, that even then ministers of the gospel might be known by their apparel, as Christ and John the Baptist, and therefore not to be so strange a matter that ministers should also differ from other men in their apparel."[21] Hooker restates this position in his *Laws* (Bk. V, ch. 28) when he sanctions the minister's attire as "but a matter of mere formality" and when he admonishes: "as we think not ourselves the holier because we use it, so neither should they with whom no such thing is in use think us therefore unholy, because we submit ourselves unto that which . . . the wisdom of authority and law hath thought comely. To solemn actions of royalty and justice their suitable ornaments are a beauty. Are they only in religion a stain?" (*Works* I, 347–48). But the most telling defense may be found in Joseph Hall's *Episcopacie by Divine Right. Asserted* (1640). Reflecting a major tendency of the organicist impulse, Hall causes the issue of ministerial vesture to represent his via media stance regarding the problem of ornaments in general. In doing so, he reveals an essential aspect of the Anglican mind in its understanding of the relationship between external things and what they represent: "The accession of honourable titles, or (not incompatible) priviledges, makes no difference in the substance of a lawfull and holy calling: These things, being merely externall, and adventitious, can no more alter the nature of the calling, than change of suits, the body. Neither is it otherwise with the calling, than with the person whose it is; the man is the same whether poore or rich. . . . As a wise man is no whit differently affected with the changes of these his outward conditions, but looks upon them with the same face . . . so the judicious beholder indifferently esteems them in another . . . valuing the calling according to its own true worth, not after the price or meanenesse of the abiliments wherewith it is cloathed; if some garments be coarse, yet they may serve to defend from cold; others, besides warmth, give grace and comelinesse to the body; there may be good use of both; and perhaps one and the same vesture may serve for both purposes" (pp. 66–68).

Essentially, what Hall is doing in this statement (through his recourse to the organicist idea of changing clothing) is invoking the concept of adiaphorism or indifferency. Derived from Saint Paul, the concept became important to such reformers as Luther and Calvin and emerged in the sixteenth- and seventeenth-century disputes between the Puritans and the Anglicans.[22] Hall voices the Anglican point of view when he says that externals like titles and privileges cannot alter the nature of a calling, that outward conditions are of no consequence to inward makeup. Milton would respond by saying that outward conditions are of absolute importance to inward makeup, that the form a thing assumes is integral to its nature (the matter of which it consists).[23] By extension, to call the form of something indifferent, as the prelates do, is to violate that matter which it manifests. With respect to the liturgy, for example, Milton felt that since the form of it had been tainted by its Romish use, its matter had been likewise tainted, so that we could not assume the form of the liturgy without being subject to its corruptions: " 'Tis not the goodnesse of matter therefore which is not, nor can be ow'd to the *Liturgie*, that will beare it out, if the form, which is the essence of it, be fantastick and superstitious, the end sinister, and the imposition violent" (YP, I, 688).

Such assumptions led the Puritans to remove root and branch all vestiges of Romish use from their church. They sought to purge their church of all those corruptions brought upon by forms that smacked of popery, forms that were imposed, as Laud's *Constitutions and Canons Ecclesiastical* (1640) makes clear, for the sake of "decency" (YP, I, 992). As an example of the way in which that need for purification was expressed, we might recall that the Commons, on 1 September 1641, "issued resolutions for the reform of ceremonies" previously attacked, "with fanatical fervor," by the Puritans: "the communion table to be removed from the east end of the church; rails around the communion table to be taken away; crucifixes and images of the Virgin Mary to be removed; candlesticks and tapers not to be used on the communion table; bowing at the name of Jesus to cease."[24] Even more to the point, however, was the "unauthorized destruction of images in many cathedrals" in the summer of 1642 by the Puritan troops. "On 26 August 1642 Colonel Sandys led his men into Canterbury Cathedral where 'were demolished that day . . . many Idolls of stone, thirteen representing Christ and his twelve Apostles standing over the West doore of the Quire, which were all caste doune headlong and some fell on their heads and their Myters brake their necks.' "[25] With all ornaments purged away, the Puritans worshipped in unadorned places. As Donne complains, the Puritans "think they cannot . . . call upon God out of the depth, except it be in a Conventicle in a cellar [or] . . . in a garret, and when they are here [in the Anglican service] wink at the ornaments, and stop their ears at the musique of the Church."[26]

What relationship this iconoclastic, purgative impulse has to the organicist idea will become clear if we examine the rhetoric with which the Puritans justified their activities and with which the Anglicans responded to that justification. In Book 5, chapter 15, of his *Laws*, Hooker records the Puritan view that unadorned places are most "suitable unto the nakedness of Jesus Christ and the simplicity of his Gospel" (*Works* I, 312). Undoubtedly, Hooker's understanding of the Puritan view is accurate. An integral part of the Puritan impulse is the need to divest the body of its trappings, a need that we have already witnessed in those fellows of Saint John's College, Cambridge, who appeared in church without their surplices. The embodiment of this impulse in polemic is discernible in Milton's desire, expressed through a language of divestiture, to purge the church of its corruption. He first accuses the prelates of investing "*Christs* Gospell," that "thredbare Matron," with pompous attire, of overlaying "with wanton *tresses*" her "chast and modest vaile surrounded with celestiall beames," and of bespeckling her "in a flaring tire" with "all the gaudy allurements of a Whore" (YP, I, 557). Then, he reproaches them: "Tell me ye Priests wherefore this gold, wherefore these roabs and surplices over the Gospel? is our religion guilty of the first trespasse and hath need of cloathing to cover her nakednesse?" (YP, I, 828). Milton's impulse is to divest the prelates themselves, "undresse them of all their guilded vanities" (YP, I, 853), in order to have their "inside nakednesse thrown open to publick view," thereby revealing their "deformed barenesse" (YP, I, 668, 765).

It is precisely this attitude that the Anglicans saw as a primary Puritan characteristic: the need to divest, to lay bare. Appropriately, they responded through a language that drew upon the same organicist concept of divestiture and investiture to defend their position. Thus, Donne justifies the Anglican via media by saying: "we stript not the Church into a nakedness, nor into rags; we divested her not of her possessions, nor of her Ceremonies" (*Sermons* IV, 106). Rather, like his Anglican counterparts, Donne saw the necessity of clothing the church lest it be unseemly: "God is said in the Scriptures to apparell himself gloriously; (*God covers him with light as with a garment*). And so of his Spouse the Church it is said, (*Her clothing is of wrought gold, and her raiment of needle worke*) and, as though nothing in this world were good enough for her wearing, she is said *to be cloathed with the Sun*. But glorious apparell is not pride in them, whose conditions require it, and whose revenews will beare it" (*Sermons* II, 290).

Organicist in import, such a defense of the Anglican via media represents only one aspect of the way in which the body was incorporated into the Puritan-Anglican disputes. Intimately associated with the Anglican accusation that the Puritan impulse is one of divesting appears the accusation that that impulse, in its zeal, expresses itself in terms of tearing as well. Thus, we find the following statement in Donne: "To a *Circumcision* of the *garment*, that is, to a paring, and taking away such *Ceremonies*, as were superstitious, or superfluous, of an ill use, or of no use, our *Church* came in the beginning of the *Reformation*. To a *Circumcision* we came; but those *Churches* that came to a *Concision* of the *garment*, to an absolute taking away of *all ceremonies*, neither provided so safely for the *Church* it self in the substance thereof, nor for the exaltation of *Devotion in the Church*" (*Sermons* X, 116). The pervasiveness of these ideas is indicated by the fact that, as late as *A Tale of a Tub*, they may be found in Swift's satirical thrust at Jack: "Having thus kindled and enflamed himself as high as possible, and by Consequence, in a delicate Temper for beginning a Reformation, he set about the Work immediately, and in three Minutes, made more Dispatch than *Martin* had done in as many Hours. For . . . *Zeal* is never so highly obliged, as when you set it a *Tearing*. . . . Thus it happened, that stripping down a Parcel of *Gold Lace*, a little too hastily, he rent the *main Body* of his *Coat* from Top to Bottom."[27]

That the association of divesting and tearing does indeed reflect the Puritan attitude is discernible in Milton's castigation of the prelates in *The Reason of Church-Government*: "As for the rending of the Church, we have many reasons to thinke it is not that which ye labour to prevent so much as the rending of your pontificall sleeves; that schisme would be the sorest schisme to you" (YP, I, 786). Milton's statement is especially revealing because it relates the rending of clothing to the rending of the body, that is, the church itself. That form of rending is precisely what Donne warns against when he says: "they pretend *Reformation*, but they intend *Destruction*, a tearing, a renting, a wounding the body, and frame, and peace of the Church." Further, those who pretend Reformation enact a "*Concisionem corporis*, the shredding of the *body* of Christ into fragments, by unnecessary wrangling in *Doctrinall points*; and then *Concisionem vestis*, the shredding of the *garment* of Christ into rags by unnecessary wrangling in matters of *Discipline*, and *ceremoniall* points; and lastly *Concisionem spiritus* . . . the concision of thine own spirit, and heart, and minde, and *soule*, and *conscience*" (*Sermons* X, 104, 105).

The Anglican ideal is to keep the body intact at all costs, to beware of "*Concisio corporis*," as Donne says, lest we "break Jesus in pieces" by departing from "any fundamentall Article of faith, for that is a skin that covers the whole body, an obligation that lies upon the whole *Church*" (*Sermons* X, 115). For this reason, we find such writers as Edward Forsett advocating a via media approach, an encouraging of what is good before a severing of what is bad: "That as in the bodie it is a greater mischiefe not to nourish and sustaine the sound and seruiceable parts, then not to cut off the diseased and corrupted: so in the Commonweale, not to reward and aduaunce the worthie, is more pernicious and of more dangerous consequence, than to afflict, punish, or pare away the hurtfull and infectious: for where the one is but spared awhile by lenitie and impunitie in some hope of amendment, the other vnrespected in his goodnesse, is so pinched by that coldnesse of entertaynment, as hee seldome or neuer can come forward and put forth any shoots of vertue" (*Comparative Discourse*, pp. 46–47). Forsett's statement introduces a new point of reference into our discussion, and in order to appreciate the full impact of the Puritan impulse to tear and sever one part of the body from the other we must take careful note of that point of reference.

Obviously, the organism to which Forsett refers in his via media approach is that of the state. The reference to the body politic at this point is hardly arbitrary, first because its use is universally sanctioned. Otto Friedrich von Gierke states quite unreservedly that "there was

hardly a single system of political theory which entirely escaped this
'organic' tendency of thought."[28] We are perhaps most familiar with
the idea from Book 5 of Plato's *Republic* (V, 462, d), in which the state
is compared to "an individual man," an "organism."[29] But even more
important for our immediate purpose is the intimate association of the
state as political organism with the church as ecclesiastical organism.
The association has a long tradition going back at least as early as the
thirteenth century, when Vincent of Beauvais, in his *Speculum doc-
trinale*, used the term *corpus reipublicae mysticum*.[30] The idea received juristic emphasis when "the venerable image of *sponsus* and
sponsa, Christ and his Church, was transferred from the spiritual to the
secular and adapted to the jurist's need for defining the relations between Prince and State." As a result, "the Church as the supra-individual
collective body of Christ, of which he was both the head and the husband, found its exact parallel in the state as the supra-individual collective body of the Prince, of which he was both the head and the husband." Appropriately, as late as 1603, we discover James I drawing upon
precisely that association in the speech to his first Parliament: "What
God hath conjoined then, let no man separate. I am the husband, and
all the whole island is my lawful wife; I am the head, and it is my body;
I am the shepherd, and it is my flock."[31] Moreover, in line with this idea
was the belief that the king was the single head not only of the civil
realm (political organism) but of the religious realm (ecclesiastical
organism) as well. That is, he was one head over two bodies. His power
over the second realm was explained by the fact that, as ruler, he had
dominion (at least within a temporal context) over the visible church.[32]
Defending precisely that idea, Whitgift voiced the Anglican point of
view when he argued that he was able to "perceive no such distinction
of the commonwealth and the church that they should be counted, as
it were, two several bodies, governed with diverse laws and diverse
magistrates."[33]

     Countering the Anglican impulse to unite the two bodies under
one head, the Puritan impulse sought to separate the two bodies. Specifically, the Puritans maintained that the jurisdiction of church and
state was different, the church concerning itself with inner things, the
state with outer. That is exactly the point of view Milton assumes in
The Reason of Church-Government, where he argues that man, "con-

sisting of two parts, the inward and the outward," is left by "the eternall
providence" "under two sorts of cure, the Church and Magistrat." To
prove that "the magistrat hath only to deal with . . . the outward man,"
Milton sets out "to shape and fashion this outward man into the similitude of a body, and set him visible before us; imagining the inner man
only as the soul." But even "the inner man" takes the form of what
Milton calls "the ecclesiastical body" (YP, I, 835, 839). When these
bodies are unnaturally joined, a monstrosity results. As Milton says in
*Considerations touching the likeliest means to remove hirelings out of
the Church*, "And for the magistrate in person of a nursing father to
make the church his meer ward . . . is neither just nor pious . . . and
upon her [the church], whose only head is in heaven, yea upon him,
who is her only head, sets another in effect, and, which is most monstrous, a human head on a heavenly, a carnal on a spiritual, a political
head on an ecclesiastical bodie; which at length by such heterogeneal,
such incestuous conjunction, transformes her oft-times into a beast of
many heads and many horns" (CM, VI, 82–83). Such is the basis of the
organicist impulse as it expresses itself in Puritan polemic.

With that idea in mind, we can more readily understand the Puritan need to tear and sever one part of the body from the other. The
Puritans saw themselves in that act not as destroying what was healthy
but as curing (by radical means, to be sure) what was unhealthy. That
is, they saw themselves as physicians enacting treatment and cure. That
attitude is apparent in the very titles of their pamphlets, such as Anthony Tuckney's *The Balme of Gilead, For the Wounds of England*
(1643).[34] Moreover, in the passage we have just considered from *The
Reason of Church-Government*, Milton looks upon both the civil magistrate and the clergyman as physicians who cure the body according to
the nature of their office. While the clergyman applies "phisick" to the
"inward bed of corruption," the civil magistrate "seres," "cauterizes,"
and even "cuts off" the corrupt limbs of the outward body if the treatment warrants it (YP, I, 835–36).

Such an attitude is made dramatically apparent in *Of Reformation*. In that tract, Milton presents us with a little self-contained drama,
in which a body summons "all the Members to meet in the Guild for
the common good" in order to contest the presence of "a huge and
monstrous Wen little lesse than the Head it selfe, growing to it by a

narrower excrescency." The wen defends his position by saying "that as in place he was second to the head, so by due of merit; that he was to it an ornament, and strength, and of speciall neere relation, and that if the head should faile, none were fitter than himselfe to step into his place; therefore hee thought it for the honour of the Body, that such dignities and rich indowments should be decreed him, as did adorne, and set out the noblest Members." The body responds by sending for "a wise and learned Philosopher," who examines the wen's "claime and Petition of right" and then says disdainfully: "Wilt thou . . . that art but a bottle of vitious and harden'd excrements, contend with the law-full and free-borne members? . . . Lourdan . . . thy folly is as great as thy filth. . . . thou containst no good thing in thee, but a heape of hard, and loathsome uncleannes, and art to the head a foul disfigurment and burden, when I have cut thee off, and open'd thee, as by the help of these implements I will doe, all men shall see" (YP, I, 583–84). Freely adapting the popular fable of the belly and the bodily members found in Livy's *Historiarum . . . Libri* (II, xxxii) and elsewhere, Milton causes his satiric drama to embody succinctly his organicist assumptions regarding church and state and the need for their separation. By doing so, he ironically inverts the fable to suit his own needs. Customarily used to placate those who criticize policy, the fable, as Milton conceives it, serves to bolster that criticism. In order to appreciate how Milton does this, we will discuss briefly the way in which he adapts to his own polemical purposes the fable as it was commonly understood.

A glance at the version appearing in North's *Plutarch* should provide the needed perspective. The belly, charged by the mutinous bodily members of only remaining "in the midst of the body, without doing anything," defends its usefulness in this manner: "It is true, I first receive all meats that nourish man's body; but afterwards I send it again to the nourishment of other parts the same."[35] What the Renaissance gathered from the fable is discernible in Forsett's statement in his *Comparative Discourse*: "This similitude was both fitly and fortunately enforced by *Menenius Agrippa*, who being imployed in the appeasing and persuading of the seditious reuoulting commons of Rome, did . . . so sensibly shew them their errour, that surseasing their malignant enuy wherewith they were inraged against their rulers (whom they accounted as the idle belly that swallowed the labors of their hands) they discerned at the last, that their repining against, and their pining of that belly, whence was distributed unto them their bloud and nourishment, necessarily tended to their owne destruction; and were thereupon forthwith reclaymed into their bounds of obedience" (p. 3).

The thrust of the fable is ironically the exact opposite in Milton. As Milton interprets the fable, the wen (that is, the belly become episcopal encumbrance) is shown to be not only completely useless, but destructive, despite his protestations that his "Office" is the body's "glory" and that "so oft as the soule would retire out of the head from over the steaming vapours of the lower parts to Divine Contemplation, with him [the wen] shee found the purest, and quietest retreat, as having been most remote from soile, and disturbance." The "wise and learned Philospher" counters that argument like a true organicist by maintaining that "all the faculties of the Soule are confined of old to their severall vessels, and *ventricles* from which they cannot part without dissolution of the whole Body" (YP, I, 584). A self-sustaining entity, complete unto itself, the body should not be joined with or encumbered by any other organism at the risk of creating something unnatural, even monstrous. Thus, Milton concludes that the wen must be severed from the head in order to restore comeliness and health to the body. As he states later in *Of Reformation*, "if we will now resolve to settle affairs either according to pure Religion, or sound policy, we must first of all begin roundly to cashier, and cut away from the publick body the noysom, and diseased tumor of Prelacie" (YP, I, 598).

That Milton's language reflects prevailing Puritan attitudes may be seen in William Prynne's *Lord Bishops, None of the Lord Bishops* (1640), which distinguishes between "the Body it selfe of the Church" and the prelates. The second are "but *wennes,* or *swellings* grown up, and so incorporated into the Body, as overspreading it like a Leprosie, it assumes the denomination of the Body." As such, continues Prynne, they are "great *Swellings*, like the Kings Evill, which are commonly next the Head, or about the necke, in the most principall parts of the Body" (p. 25). Our only recourse, as Alexander Leighton says, in *An Appeal to the Parliament; or Sions Plea against Prelacie* (1628), is surgery: "as a knob, a wen, or any superfluous bonch of flesh, being no member doth not onely overburthen the body, but also disfigureth the feature, yea killeth the body at length except it be cut; so these Bishops be the knobs & wens and bunchie popish flesh which beareth down, deformeth & deadeth the bodie of the Church, that ther is no cure . . . but cutting off" (p. 11).

Finally, the decorousness of Milton's adaptation of the fable of the belly and the bodily members to suit his own purposes is even further enhanced if we consider the following observation by E. K. Chambers: "St. Paul probably had [the fable] in mind when he wrote I Cor. XII: 12–26."[36] Chambers' observation implies the existence of an intimate correspondence, possibly conceived at the very root of organicist thinking, between the body of the state, as represented by the fable, and the body of the church, as represented by the biblical source. If accurate, such an observation would go far to reinforce Milton's political application of the fable to his antiprelatical argument, an argument, as we have seen, based upon fundamental organicist relationships. Whether accurate or not, Chambers' observation at least underscores the Renaissance predisposition to think of the fable and the passage from 1 Corinthians in the same terms. For example, immediately after speaking about the moral import of the fable, Edward Forsett states: "The like comparison is most diuinely enlarged by a much better Orator, and in a much more important poynt of the vnseparable union of the members of Christ with their head, and of the necessary communion of their distinct gifts and works amongst themselves" (*Comparative Discourse*, pp. 4–5).

In the context of Milton's organicist concerns, Forsett's statement throws a good deal of light upon the attitudes embodied in Milton's prose. It allows us to see the underlying unity of Milton's use of the body for polemical purposes: the body of the church, with all its ramifications, finds appropriate correspondence in the body of the state. Unlike what Forsett would maintain, however, the two bodies, in Milton's thought, are to be brought into conjunction only to reveal their essential disparities. Complete unto themselves, they must not be joined for fear of creating a monstrosity. An unnatural joining necessitates a forcible disjoining, a disjoining enacted not for the sake of mutilating the body but for the sake of restoring it to its health. For that reason, the thrust of Milton's reforming zeal is ultimately, in his terms, constructive rather than destructive. His final vision involves not the tearing down of the body but the re-forming of it.

That is the impression one receives from Milton's apocalyptic vision of Truth in *Areopagitica*:

Truth indeed came once into the world with her divine Master, and was a perfect shape most glorious to look on: but when he ascended, and his Apostles after him were laid asleep, then strait arose a wicked race of deceivers, who . . . took the virgin Truth, hewd her lovely form into a thousand peeces, and scatter'd them to the four winds. From that time ever since, the sad friends of Truth . . . imitating the carefull search that *Isis* made for the mangl'd body of *Osiris*, went up and down gathering up limb by limb still as they could find them. We have not yet found them all . . . nor ever shall doe, till her Masters second comming; he shall bring together every joynt and member, and shall mould them into an immortall feature of lovelines and perfection. Suffer not these licencing prohibitions to stand at every place of opportunity forbidding and disturbing them that continue seeking, that continue to do our obsequies to the torn body of our martyr'd Saint. (YP, II, 549–50)

The import of this passage for our discussion is quite significant, especially as it comments upon the way Milton incorporated the organicist idea into his outlook as a reformer. For him, the Reformation itself, as J. Max Patrick suggests, implied a re-forming of the bodily members.[37] Philosophically, in his impassioned plea for the toleration of those who desire "to unite those dissever'd peeces that are yet wanting to the body of Truth" (YP, II, 551) Milton was inclined to see the fulfilling of the Reformation as the attempt to approach bodily wholeness. This idea would seem not only to substantiate still further the argument that, as a polemicist, Milton viewed the world in decidedly organicist terms, but also to indicate that, when called upon, he could rise above the immediate contentions of the time and envision a body that must be called transcendent.

University of Illinois at Chicago Circle

NOTES

1. Don A. Martindale, *The Nature and Types of Sociological Theory* (Cambridge, Mass., 1960), p. 78.
2. Ibid., p. 79.
3. Edward Forsett, "To the Reader," *A Comparative Discourse*, reprinted in *Two Tracts* (Farnsborough, Hants., 1969), p. 1; hereafter cited in the text as *Comparative Discourse*.

4. Michael Walzer, *The Revolution of the Saints: A Study in the Origins of Radical Politics* (Cambridge, Mass., 1965), p. 156.

5. Cited in ibid., pp. 156–57.

6. Richard Hooker, *The Works*, ed. John Keble (New York, 1845), II, 247; hereafter cited in the text as *Works*.

7. The Columbia *Works of John Milton*, ed. Frank Allen Patterson et al. (New York, 1931–1938), XVI, 61; hereafter cited in the text as CM, with volume and page number.

8. See also Rom. xii, 4–5; 1 Cor. x, 16–18, xi, 3, xv, 44; Eph. i, 22–23, iv, 15–16, v, 23, 30, 32; Col. i, 18, ii, 9, 10, 11, 19.

9. Ernst H. Kantorowicz, *The King's Two Bodies* (Princeton, 1957), pp. 195–96.

10. Ibid., pp. 199–200.

11. *The Reason of Church-Government*, in the Yale *Complete Prose Works of John Milton*, ed. Don M. Wolfe et al. (New Haven, 1953–), I, 757; hereafter cited in the text as YP, with volume and page number.

12. Malcolm Ross, *Poetry and Dogma: The Transfiguration of Eucharistic Symbols in Seventeenth Century English Poetry* (New Brunswick, N.J., 1954), p. 189.

13. *The Complete English Poetry of John Milton*, ed. John T. Shawcross (New York, 1963).

14. Darwell Stone, *A History of the Doctrine of the Holy Eucharist* (New York, 1909), I, 94.

15. *The Rationale of Ceremonial*, ed. Cyril S. Cobb, Alcuin Club Collections, XVIII (London, 1910), pp. 41–42.

16. Donald J. McGinn, *The Admonition Controversy* (New Brunswick, N.J., 1949), p. 9.

17. Ibid., pp. 15–16.

18. John Wyclif, *The English Works*, ed. F. D. Matthew, Early English Text Society, LXXIV (London, 1880), p. 471.

19. Cited by Hooker, *Laws* (Bk. V, ch. 29), *Works*, I, 351.

20. In *English Puritanism from John Hooper to John Milton*, ed. Everett Emerson (Durham, N.C., 1968), p. 265.

21. Cited by McGinn, *The Admonition Controversy*, p. 256.

22. Ernest Sirluck, ed., "Introduction," YP, II, 69.

23. See Milton's Ramistic formulations in Bk. I, ch. 7, of *The Art of Logic*, CM, XI, 55–63.

24. Don M. Wolfe, ed., "Introduction," YP, I, 129.

25. Lawrence Stone, *Sculpture in Britain* (Baltimore, 1955), p. 2.

26. John Donne, *Sermons*, ed. George Potter and Evelyn Simpson (Berkeley, 1953–1962), X, 221–22.

27. *Jonathan Swift: Selected Prose and Poetry*, ed. Edward Rosenheim, Jr. (New York, 1959), p. 99.

28. Otto Friedrich von Gierke, *Natural Law and the Theory of Society*, trans. Ernest Barker (Cambridge, 1934), I, 51–52.

29. Plato, *The Collected Dialogues*, ed. Edith Hamilton and Huntington Cairns, Bollingen Series, LXXI (New York, 1961), p. 701.

30. Kantorowicz, *The King's Two Bodies*, p. 208.

31. Ibid., pp. 216, 223.

32. Cf. Walzer, *Revolution of the Saints*, pp. 171–72.

33. Quoted by Charles and Katherine George, *The Protestant Mind of the English Reformation, 1570–1640* (Princeton, 1961), p. 194.

34. For the Anglican point of view, see John Taylor's satiric tract *The Causes of the Diseases and Distempers of this Kingdom; Found by Feeling of her Pulse, Viewing her Urine, and Casting her Water* (1645).

35. "The Life of Martius Coriolanus," *Shakespeare's Plutarch*, ed. T. J. B. Spencer (Baltimore, 1964), p. 303.

36. E. K. Chambers, "Appendix B," *The Tragedy of Coriolanus* (Boston, n.d.), p. 195. According to Chambers, the fable is over three thousand years old.

37. In his edition of *Areopagitica*, in *The Prose of John Milton*, ed. J. Max Patrick (New York, 1967), p. 317, n. 326.

MILTON'S *AREOPAGITICA*: ITS ISOCRATIC AND IRONIC CONTEXTS

Joseph Anthony Wittreich, Jr.

Milton's ambivalent attitudes toward both the English Parliament and Isocrates suggest that his title for this, his most famous, prose work possesses more precise imaginative connections with its substance than is usually supposed. Through his title—and then in his exordium—Milton equates himself with Isocrates and Parliament with the General Assembly. But those equations are shaken by the allusion to St. Paul, who is clearly to be admired for his toleration and whose audience is to be rebuffed for its lack of it. Milton allows the initial correspondences to remain intact until he fulfills the rhetorical demands of his exordium (eliciting the good will of his audience) and then allows ironic inconsistencies to tumble forth. *Areopagitica*, then, is written from two perspectives (the one serious, the other ironic)—a conclusion that is supported by both the allusion to St. Paul and the reference to Euripides' *The Suppliants*. A "perpetual stumbling block" to generations of readers, the title of Milton's oration proves to be an important source of meaning and unity for the work.

THE TITLE for "A Speech of Mr. John Milton for the Liberty of Unlicensed Printing" has been a perpetual stumbling block for those who have tried to decipher it. The point is deftly illustrated by John W. Hales. Finding but "slight resemblance" between Milton's *Areopagitica* and Isocrates' *Areopagiticus*, he maintains that Milton's title makes "the ordinary Briton 'stare and gasp'! It is an unpopular title, and may be taken as a sign of Milton's indifference to merely popular approval."[1] Milton's title continues to perplex more recent editors. Ernest Sirluck, the most notable of them, feels that "in purpose, Isocrates differs so strikingly from Milton that the latter's choice of title is rather curious."[2] Though superficial resemblances between the two orations always have been noted, chiefly in their form and situation, Milton's editors have customarily stressed the violent discrepancies in style and aim. With sustained eloquence, Isocrates implores the General Assembly to restore controls to the Court of Areopagus, while Milton nervously pleads with Parliament to lift controls. Thus it has been proposed, first by Sirluck, then by Michael Davis, that Milton intended his title to recall Saint Paul's speech to the Athenians (Acts xvii, 18–34), which, in its assault on religious conformity and in the urgency with which it presses for toleration, approaches the spirit of *Areopagitica*.[3]

Milton's title, however, possesses more precise imaginative connections with the substance of his oration than has been supposed. Through his title, Milton means to establish a set of correspondences between himself and Isocrates, between Parliament and the General Assembly. But he also challenges those correspondences soon after they are made, by the induction of a Biblical allusion wherein Saint Paul is clearly to be admired for his toleration and his audience rebuffed for their lack of it. Significantly, both allusions are introduced early in the oration. But whereas the one involving Paul is only vaguely formulated, the one involving Isocrates is clearly articulated. Moreover, through the Biblical allusion Milton sets up the basis for an ironic inversion of his initial equation: Milton $=$ Isocrates, Parliament $=$ General Assembly becomes Milton $=$ General Assembly, Parliament $=$ Isocrates —an inversion suggested here but encouraged later. Milton's technique in *Areopagitica*, therefore, is not unlike the one he employs in *Paradise Lost* with the Promethean allusion. There he retains the similarities between Satan and Prometheus just long enough to create the illusion of Satan as a power coequal with God (that is, to fulfill the narrative demands of his story); then he allows their differences to emerge. Here he exploits the initial equation just long enough to elicit the good will of his audience (that is, to fulfill the rhetorical demands of his exordium); then he allows the Pauline allusion to emerge and ironic inconsistencies to tumble forth.

I

In his initial sentence, Milton suggests various attitudes one *might* assume toward the task he is about to embark on: "Some will doubt of what will be the success, others will fear of what will be the censure; some with hope, others with confidence of what they have to speak."[4] In his second sentence, admitting that he has variously assumed each of these attitudes, Milton invites us to consider what his own disposition is toward those whom he addresses and to consider which of these attitudes "swayed most" (718). Such an invitation, alongside Milton's admission that he has "variously affected" each of these attitudes, encourages us to question how seriously he means us to take the self-deprecation and flattery in his exordium and calls attention to his willingness, in the exordium, to juggle, even to misrepresent, crucial details. Milton describes Isocrates' oration as "that discourse to the parliament of Athens that persuades them to change the form of democraty which was then established" (719). Like Milton's oration, Isocrates' was intended to persuade, but it did not. But unlike Milton's discourse, it urges imposing restraints rather than relaxing them, and the vote of the Athenian assembly against his proposal was a vote for liberty, a vote against censorship. However, the forthcoming vote of the English Parliament, despite Milton's appeal, was to be a vote for the continuation of censorship, a vote for ignorance and against liberty. Milton's misrepresentation of an essential fact concerning the effect of Isocrates' oration is especially curious when we recall his painstaking effort in the formal argument not to offend any faction by misrepresentation of detail or by offensive arguments.[5] This curiosity is compounded by Milton's own statement in the First Prolusion that "the first and most important duty of the orator" is to elicit, in his exordium, "the good will of the audience" without which the auditors will be unreceptive to his cause, as well as his assertion in the Seventh Prolusion that oratory is not "merely specious eloquence" and that the orator, therefore, should have a full knowledge of what he says (595, 622). But the curiosity is just as quickly dispelled when we recall that in the First Prolusion, after explaining what an exordium should be, Milton launches into an assault on his audience, telling us he prefers the approval of the learned few to that of the "countless legions of ignorant fellows who have no mind, no reasoning faculties, no sound judgment" (595).

Milton, to be sure, knew what he was talking about in *Areopagitica*. He read Isocrates' *Areopagiticus*, and we may fairly assume that his statement about it is calculated rather than ill informed. Milton was not an incurable idealist, as he is ordinarily depicted at this stage in his intellectual development. His attitudes toward Parliament were more equivocal than customarily thought.[6] It is usually assumed that Milton believed unreservedly in the wisdom of Parliament; however, his daring in misrepresenting an essential fact to them reveals his estimate of their intellectual level. Through his title, Milton has, as it were, locked the ironic context and thus the full implications of his discourse from the members of Parliament who presumably would be unequipped to decipher the allusion. Milton's full meaning is reserved for the esoteric few who can read and comprehend.

Areopagitica is at once a serious statement on the nature of liberty and a tour de force on Parliament, which Milton suspects, for all he says, is about to deny that liberty. As we have seen in the First Prolusion, the streak of playful perversity was not unprecedented in Milton.[7] To disregard the ambivalence of Milton's attitude toward Parliament is to miss the grim irony in *Areopagitica* and to reduce the significance Milton assigned to England at this moment in her history. He envisions a regenerate England *in the future*, but the England of the present is not as yet regenerate.[8] She is wallowing in ignorance, and the "rottenness and gangrene" that Milton describes in *Of Reformation* are, he tells us, "universal" (YP, I, 538). Parliament, presumably, is not uninfected. Milton "implies that Parliament *should* be like the Areopagus," not that it *is* like the Areopagus.[9] Like the ancient governing body, Milton is saying, Parliament *should* aim at educating men, thereby freeing them from bondage; it *should* attempt to build moral character rather than to legislate it.

Milton possessed a heightened awareness of the world he lived in. The artist who wrote *Areopagitica*, while he nurtured the hope that Parliament would rescind the licensing act, was not convinced they would actually do so; thus the strain of irony, as well as the uneven and nervous style, which mirrors the conflict between the idealist who hopes for rescission and the realist who doubts it will occur. There are two perfectly synchronized contexts in which *Areopagitica* may be read —the one serious, the other ironic. Milton's title functions largely within the latter context, making what is necessarily cryptic apparent to the sagacious reader whom Milton would no doubt turn to, rather than to Parliament, as the fit audience for his oration. In the exordium, Milton speaks tongue-in-cheek. What he says about himself and Parliament is the opposite of what he really means. The energy of *Areopagitica* derives largely from the obliqueness of Milton's method which, giving the impression of great restraint, uses praise to imply blame and blame to imply praise.

Milton's attitude toward Isocrates is, likewise, more ambivalent than customarily thought. The differences between *Areopagitica* and *Areopagiticus* are readily apparent, though there are equally striking resemblances and, interestingly, some verbal echoes. Just as peace brought to Athens joy accompanied by complacency, the transference of authority from king to Parliament brought to England a false sense of security. Milton's *Areopagitica* may be read, like *Areopagiticus*, as a warning that the strength of the nation consists not in physical strength alone but in the quality of the citizenry and in the spirit that animates them. In Athens and England alike political well-being seemed to be accompanied by degeneracy, the cause of which, Isocrates explains in his exordium, is "that nothing of either good or of evil visits mankind unmixed."[10] The thought is echoed, with somewhat different implications, in *Areopagitica*: "Good and evil we know in the field of this world grow up together almost inseparably; and the knowledge of good is so involved and interwoven with the knowledge of evil, and in so many cunning resemblances hardly to be discerned, that those confused seeds which were imposed on Psyche as an incessant labor to cull out and sort asunder, were not more intermixed" (728). Isocrates, furthermore, explains that "after our city had been laid waste by the barbarians, we became, because we were anxious about the future and gave attention to our affairs, the foremost of the Hellenes; whereas, when we imagined that our power was invincible, we barely escaped being enslaved" (Norlin, II, 107). If we substitute for *the barbarians* the words *popery and royalism* we convert the Isocratic statement into one which describes the hypothetical situation Milton is trying to avert. Isocrates sees the very "hatred . . . which then brought disaster" being revived (Norlin, II, 109). Just as the General Assembly, to which Isocrates addresses himself, was prostituting its talents and provoking hostility, taking on the image of the barbarians whom it detested, so the English Parliament was casting itself in the image of the Anti-Christ, employing the tactics of the papists and becoming itself what it most deplored.

Thus both Isocrates and Milton wonder how men can tolerate tyranny and suggest—Isocrates more blatantly than Milton—that "we may finally run aground on rocks more perilous" than those which at one time loomed before us (Norlin, II, 115). Despite the obvious tactical differences (Isocrates encouraging new restraints, Milton urging that old ones be lifted), both orators are trying to avert anarchy and preserve democracy. Milton and Isocrates, moreover, share a belief in a natural hierarchy and apprehend the truth afforded to them by experience, namely that when those best fit to rule are not ruling, or are not ruling well, democracy becomes tyranny. Correspondingly, Milton concurs in Isocrates' view that "it is not by legislation, but by morals, that states are well directed, since men who are badly reared will venture to transgress even laws which are drawn up with minute exactness, whereas those who are well brought up will be willing to respect even a simple code" (Norlin, II, 131). In Milton's words, "real and substantial liberty . . . is rather to be sought from within than from without" (830).

For Milton and Isocrates, then, education is tantamount to attaining and preserving real liberty, and while the latter elects to detail and demonstrate the value of education within *Areopagiticus*, Milton does so in a separate essay, *Of Education*. Whereas Isocrates chooses to embody in a single discourse the ideal and the way that ideal is, through education, to be achieved, Milton prefers to envision the ideal and allow *Of Education* to elaborate how that postulated ideal is to be realized. Isocrates and Milton attribute to the educated man the capacity for distinguishing between good and evil and the perspicuity for selecting the former. Isocrates contends that education removes "the root of evil," delivers "the young man from the sins that spring from it," and prepares those "educated liberally and trained in high-minded ways" for private and public life (Norlin, II, 133). Milton, in parallel statements, asserts that the aim of education is "to repair the ruins of our first parents" and to prepare a man "to perform justly, skilfully, and magnanimously all the offices, both private and public, of peace and war" (631–32).

At the same time, a thread of nationalism runs obtrusively through the latter parts of both orations. Isocrates exclaims, "our own country is able to bear and nurture men who are not only the most gifted in the world but in the arts and in the powers of action and speech, but we are also above all others in valour and in virtue." And he concludes, "we shall both deliver ourselves from the present ills and become the saviour not of Athens alone, but of all the Hellenes" (Norlin, II, 150, 157).

Milton, in another parallel statement, sees "a noble and puissant nation rousing herself like a strong man after sleep, and shaking her invincible locks. Methinks I see her as an eagle muing her mighty youth, and kindling her undazzled eyes at the full midday beam, purging and unscaling her long-abused sight at the fountain itself of heavenly radiance" (745).

There is, then, an intellectual kinship between Milton and Isocrates—a kinship clearly evident when their orations are set side by side. But despite this interlocking of minds at many points, there are, likewise, many Isocratean notions that Milton either rejects or extends to new conclusions.

The extravagant praise that Milton heaps on Isocrates in *Areopagitica* is not unprecedented in his other works. In *Of Education*, Milton identifies Isocrates with the great educators of antiquity; in Sonnet X, he describes him as "Old man eloquent." It is important to note, however, that in each instance the praise comes parenthetically and may, if taken by itself, be misleading. Milton looked to Isocrates as a symbol of the classical rhetorical tradition, encompassing Aristotle, Plato, and Cicero, all of whom he admired and by whom, in his rhetorical habits, he was profoundly influenced. Like Isocrates, Milton was interested in cultivating the whole man and would concur with the ancient that the true orator at once should unite in himself the qualities of rhetorician, statesman, and philosopher, and should himself be a virtuous man if he is to be a purveyor of moral truth. Milton, moreover, would have received quite amiably the Isocratic notion that from the orator spring the forces that create noble civilizations and governments. Unlike Isocrates, however, for whom ἰδέα referred to both thought and the rhetorical patterns out of which speech is composed, but primarily to the latter, Milton, when using the word, refers exclusively to the former, as in the Seventh Prolusion (623).

These observations, particularly the last, lead into a fundamental discrepancy between the educational aims of Isocrates and Milton.[11] From Isocrates' point of view, three things—natural ability, practice, and education—combine to make a successful orator, but of these education is the least important. Milton, however, makes education primary and knowledge a means to spiritual rather than practical fulfillment. Isocrates' scheme of education, though in its particulars impossible to reconstruct from his writings, clearly begins with rhetorical training and may move on to other matters. Milton's scheme, on the other hand, begins with the acquisition of knowledge and ends with the formulation of it—a function of rhetoric. Thus, Milton would resist the Isocratic notion that the orator should be able to speak on any subject but need not know the details of that subject. In the Seventh Prolusion, Milton makes it abundantly clear that he should indeed know his subject.

The most conspicuous difference between Isocrates and Milton is one of temperament, a difference illustrated by their respective attitudes toward freedom. For Isocrates, essentially an authoritarian, true freedom implies the right to entertain certain ideas, not the privilege to examine erroneous ideas. For Milton, essentially a liberal, moral choice is the essence of freedom. Whereas Isocrates, a conservative temperament, recoils into the past as he attributes the weakness of Athens to an excess of freedom, Milton, a revolutionary temperament, hurls himself into the future as he ascribes the infirmities of his age to a surfeit of restraints.

Correspondingly, the styles of the two orators differ. Isocrates' eloquence, more sustained than Milton's, is always tamed and muted. Milton's style, on the other hand, nervous and uneven, continually rising and falling, reaches emotional temperatures and soars to titanic heights unprecedented in Isocrates. This stylistic discrepancy was doubtless realized by Milton. In his oratorical habits, Milton follows his own precedent of sometimes scrupulously observing, other times deliberately violating, convention. Milton's rigorous adherence to Isocratic structure coupled with his conspicuous departure from Isocratic style involves a trenchant criticism of his predecessor, and Milton's deprecation of "specious eloquence" makes his praise of Isocrates subject to qualification. Milton surely would imagine his own efforts as surpassing those of his predecessors. He would hope that his own *Areopagitica* would excel the *Areopagiticus* of Isocrates.[12] Milton, it seems, intentionally employs a style unlike that of Isocrates, in part to define their intellectual differences. In defining them, Milton distinguishes Isocrates, who makes philosophy the servant of rhetoric, from himself, Milton being inclined to underplay rhetorical devices with those of poetry to emphasize his ideas.[13] While Isocrates regarded rhetoric as a purely verbal art not fundamentally related to knowledge, Milton seems to follow the concept of symbolic style which, Ruth Wallerstein observes, derives from Tertullian and combines with the Christian rhetorical tradition in the epistles of Paul. For Milton, then, style is inseparable from thought and is, therefore, "translated into thought symbols."[14]

Moreover, while Isocrates immerses himself in the classical oratorical form and perfects it, Milton elects to approach that form "analytically and externally, tearing [it] to pieces and putting [it] together again in a way that expresses his genius," not that of his models.[15] Milton's attitude toward Isocrates, a symbol of the classical rhetorical tradition, is therefore not unlike his attitude toward Homer and Virgil, symbols of the classical epic tradition. Through the various forms Milton elects to write in he is linked with their practitioners (ancient poets and classical rhetoricians), but his own revolutionary temperament impels him to dissect those forms in order that he may recreate them. Thus just as Milton finally rejects much that comprises epic tradition—its vapid machinery and secular values—he similarly repudiates the "specious eloquence" of Isocrates and the tradition that he represents, as well as the pernicious values that such eloquence dresses. Milton simultaneously pays homage to those, like Isocrates, who created and perfected the literary forms he is heir to and seeks to undermine the uncongenial values those forms characteristically embodied.

II

Through these ambivalences Milton prepares the way for the ironic inversion that comes in his peroration and that is signaled by the often cited passage in which he exempts "popery and open superstition" from toleration (747). The passage is well known and by some regretted. It is, nevertheless, a crucial passage. At this point the serious and ironic contexts of *Areopagitica* conflate, and the exemption of Catholic books relates significantly to both contexts. There is clearly a problem regarding how we are meant to read this passage. In many passages throughout *Areopagitica* Milton makes it quite clear that his argument for unlicensed printing applies to *any book whatsoever* (for example, 725, 726, 727, 729, 730). That Milton's concession involves a flagrant contradiction of his main argument relating to *any book whatsoever* is so obvious that it is difficult to be patient with those who believe Milton himself was impervious to the inconsistency.

The business of the orator, Milton knew, was "to inform, to regale, and to convince" (604). He knew, as well, that arguments "fortified with impregnable logic" could unwittingly be shattered by "the speaker's fault" (596). Milton was not disposed to let a careless inconsistency reflect invidiously on a carefully devised argument. Apprehending the subtleties of irony, Milton contends that it "was born out of Tragedy" and "ought to resemble his parentage, to strike high, and adventure dangerously at the most eminent vices among the greatest persons" (YP, I, 703). The irony Milton describes is clearly "the non-heroic residue of tragedy," that sort of irony which derives from a poet who, from the state of experience, looks at tragedy from below.[16] Milton sagaciously chooses irony as the most effective vehicle for lending form to the ambiguities of human experience, a mode which, Kenneth Burke reminds us, "aims to give a representation by use of mutually related or interacting perspectives." Burke ascribes the double perspective and uncertainties of attitude manifested in true irony to "a sense of fundamental kinship with the enemy [in this case, Parliament], as one needs him, is indebted to him, and is not merely outside him as an observer but contains him within."[17] And Frye, after quoting Burke, explains further that "whenever the reader is not sure what the author's attitude is or what his own attitude is supposed to be" we have high irony of the sort Milton describes and, presumably, uses in the peroration of *Areopagitica*.[18]

Insofar as Milton nurtured the hope of persuading Parliament to repeal the licensing act, his concession may be politically expedient, at the same time that it reveals Milton's grim realization of the low tolerance level of the masses whom Parliament represents. Even more significantly, the concession, rather than being introduced in the formal argument, is relegated to the peroration and buried in its emotional extravagance. The equivocation, then, is politically expedient and, in that sense, functions within the serious context of the oration. But its most important function is to reveal and make explicit the ironic context. To the ordinary reader, inimical to the profound liberal principles of the main argument, there would be no contradiction. However, Milton's fit audience, following the ambivalences suggested by Milton's title, would at this point be prepared to decipher the irony Milton presents: men of principle will comprehend the incongruity between this concession and Milton's earlier assertion that *any book whatsoever* should be exempt from the licensing order; men of expediency will ignore, indeed they probably will not even grasp, the incongruity. The initial equation (Milton = Isocrates, Parliament = General Assembly), shaken during the course of *Areopagitica*, is inverted here as Milton likens himself to the General Assembly and Parliament to Isocrates. While the former oppose restrictions to freedom, the latter encourage, even require, them. The reigning principle to which Isocrates and Parliament adhere is authoritative and, from Milton's point of view, wrong. It assumes that men should be diverted from error and directed toward truth by force, not reason. But reason, Milton tells us, "is but choosing" (733), choosing between good and evil, between those books that propound virtue and those that seek to pervert it. Milton and the General Assembly, on the other hand, represent the value of true and unrestricted freedom, which unbinds men from chains rather than shackling men into them. Milton's concession, then, which comes as a calculated afterthought, infuses his argument with cogency for the ordinary reader at the same time that, for the fit reader, it reveals his suspicions of the general character of the Parliament which he is fictitiously addressing. Moreover, Milton reveals the true dramatic center of his oration, which is not so much a battle of the books as a contest of wills.[19] In *Areopagitica*, the indomitable will of Milton relentlessly opposes and is opposed by the collective will of Parliament. Milton, on the one hand, the liberator of a Promethean nation, seeks to unbind the Titan, while the Hephaestean Parliament seeks to shackle him in chains.

The predications of this argument—that Milton reads the signs of his time incisively, that through his title he means to create an ironic context from which his oration may be read, a context which significantly qualifies the exemption of Catholic books and goes a long way toward explaining it—are supported by the inexplicit Biblical allusion to Paul speaking to the Athenians in the Court of Areopagus. Paul (Milton) is speaking to the Athenians (Parliament), propounding a "new doctrine" as he reflects upon the Areopagus whose members spent "all their leisure telling or listening to something new" (Acts xvii, 18–34), thereby avoiding the iron yoke of conformity. The present Athenians (Parliament), Paul (Milton) notes, are promulgators of ignorance. Reproved by the masses, Paul (Milton) is approved by a few who join him and become believers. Paul's situation and that of Milton in *Areopagitica* are analogous to one in which Milton found himself in the First Prolusion. There Milton addresses "an utterly unsympathetic au-

dience" and makes it clear that he, nevertheless, prefers the approval of
the few learned men (595). The implied allusion to Paul is doubly interesting in that Paul maintains an ambivalent attitude toward those
whom he addresses and, like Milton, uses praise to imply blame.[20]
Paul at once hopes to convince the multitudes and realizes those hopes
are vain. Milton sustains this double attitude toward audience throughout his oration. The jeering masses and few believers among the Athenians nudge Milton into a recognition that Parliament was likely to
confirm itself in error and consign the nation to ignorance. Milton is
saying, as he said in the Seventh Prolusion, that to tolerate censorship
is to tolerate ignorance and for Parliament to tolerate ignorance is for
Parliament to tolerate "the most despicable of all things" (628). Through
his wit, Milton converts a whole arsenal of arguments into weapons that
he uses against ignorance to destroy her.

Milton's quotation from Euripides' *The Suppliants,* which appears
on the title page of *Areopagitica,* brings further support to this interpretation. Milton quotes from Theseus' speech about "true liberty," first
in the original Greek, then in English. In the first instance, he at once
attracts the learned and impresses the unlearned, while through the
translation he makes the essence of the speech accessible to all.[21] That
quotation has a context, and that context—comprehensible to Milton's
fit audience—reinforces the ironic implications of the title. Despite the
seemingly fierce patriotism and the unconditional compliment Theseus seems to pay the Athenians, the play itself cannot be described as a
eulogy of Athens. It is too full of grimness for that, and like *Areopagitica,*
is "as much a national warning as a national eulogy."[22] Thesus, like
Milton, describes not what is but what may be. And like *Areopagitica,*
The Suppliants deals with what is for Euripides and Milton the central
paradox of man—his capacity for intelligence and self-control on the
one hand, his domination by irrationality and folly on the other. Milton
and Theseus alike represent the perfect leader who gives full rights and
liberties to all, and both reveal their own slackening confidence in those
who are the leaders of the nation but who are not in tune with its temper
and needs.

To conclude: Milton's *Areopagitica* crystallizes an attitude toward
life that by 1644 had been galvanized into a vision, but it is an attitude
retrospectively evaluated and significantly revised. Besides replacing
the vision of a paradise on earth with the hope for a paradise within,

Milton's theory of retaliation deepens and his psychology of hatred undergoes refinement. The intellectual sanction that Milton, sagacious politician, gives to bigotry is one he comes to regret, as he learns that the idealist cannot afford to prostitute his values in order to make them palatable to the untutored masses. In *Areopagitica*, we see Milton struggling, and struggling heroically, with a question vital to his age and to all time. To see Milton's title as an inextricable part of his oration is to explain many baffling problems in this, his most famous, prose work. And it is, incidentally, both to pay Milton the overdue compliment of having unified his work imaginatively and to remove any suspicion that he was embarrassingly ignorant of the full implications of his argument. To see Milton grappling with the timeless question of censorship is, finally, to see him, in William Empson's words, as "a broader and more adroit kind of man than is usually thought, less pedantic and self-enclosed, more humane, more capable of entering into other people's motives and sentiments."[23]

University of Wisconsin, Madison

NOTES

1. *Areopagitica* (Oxford, 1894), p. xxxii. See also C. W. Crook, ed., *Areopagitica* (London, 1906), p. xxi.

2. *Complete Prose Works of John Milton*, ed. Don M. Wolfe et al. (New Haven, 1953–), II, 486, n. 1; hereafter cited as YP, with volume and page number.

3. Sirluck, ibid.; Davis, *Areopagitica and Of Education* (London, 1963), p. 5.

4. *John Milton: Complete Poems and Major Prose*, ed. Merritt Y. Hughes (New York, 1957), p. 717; cited hereafter by page number in the text.

5. See Sirluck's discussion of Milton's carefully devised strategy (YP, II, 170–78), and Michael Fixler, *Milton and the Kingdoms of God* (London, 1964), p. 126.

6. Cf. Arnold Williams, "*Areopagitica* Revisited," *University of Toronto Quarterly*, XIV (1944), 74, and Zera S. Fink, "The Theory of the Mixed State and the Development of Milton's Political Thought," *PMLA*, LVII (1942), 705–36.

7. In the Third Prolusion, after delivering an assault on scholastic philosophy, Milton praises Aristotle, the fountainhead of scholastic philosophy, in his peroration. One may recall, moreover, that Milton prefaces *Comus*, his celebration of chastity, with a line from Virgil's Second Eclogue, a celebration of homosexuality, and that he toyed nastily with an engraver in a Greek inscription he affixed to a portrait he despised.

8. See Edgar F. Daniels, "Samson on *Areopagitica*," *N & Q*, XI (1964), 92–93.

9. Hughes, *Complete Poems and Major Prose*, p. 716.

10. *Areopagiticus* in *Isocrates*, trans. George Norlin (Cambridge, Mass., 1962), II, 107; hereafter cited in the text.

11. Donald L. Clark, *John Milton at St. Paul's School* (New York, 1957), esp. pp. 1–10, provides the most extensive discussion of the intellectual kinship between Isocrates and Milton. He is surely wrong, however, when he says that "Milton's school would be more like that of Isocrates . . . for Isocrates oriented his school toward preparing his pupils 'to speak in Parliament or Counsel,' by making all liberal knowledge function through rhetoric" (p. 252).

12. In *Apology for Smectymnuus*, written two years and eight months before *Areopagitica*, Milton dedicates himself to surpassing his classical oratorical models, an intention he reaffirms in *Defensio Secunda*.

13. See Crook, ed., *Areopagitica*, p. x; E. N. S. Thompson, "Milton's Prose Style," *PQ*, XIV (1935), 1–15; Alan F. Price, "Incidental Imagery in *Areopagitica*," *MP*, XLIX (1952), 217–22; John X. Evans, "Imagery as Argument in Milton's *Areopagitica*," *TSLL*, VIII (1966), 189–205—all of whom make his point and elaborate it convincingly.

14. Ruth Wallerstein, *Studies in Seventeenth-Century Poetic* (Madison, 1950), p. 31.

15. Northrop Frye, *The Return of Eden: Five Essays on Milton's Epics* (Toronto, 1965), p. 91.

16. Northrop Frye, *Anatomy of Criticism* (Princeton, 1957), pp. 224, 237.

17. Kenneth Burke, *A Grammar of Motives* (Cleveland, 1962), pp. 503, 512.

18. Frye, *Anatomy of Criticism*, p. 223.

19. See Price, "Incidental Imagery in *Areopagitica*," p. 217.

20. Paul's opening address has been interpreted in two ways: (1) Men of Athens, I see that in every respect you are extremely *religious*; (2) Men of Athens, I see that in every respect you are extremely *superstitious*. In either case Paul's meaning is the same; the only difference is that in the second instance it is conveyed directly and in the first through irony. The Greek word δεισιδαιμονεστεροι is ambiguous, as noted by John Calvin, *Commentary Upon the Acts of the Apostles*, ed. Henry Beveridge (Edinburgh, 1844), II, 154–56. However, "most interpreters . . . whether regarding the speech as Pauline or as Lukan, accept the verse as a true *captatio benevolentiae*, and the word as meaning 'religious' (favorable sense)" as opposed to "superstitious" (unfavorable sense); see *The Interpreter's Dictionary of the Bible*, ed. George Arthur Buttrick et al. (New York, 1962), IV, 465.

The Text of the New Testament of Jesus Christ, trans. William Fulke (London, 1589) reveals that Acts xvii, 22, is the basis of a controversy between Protestant and Catholic theologians that has a direct but undetected bearing on *Areopagitica*. The Latin Vulgate translates the Greek word as "superstitious" rather than "religious." The reluctance of Protestant theologians and translators to correct the mistranslation is polemical rather than scholarly: the Protestants continually use the passage to remind the papists that Paul openly opposed the sort of superstition and idolatry they see the Catholic church representing.

There is, then, a double propriety in Milton's use of Paul's address. First, Paul's speech provides him with a precedent for rebuking rather than praising his audience, an exact parallel for his own ironic exordium. Second, in boldly attacking open superstition and idolatry Paul provided militant Protestants with justification for their equally bold attacks on popery (see, for instance, Fulke's notes to verse 22 in *The Text of the New Testament*, p. 217ᵛ). Paul's speech, then, illuminates both the ironic and the serious contexts of *Areopagitica*.

21. Wilbur Elwyn Gilman, *Milton's Rhetoric: Studies in His Defense of Liberty* (New York, 1939), p. 11.

22. See H. D. F. Kitto, *Greek Tragedy* (New York, 1950), p. 239. Edgar Daniels, "Samson on *Areopagitica*," has suggested that in the famous passage, beginning "Methinks I see a noble and puissant nation rousing herself like a strong man after sleep" (745), Milton intentionally does not identify Samson, thereby preventing the reader "from pursuing the comparison to its catastrophic ending, which is hardly appropriate to his prophecy for England" (p. 93). To the extent that Milton does not wish to prophesy doom for his nation, Daniels is correct; but to the extent that Milton may wish to win his audience, even if out of fear, Daniels misses the rhetorical force of this passage. Both Cicero and Quintilian acknowledged that the orator may, indeed, have to rely upon fear to win the sympathy of some members of his audience, in which case they counsel the orator to confine the tactic to the peroration and to veil the threat so as not to alienate members of the audience whose sympathies have already been won.

23. William Empson, *Milton's God*, 2d. ed. (London, 1965), pp. 317–18.

MILTON AND TACITUS

Edwin B. Benjamin

The political and historical literature of the seventeenth century was greatly influenced by the study of Tacitus. Milton, though not the Tacitean that some professed to be, drew frequently on this material. In the antiepiscopal and antimonarchical tracts, he presents the Stuart government as trying to establish a repressive and enervating tyranny in England, and consistently draws parallels (not all from Tacitus) with the process by which Roman liberty was extinguished under the empire. In the *First Defence*, he objects to Salmasius' interpretation of Tacitus, calling Tacitus much more the republican than the friend of kings. The recovery of Tacitus had increased knowledge of Roman Britain, and, like other English Renaissance historians, Milton uses him in his *History of Britain*. Milton also appears to have been influenced by the much discussed Tacitean style. His adaptations of passages from Tacitus in the *History* seem at times to imitate directly the wit and concision of the Latin, and it is likely that some of these features are carried over into the style of the epics.

TACITUS HAS always been a popular author, but he has probably never been more popular than during the century following the publication of Lipsius' famous edition of 1574. He was drawn on by dramatists (Jonson's *Sejanus*, Racine's *Britannicus*), painters (Rembrandt's *Civilis among his Batavians*), musicians (Monteverdi's *Poppaea*), was even made the subject of a sonnet sequence (Adimare's *La Polinnia*), but he was best known to the increasing number of those interesting themselves in matters of politics and statecraft. He was an important authority for such social theorists as Bodin, Lipsius, Botero, Bacon, Sir John Eliot, to name but a few; and beginning with the first political commentary, by Carlo Pasquale in 1581, he was made the subject of numerous others, on the order of Machiavelli's *Discorsi*.

The whole intricate structure of *ragione di stato,* as it was developed in political commentaries, essays, histories, was heavily indebted to Tacitus; in particular he was thought to be the repository of the *arcana imperii,* the secrets of ruling (the phrase itself seems to come from Tacitus),[1] the "Patriarch, and Oracle of States-men," the "Arch-Flamming of Modern Policy,"[2] who has looked behind the curtain and who can therefore disclose to those intelligent and subtle enough to follow him the intricate processes by which states and men are governed and controlled.

The intellectual effort represented by this body of writing was considerable, and though to some extent the point of view is objective and even scientific—an analysis of what men are rather than what they should be—it was sufficiently weighted on the side of power politics to attract widespread odium. "Happy had the world been, if Tacitus had alwaies been Tacit."[3] It was not only that Tacitus was thought to reveal too much of the inner workings of statecraft; he was thought to encourage, implicitly at any rate, unlawful seizure of power and tyrannical repression once power is seized—two things that were customarily connected. These of course were the charges most commonly levelled against Machiavelli as well, and the two were often identified and considered equally dangerous.[4] When, for example, in Boccalini's *Ragguagli di Parnaso,* Tacitus is elected ruler of the island of Lesbos, he unsuccessfully attempts by the approved methods of power politics to turn an elective monarchy into a tyranny, and the implication of the elegant fiction is that contemporary politicians are studying Tacitus with the same purpose in mind. Boccalini's extensive political commentary on Tacitus was not allowed to be published in Venice, nor was it published during his life; permission was refused for lectures on Tacitus at Oxford in 1627–28;[5] and though such reactions probably seemed extreme to most educated men of the time, they indicate a widely held stereotype.

The Machiavellian, so-called black Tacitism, was based largely on the *Annals* and *Histories,* especially those parts describing the machinations of Tiberius and Sejanus or the brutal scramble for the empire that took place after the death of Nero, and though this was the image of Tacitus that was best known to the seventeenth century, there was also the libertarian Tacitus that, as Renaissance merged into Enlightenment, increasingly recommended itself to the learned world. Tacitus is always mindful of the republican, senatorial Rome that was swept away by the civil wars and the establishment of the empire, and the treacheries and subserviences of Tiberian or Neronian Rome are always measured against the Stoic virtue of a Brutus, a Cassius, or a Cato—or their less effective imitators Thrasea and Helvidius Priscus—who haunt the pages of the *Annals* and *Histories* as surely as the ghost of the elder Hamlet haunts the corrupted castle of Elsinore. Nor does Tacitus only look backward; he also looks to the barbarian peoples surrounding Rome, particularly the Germanic tribes, for traces of a liberty and morality that had been lost to the more cultivated Romans. This was the Tacitus that appealed to the eighteenth and nineteenth centuries more than to the order-centered Renaissance, but as early as la Boétie's *Discours de la servitude volontaire* (1548) we can find this interpretation developing.[6] Tacitus' influence on la Boétie, though not major, is by no means insignificant, and in the republican and antimonarchical literature that begins to emerge with the wars of the Reformation, particularly in France, we find Tacitus playing something of a part. Hotman's *Franco-Gallia*, the *Vindiciae contra Tyrannos*, and the *Brutus*, all make some use of Tacitus, in idealizing ancient opponents of tyrannical rule and in appealing to a tradition of native institutions as opposed to those inherited from Rome. Although Tacitus is better known for his interest in ancient Germany, he pays some attention to Gaul, and if his vein of republicanism seems at times spurious, it at least serves as an effective counterimage to the tyrannical methods of a Tiberius or a Nero.

It is not easy to know how well Milton knew Tacitus. He was enough of an individualist not to feel it necessary to follow current fads, and he certainly preferred the great Greek writers of the classical age, and among the Romans Cicero and the great Augustans, to the Silver Age writers who were so popular in certain seventeenth-century circles. Although Tacitus would undoubtedly be accorded a place among "those authors which are most commended; whereof some were grave Orators & Historians," in which Milton says he was "not unstudied" in his earlier years,[7] he never singles him out by name as he does Plato and Xenophon, nor does he mention him in *Of Education*. In the *First Defence*, he praises him as a "grave and judicious writer," but on the other hand, in the exchange with Henry de Brass in 1657, he finds him inferior to Sallust, whom he terms the best of the Latin historians.[8] Still, in *Lycidas*, he apparently adapts the famous tribute to Helvidius Priscus from the *Histories*: "That last infirmity of Noble mind";[9] and references are frequent enough to suggest that if not the professional Tacitean, Milton made use of the language of Tacitism and its insights. It is likely, although the matter is never clearly formulated, that what Milton objected to was the rather narrow interpretation given Tacitus by the statists, and that he responded sympathetically, as in the *First Defence*, to the broader, more libertarian aspects.

Milton's acquaintance with the distinctions of the politicians, those "acute wits of Europe," as Swift calls them in *Gulliver's Travels* (Part II, ch. 7), who have "reduced politics into a science," can be seen from the *Index Politicus* of the *Commonplace Book* and the seven pages of marginalia jotted down, perhaps by Milton, in Sir Richard Baker's translation of Vergilio Malvezzi's political commentary on Tacitus (London, 1642).[10] Like most men of his age, Milton was interested in the operations of political power—the shifting forms of government, the role of Parliament, the secrets of court and state. His entries in the *Commonplace Book*, and his annotations of Malvezzi (if the latter are his), show his familiarity with the more or less technical language of politics then in vogue. Tacitus plays a part here, if not a large one, along with Machiavelli, Guicciardini, de Thou, and Bacon. In the *Commonplace Book*, he is quoted directly once, and then in a quotation from Bacon, but the idea expressed—the connection between tyrannical rule and a subservient populace—recurs often in Milton. A related passage is Milton's analysis of the reason why Rome shifted from republic to empire, a question of great interest to those in the seventeenth century who wanted England to shift from kingdom to republic, and his pointing to a weakening of moral fibre is at least Tacitean, if not directly traceable to any one passage in Tacitus: "The form of state to be fitted to the peoples disposition some live best under monarchy others otherwise. so that the conversions of commonwealths happen not always through ambition or malice. as amoung the Romans who after thire infancy were ripe for a more free government then monarchy, beeing in a manner all fit to be K[ing]s. afterward growne unruly, and impotent with overmuch prosperity were either for thire profit, or thire punishment fit to be curb'd with a lordly and dreadfull monarchy; which was the error of the noble Brutus and Cassius who felt themselves of spirit to free an nation but consider'd

not that the nation was not fit to be free, whilst forgetting thire old
justice and fortitude which was made to rule, they became slaves to
thire owne ambition and luxurie" (YP, I, 420). A version of these ideas
will occur later in Milton's attack on what he considers Salmasius'
misinterpretations of Tacitus.

The marginalia to Malvezzi's commentary show much more directly the part played by Tacitus in the world of politicians. Here we
catch something of the atmosphere—the mystery, the dissimulation,
the irony—as well as the jockeying for power that links Tacitus and the
Machiavellians. Notable, and typical, is Milton's apparent acceptance
as valid of the *arcana imperii*, the secrets of ruling that occur so often
in the literature of the politicians. The thought that there were such
secrets to be learned by a ruler was always somewhat shocking to the
age (the king of Brobdingnag in his naiveté cannot imagine what they
could be, apart from common sense and reason, justice and lenity), and
in utilizing them Milton is showing his acquaintance with the most
sophisticated thought of the time. The first use of the phrase in English
seems to be in the notes to Sir Henry Savile's translation of the *Histories*
and *Agricola*, the first translation of Tacitus in English (Oxford, 1591),
and it is interesting to note that in one of his marginalia Milton harks
back to the court of Elizabeth in the 1590s, to the time when Tacitism
had its first impact on English thought:

Sub Tiberio fuerunt Germanicus et Drusus: hic erat filius principis et pollebat
amore patris. Germanicus progener Augusti, adoptatus a Tiberio, cui accedebat
amor populi ex patrui alienatione: itaque Tacitus de Tiberio dixit eum
sustinuisse iudicium. quod enim alterum peroptabat ille, alterum verò populus
neminem populo ostendit, ac scilicet aut alterum firmando suum abijceret, aut
hunc preferendo, studia popularium in se concitaret: hoc arcanum imperij
non nescivit Elizabetha regina Angliae, adeoque lege cavit, ne quis sub poenâ
capitis, mentionem faceret haeredis regni, dicens sibi ante mortem non esse
fodiendum sepulchrum: rationem reddit Tiberius Macroni: orientem ab eo
solem adorari, occidentem deseri: adeoque teste Tacito. 1. Histor. suspectus
semper invisusque dominanti est, quisquis proximus destinatur.[11]

This is a good example of technical Tacitism, and narrow and petty
as such analyzing may seem to be, its moral neutrality and its air of
exposing the *real* truth gave it an appeal of irresistible novelty. This
excerpt is typical of the *Marginalia*, which themselves are no different
from hundreds of other such collections, published and unpublished.

These distinctions carry over into the prose. Although as a rule

Milton prefers where he can to ground his arguments on divine law as revealed in the Bible, rather than on natural law as manifested in history, he sees in history recurrent pattern if not demonstrable design, and as he moves from the ecclesiastic considerations of the antiprelatical tracts to the more secular defense of the Cromwell government, he relies more frequently on historical precedent. One of the periods he refers to most often is that which saw the extinction of the Roman republic and the establishment of the more or less tyrannical empire, hoping of course that England will reverse the process, throwing off the tyranny of the Stuarts and establishing a republican commonwealth. While this is not precisely Tacitus' subject, it has much in common with his interpretation of Roman history under the Julian-Claudian emperors.

In the antiprelatical tracts, Milton develops for the first time his belief that a deliberate attempt has been made—in this instance by the bishops—to impose a tyranny on England, and he sees the bishops as using among other things the methods of the politicians to thwart the proper fulfillment of the Reformation. But whereas in his private jottings Milton approached the distinctions of the politicians more or less dispassionately, here he sees them as part of the structure of power politics. He is thinking primarily of the methods of the Jesuits as furthering what he regards as the tyranny of the Counter-Reformation, and it is interesting to see Malvezzi's commentary on Tacitus appear in this context.

This is the masterpiece of a modern politician, how to qualifie, and mould the sufferance and subjection of the people to the length of that foot that is to tread on their necks. . . . To make man governable in this manner their precepts mainly tend to break a nationall spirit, and courage by count'nancing upon riot, luxury, and ignorance. . . . Alas Sir! a Commonwealth ought to be but as one huge Christian personage, one mighty growth, and stature of an honest man, as big and compact in vertue as in body; for looke what the grounds, and causes are of single happines to one man, the same yee shall find them to a whole state, as *Aristotle* both in his ethicks, and politiks, from the principles of reason layes down. . . . For certain I am, the *Bible* is shut against them, nor *Aristotle* is for their turnes. What they can bring us now from the Schools of *Loyola* with his Jesuites, or their *Malvezzi* that can cut *Tacitus* into slivers and steaks, we shall presently hear.   (YP, I, 571–73)

The "slivers and steaks" of Tacitus refer to the political commentaries, the method of which we have noted Milton himself following in the marginalia; here, however, he associates them with the Jesuits and modern politicians, whom he accuses of seeking to establish a tyranny. Milton never tires of pointing out the bond between tyranny and slavery, and, as with his attacks on Bishop Hall's Senecan style, the "tyrannous Aphorism" seems to him the badge of a servile mind: "Others betake them to State affairs, with souls so unprincipl'd in vertue and true generous breeding, that flattery, and Court-shifts, and tyrannous Aphorisms appear to them the highest points of wisdom, instilling their barren hearts with a conscientious slavery, if, as I rather think, it be not fain'd" (YP, II, 395). Though here the target is personal advancement at court rather than the establishing of dominion over others, the calculated programming involved was thought to be much the same in both processes, the *ars aulica* applying in a personal sphere the methods of the *ars imperandi.*

In the antimonarchical pamphlets, Milton extends to Charles and his advisers the accusations he had levelled against the bishops. Where modern historians see Charles as acting mainly out of desperate expediency and weakness, Milton sees him as working deliberately through a cabinet council, aided by Strafford and the prelates, to destroy the traditional native liberties and to establish the arbitrary rule of the monarchy. To "putt Tyranny into an Art" is his telling phrase, and this involves, on the part of the would-be tyrants, familiarity with the great mass of historical precedent, "court maxims," "Essays and curtal Aphorisms," empirical observations that had been built up by the writers on political subjects (YP, III, 344, 500, 496). How this process was thought to work can be seen by the description of the activities of Henry III of France given in Enrico Davila's *History of the Civil Wars of France,* a book that went through two hundred editions. Henry III had as advisers for his nefarious schemes two Florentines, "men exceedingly learned in the Greek and Latin studies"; every day after dinner he retired with them and "making them read unto him *Polybius* and *Cornelius* Tacitus, but much more often the discourses and Prince of Machiavel; which readings stirring him up, he was so much the more transported with his own secret plots."[12] Milton's version of this is the "Turkish Tyranny" he describes in the *Commonplace Book* and the *Observations upon the Articles of Peace,* which was said to have been planned by Charles IX and Catherine de Medici in secret consult at Blois: "Thuanus relates that a plan was considered at Blois by King Charles IX, the Queen Mother, and others for reducing the French

monarchy to a Turkish tyranny; and he reports at length the very good
reasons for doing this as stated by a certain Poncet" (YP, I, 457). Whatever the name, the implementation of tyranny was thought to follow a
familiar pattern: the enervating of the spirit of the people; the bringing
in of foreign troops; the use of "Spies and haunting Promooters," to
name a few of the points that Milton mentions (YP, III, 344, 578, 449,
576). For Milton the process is inevitably connected with Catholicism,
especially the Spanish Catholicism of the Counter-Reformation, and
in a notable image that conveys the atmosphere of this type of opinion,
he describes the interdependency of "Tyranny and fals Religion":
"This however must not be let pass without a serious observation; God
having so dispos'd the Author in this Chapter as to confess and discover
more of Mysterie and combination between Tyranny and fals Religion,
then from any other hand would have bin credible. Heer we may see
the very dark roots of them both turn'd up, and how they twine and
interweave one another in the Earth, though above ground shooting up
in two sever'd Branches" (YP, III, 509). "Yet dig'd the Mole," writes
Henry Vaughan describing the Machiavellian politician, and it is in
this setting that the cabinet council, whether of Charles IX or Charles
I, was thought to flourish.

Though Tacitus, as we have seen, contributed to formulating the
body of opinion Milton is drawing on, Milton does not refer to him unmistakably in the antimonarchical writings. Tacitus had been quoted
in the House of Commons, notably by Sir John Eliot in his famous
attack on Buckingham, comparing him to Sejanus. Charles is reported
to have said when he heard of the speech, "Why then I must be
Tiberius." It is likely Milton had heard of the incident and throughout
his work he makes a number of references to Tiberius—most brilliantly
in *Paradise Regained*—but although he compares Charles to Nero and
Caligula and draws the parallel (as he is to do at greater length in the
First Defence) between English liberty and the liberty of republican
Rome, he does not look to Tacitus for support. Yet Tacitism, as the
syncretic mind of the age would have understood it (the concept, not
the word), is to some degree felt. The first page of *The Tenure of Kings
and Magistrates*, for example, paraphrases a sentence from Sallust (the
original is on the title page of *Eikonoklastes*) describing the baneful
effect of tyranny: "Hence it is that Tyrants are not oft offended, nor
stand much in doubt of bad men, as being all naturally servile; but in

whom vertue and true worth most is eminent, them they feare in earnest, as by right thir Maisters, against them lies all thir hatred and suspicion" (YP, III, 190).[13] This sentence has some claim to be called Tacitean since the original appears to have been imitated by Tacitus at least twice. In a chapter of his *Politica* dealing with tyranny (*quid ea sit, & eius ingenium*), Lipsius, the famous Tacitean (who claimed that if a knife were held to his throat there was no sentence of Tacitus he could not repeat), had collected these three passages, plus a number of others more or less related.[14] The ieda of course is central both to Tacitus' picture of Rome under the Caesars and to Milton's fears for what England might become under the Stuarts. If we can not call Tacitus the direct progenitor, he could be considered at least a cousin once removed.

Tacitus, latent in the antiprelatical and antimonarchical tracts, surfaces unmistakably in the *First Defence*. Presenting a far more comprehensive theory of state than in the earlier tracts, Milton also extends the comparison between the England that changed from monarchy to commonwealth and the Rome that changed from republic to empire. He sees the true tradition of Rome as antimonarchical, as the expulsion of the early kings demonstrated; when in the first century B.C. republic was abandoned for empire, Milton feels that the Roman people yielded their rightful sovereignty "under compulsion by the Caesars, who gave the fair title of law to what was but their own violence" (YP, IV, 460). Yet even under the empire such tyrants as Tiberius and Nero made a show of submission to the Senate, and a good emperor like Marcus Aurelius did not refuse respect to the old Stoic heroes Cato, Thrasea, Helvidius Priscus, nor even to the tyrannicide Brutus. Although in this interpretation of Roman history Milton is most indebted to Cicero, especially in his attacks on Antony as main subverter of the republic, he also draws on Tacitus—possibly because he has been cited by Salmasius—and shows a greater familiarity with him than his earlier writings suggest. Tacitus is the main source of information about Thrasea and Helvidius Priscus (as we have seen, Milton in *Lycidas* had borrowed a phrase from Tacitus' description of the latter); Tacitus is also the source for Tiberius' and Nero's pretended respect for the authority of the Senate. Milton's knowledge of Tacitus comes out most clearly in his objection to a sentence Salmasius had quoted from Tacitus in support of monarchy: "The gods have given the emperor supreme authority, while the subjects are left with the glory of obedience" (*Annals*, VI, 8). Milton points out that these are the words of Marcus Terentius, a Roman knight on trial for his life, who is attempting to flatter Tiberius, and that they do not represent the real opinion of Tacitus, whom Milton calls "a noble writer most opposed to tyranny." Milton then cites two other passages (*Annals*, I, 3–4), in which Tacitus laments the moral change that took place as republic lapsed into empire: "After the victory at Actium the form of government was overthrown and no trace of the old pure manners could be found; equality was over and everyone looked to the orders of the emperor"; and "When equality was ended and self-seeking violence began to take the place of decent moderation, then despotisms appeared and among many peoples remained forever" (YP, IV, 443). The libertarian side of Tacitus has perhaps been at times exaggerated, but Milton, probably because of his own sympathies in that direction, is one of the first in England to recognize it.

As one of the few classical writers interested in non-Roman peoples, especially the Germans, Tacitus was frequently referred to during the Renaissance by antiquarians and by those who were attempting to find a historical basis for a native cultural tradition distinct from that of Rome. He was quoted by both the German reformers and by the French defenders of tyrannicide, and his idealization of the Germans undoubtedly contributed to the view, beginning to emerge, that saw northern Europe as the home of freedom, and Mediterranean and Slavic Europe as sunk in despotism and hierarchy. In the *First Defence*, Milton cites the authority of Tacitus for limitation of royal power among both the ancient Germans and Britons, and he also calls Holland the ancient home of freedom, which may well refer to the revolt of the Batavians under Civilis, for which the only account is in Tacitus (YP, IV, 448–49, 479, 311, 396). The episode was frequently referred to by the Dutch themselves in the course of their eighty-year struggle against Spanish domination. And in the *Second Defence*, which is more general and rhetorical than the first—less a barrage of texts and allusions—he refers twice to Germanic freedom (YP, IV, 555, 654). "War and liberty before peace and servitude" is a commonplace of antiquity; not last effective are Tacitus' versions of it, which he customarily put in the mouths of Germanic opponents of Rome (*Histories* IV, 17, 64, 76). Milton uses the antithesis several times in the *First Defence*, and though one of these refers specifically to Livy, it is not unlikely, in view of his interest in German liberty, that there are also lingering echoes of Tacitus (YP, IV, 390, 512, 518).

The recovery of Tacitus in the Renaissance, plus a more systematic knowledge of classical authors, had expanded somewhat the knowledge of early British history, and in his *History of Britain* Milton as a matter of course makes use of him. For pre-Saxon times, the medieval chroniclers had been content to follow the fictions of Geoffrey of Monmouth, and little actual history remained beyond a brief summary of Caesar's invasion and a garbled recollection of the conquest of Britain by Claudius, the principal features of which—both false—were his marriage with the British princess Genuissa and his circumnavigation of the island. Polydore Vergil, dismissing Geoffrey to the annoyance of English antiquarians, was the first to utilize classical sources in his account of Roman Britain. He included a more complete account of Caesar's invasion, and from Tacitus and perhaps Dion Cassius, he described subsequent Roman conquest and colonization, including the striking appearance of Caractacus in Rome, the revolt of Boadicea, and the invasion of Scotland by Agricola, which Scott's antiquary Jonathan Oldbuck was later to block out as an epic poem for his young friend Lovell. Subsequent historians followed Polydore, usually expanding him somewhat, and as a result Tacitus contributed a few new faces to the pantheon of national worthies, notably Caractacus and Boadicea. A similar process can be traced on the Continent, where a more comprehensive knowledge of the classics combined with a growing sense of national identity to create new heroes. The Batavian leader Civilis, as we have mentioned, the only account of whose rebellion against the Romans is Tacitus' *Histories*, became to the Dutch in their war against Spanish rule a symbol of national resistance to foreign domination and was commemorated by Rembrandt in a picture now in Stockholm.

Milton was of course familiar with what was known of the history of Roman Britain. His list of proposed subjects for tragedy includes a number from early British history, in particular Cartismandua, the British queen who betrayed Caractacus to the Romans, and in his *History of Britain* he follows what had become by this time the more or less standard account of Roman Britain, much of which is drawn from Tacitus. He includes only the first of the three famous speeches—Caractacus' acknowledgment of defeat on the occasion of the triumph in

Rome; Boadicea's address to her troops before the final battle; Gal-
gacus' devastating attack on Roman methods of conquest in his speech
before the battle with Agricola in the Grampian Hills, a sentence from
which is sometimes quoted today by opponents of United States intervention in Vietnam.[15] But he follows Tacitus' brief account of the
subjugation of Britain and the rule of the early governors. Like other
writers of the time, he has a somewhat ambivalent feeling toward his
ancient forebears: he has some sense of a primitive simplicity and
honesty ("thir dealing, *saith Diodorus*, plaine and simple without
fraude"), but he cannot stomach their superstition, their sexual practices and the habit of painting their bodies (YP, V, 60). He is obviously
fascinated with Boadicea, as most writers have been, and is suspicious
of the conflicting, extravagant details about her; but to him, as his
comment on the final defeat indicates, she is certainly not the Joan of
Arc figure she became to the nineteenth century: "But the truth is,
that in this Battel, and whole business, the *Britans* never more plainly
manifested themselves to be right *Barbarians*; no rule, no foresight, no
forecast, experience or estimation, either of themselves or thir Enemies;
such confusion, such impotence, as seem'd likest not to a Warr, but to
the wild hurrey of a distracted Woeman, with as mad a Crew at her
heeles" (YP, V, 80). Though aware of Roman deficiencies, Milton prefers
Roman law and civilization to an undisciplined liberty, and, like many
of his contemporaries, he accepts Rome's civilizing mission for Britain
much as he accepts English rule over the *"wild Irish."*

On the other hand, Milton is not without reservations on the subject of imperial Rome. He recognizes, as with Julius Caesar, that Roman discipline and might can only too easily lapse into tyranny, and
following Tacitus (*Agricola*, 16), he blames the excessive rigor of
Suetonius Paulinus in pacifying Britain after his defeat of Boadicea
(YP, IV, 444–46; V, 82). Tacitus' father-in-law Agricola had been gov-
ernor of Britain under Domitian, and in the short memorial life
that has survived, Tacitus gives a brief description of his admin-
istration, which Milton, like the other historians following Polydore, includes. Milton has a sharper sense of Roman rapacity than
his predecessors and praises Agricola for bringing "peace into some
credit; which before, since the *Romans* coming, had as ill a name as
Warr" (YP, V, 85). A number of sentences are adapted, including one
we will discuss below, describing the enervating effects of Roman civility

on conquered peoples. The situation of Agricola under Domitian—the good man threatened under a tyrant for doing good—is recurrent in Tacitus, and Milton's account of Agricola's recall, if not taken directly from Tacitus, is thoroughly in the spirit of Tacitus, even to his measured antitheses: "These perpetual exploits abroad won him wide fame; with *Domitian*, under whom great virtue was as punishable as op'n crime, won him hatred. For he maligning the renown of these his acts, in shew decreed him honours, in secret devis'd his ruin. *Agricola* therefore commanded home for doeing too much, of what he was sent to doe, left the Province to his Successor quiet and secure" (YP, V, 92).

As has often been noted, Milton's work is very much of a piece, and patterns once established are likely to recur. Some of those developed in the prose, associated with the Tacitean point of view, crop up again, although in greatly abbreviated form, in the later poetry. For all his show of libertarianism, Satan rules hell through cabinet council "In close recess and secret conclave" (*PL* I, 795); "dark *Divan*," (X, 457). And his destruction of Adam and Eve is not without political overtones, a hoped-for enslavement along the order of a Turkish tyranny: "with necessity, / The Tyrant's plea" (IV, 393–94). The dismal course of human history that follows humanity's rejection of Christ is summed up in a version of the Sallustian-Tacitean epigram prefixed to *Eikonoklastes*: "so shall the World go on, / To good malignant, to bad men benign" (XII, 537–38). The Roman greatness that Satan dangles before Christ in *Paradise Regained* has lost the strength and simplicity of its origins, nourished now by heartless cruelty and enervating luxury.

> That people victor once, now vile and base,
> Deservedly made vassal, who once just,
> Frugal, and mild, and temperate, conquer'd well,
> But govern ill the Nations under yoke,
> Peeling thir Provinces, exhausted all
> By lust and rapine.   (IV, 132–37)

The words are Christ's, but the ever-receding glimmerings of a lost innocence could easily come from the writers of the Silver Age. Almost as a rule in Milton's later poems, the world is so unfriendly to right action that a generous nature can only stand against the tide with an Abdiel, Enoch, or Samson, or cultivate an inner serenity. Such a predicament has much in common with Stoic, or exilic, attitudes in general and is not necessarily confined to Tacitus, but it fits his melancholy vision of a society in which, as a Germanicus or an Agricola found out, to do well is to do ill, and for doing nothing no man is called to account.

Is there anything in seventeenth-century English that can be called a Tacitean style? If so, was Milton influenced by it? The economy and weight possible in an inflected language such as Latin make analogy between Latin and English ultimately suspect, but there can be little question that writers themselves distinguished a Ciceronian from a Senecan or Tacitean style and at times deliberately attempted to reproduce certain characteristic features. In his epigram "To Sir Henrie Savile," Tacitus' first English translator, Jonson, for example, praises Savile for rendering Tacitus' "numbers, both of sense, and sounds,"[16] and though a poetic tribute should perhaps not be taken too literally, it is likely that he is accepting stylistic imitation as part of a translator's task. And Savile's volume bears out Jonson's verdict. Although on one occasion Savile attacks the style of Tacitus (pp. 205–06), he himself at times appears to be consciously imitating it—not always with happy results—both in his translation and in his brief original composition, *The Ende of Nero and Beginning of Galba*, which he wrote to fill in the gap between where the *Annals* break off and the *Histories* begin. What this imitation consisted of we shall see in a later example.

The style of Tacitus was most commonly attacked or praised for its obscurity. Those who attacked it felt that in his choice of words, his rather unusual constructions, and his avoidance of the kind of balance and symmetry that helps the reader of Cicero and Livy, he was deliberately obfuscating his subject matter; his defenders, on the other hand, felt that it was precisely these qualities that made possible the penetration of his vision, that only by being difficult can one be profound. There is in the Renaissance a tradition of the enigmatic—a well-known English example is George Chapman—according to which the writer, whether poet, philosopher or politician, is a kind of keeper of mysteries, addressing himself to a group of initiates, above and beyond the capacities of the vulgar. Tacitus himself was given this character, one who will take the knowing reader behind the veil and reveal to him the mysteries of statecraft. The very difficulty of his Latinity, which seems not to have been always well understood by the earlier generations of the Renaissance, probably helped in creating such a belief; there is also his insistence on the hidden springs of things, whether of character, as in his portrait of Tiberius, or of the famous *arcana imperii* that we have already discussed. His interest in the German forests and the uncharted reaches of the northern seas is a more literal manifestation of this feeling, and it is thoroughly characteristic that when Agricola pushes up into Scotland with his army, Tacitus describes the inhabitants as terrified, the secret of their sea having been exposed, the last refuge to the conquered shut off (*Agricola,* 25).

Although to the seventeenth century Tacitus' description of the mysterious was largely confined to the mysteries of statecraft, the example of his style undoubtedly led to experiments in the enigmatic and cryptic, and stimulated greater attention to paradox and irony. Tacitus can be like Seneca, brief and pungent, but more typically he is asymmetrical, deliberately twisting and imbalancing the normal regularities of the Latin period. It is not always easy to decide when the involutions of seventeenth-century style are deliberately planned or merely careless, but in addition to Savile, the labored style of such writers as Henry Wotton and Robert Naunton, both of whom had reputations as *politiques,* is probably an attempt to imitate the arcane and enigmatic associated with the Taciteans. In Jonson's *Sejanus,* the letter that Tiberius sends to the Senate sealing Sejanus' fate is another example, certainly with its twistings and turnings very different from Jonson's usual prose. In a brilliant passage, Morris Croll has called attention to the broader implications of the vogue for Tacitus, though I am not sure that the prose of Bacon really fits his case:

But the desire for wit and ingenuity was only one phase of seventeenth-century taste. Combined with it was a desire for ceremonious dignity, an ideal of deliberate and grave demeanor, which was partly, no doubt, an inheritance from the courtly past, but was modified and indeed largely created by the profound moral experience which the new age was undergoing. . . .

Seneca—its favorite author—might *suggest* the ideal manner; but he was too superficial, too familiar . . . Tacitus, if he had not been too difficult . . . would have been the usual exemplar of English prose style. Bacon's great service to English prose was that he naturalized a style in which ingenious obscurity and acute significance are the appropriate garb of the mysteries of empire, and by means of his example the Tacitean strain became familiar.[17]

Provocative as Croll's distinctions are, they are too general to be applied meaningfully to Milton's style, and it is equally certain that Milton has little of the rather technical imitation of Tacitus found in Savile and perhaps a few others. Milton was contemptuous of the English imitators of Seneca and he probably felt similarly about the Sir Politick-would-bes of the time. Yet that his own satirical vein must certainly have responded to the wit and irony of Tacitus can be seen from the occasional passage that we can set directly against Tacitus. From his version of a short passage from the *Agricola* which had been used in abbreviated form by Polydore Vergil and repeated in fuller versions by subsequent chroniclers, we can see that Milton is able to convey, perhaps more successfully than any of his predecessors, the point and wit so characteristic of the Latin. In addition to Tacitus and Milton, I have included the versions of Polydore, Holinshed, Savile, and Daniel. Holinshed seems to have bypassed Polydore and gone in his own way to the original; with Savile, who was one of the first Englishmen to gain an international reputation for classical scholarship, we see emerging a different relationship to the text, one that I believe is followed to some degree by Daniel and Milton. The three are attempting to imitate a manner as well as to transmit relevant facts.

Tacitus

Sequens hiems saluberrimis consiliis absumpta. namque ut homines dispersi ac rudes eoque in bella faciles quieti et otio per voluptates adsuescerent, hortari privatim, adiuvare publice, ut templa fora domos extruerent, laudando promptos, castigando segnis: ita honoris aemulatio pro necessitate erat.

Polydore Vergil (1513)

Item Britannos generatim ut rudes, bonus pariter moribus ac institutis honestandos curabit, hortando, vt Templa, fora, sedes sibi extruerent, laudando promptos, castigando segnes, quò honoris aemulatione excitarentur ad ciuiles mores: quia ubi virtutis honos publice non est, haud ibi virtutis vel gloriae cupiditas esse potest.

Holinshed (1578)

In the winter following, Agricola tooke paines to reduce the Brittains from their rude manners and customs, unto a more ciuill sort and trade of liuing, that changing their naturall fiercenesse and apt disposition to warre, they might through tasting pleasures be so inured therewith, that they should desire to liue in rest and quietnesse: and therefore he exhorted them priuilie, and holpe them publiklie to build temples, common halls where plées of law might be kept, and other houses, commending them that were diligent in such dooings, and blaming them that were negligent, so that of necessitie they were driuen to striue who should preuent ech other in ciuilitie.

Savile (1591)

The winter ensuing was spent in a most profitable and pollitike deuise. For whereas the Britans were rude and dispersed, and therefore prone vpon euery occasion to warre, to induce them by pleasures to quietnesse and rest, he exhorted them in priuate and helpt them in common to builde temples and houses, and places of publicke resort, commending the forward and checking the slow, imposing thereby a kind of necessitie vpon them, whilest ech man contended to gaine the Lieutenants goodwill.

Daniel (1612)

Aduice was taken, *sayth he,* that the people, dispersed, rude and so apt to rebellion, should bee inured to ease and quiet by their pleasures: and therefore they exhorted priuatly, and ayded them publikely to the building of Temples, Bources, Pallaces: commending whom they found forward, and correcting the unwilling, so that the emulation of honor was for necessity.

Milton (1647)

The Winter he spent all in worthie actions; teaching and promoting like a public Father the institutes and customes of civil life. The Inhabitants rude and scatter'd, and by that the proner to Warr, he so perswaded as to build Houses, Temples, and Seats of Justice; and by praysing the forward, quick'ning the slow, assisting all, turn'd the name of necessitie into an emulation.[18]

Polydore retains a few phrases from the Latin, but the Tacitean flavor is carefully removed. Tacitus had been somewhat ambivalent about the civilizing mission of the Romans. His admiration for Agricola is great, but the passage clearly implies that the warlike spirit of the Britons is to be undermined as they are accustomed "per voluptates" to quiet and leisure, and the emulation of honor that is encouraged by the example of Agricola does not conceal the iron hand of necessity. In Polydore this sense of deliberate policy is lost; he sees the Romanizing of the Britons as a simple triumph of civilization, and in summing up the process, he turns as if by instinct to the virtue, honor, and glory of the humanist educators. His sentence, like Tacitus', concludes with a kind of epigram, but there is a great difference between Tacitus' ambiguity and Polydore's rather facile moralizing. Holinshed includes more of the original than Polydore, but he expands and adapts, somewhat in the manner of the earlier Tudor Englishings. In describing the Britons, for example, he omits Tacitus' carefully chosen "dispersi" and adds somewhat gratuitously "their naturall fiercenesse." A phrase such as "desire to liue in rest and quietness" has none of the political overtones of "quieti et otio," but rather suggests the sweetness and tranquility of the older language that was rapidly giving way before the harder and more critical values of the Renaissance. Holinshed imitates the economy of "hortari privatim, adiuare publice," but not that of "laudando promptos, castigando segnis," and he really cannot cope with the sharpness and cynicism of "ita honoris aemulatio pro necessitate erat." He is admirable in his own way, but it is not the way of Tacitus.

Savile, Daniel, and Milton are not only much more alive to the ironical and political overtones of the passage, Savile frankly labelling Agricola's policy as "a most profitable and pollitike deuise," but they also make something of an effort to imitate its rhetorical turns. None, it is true, quite gets the irony of "quieti et otio per voluptates adsuescerent"—Milton in fact omits the clause completely—but they all retain the Tacitean "dispersi," with its important suggestions of barbarian absence of civil order, and preserve something of the ironic distinction between "aemulatio" and "pro necessitate." Savile perhaps follows the Latin sentence structure too closely. His sentence, like that of Tacitus, is constructed around a pair of main verbs ("hortari . . . adiuvare"; "exhorted . . . and ayded"), with a series of subordinate elements at either end. The result is less happy in English than in Latin, and in Savile the subordinate phrases hang rather loosely together and never come to a proper climax. On the other hand, as other passages in Savile suggest, there may well be an element of experimentation here; increasing use of participial and absolute constructions was one of the devices used by the prose writers of the 1590s to attain a greater complexity of style. Daniel's reaction to the Latin seems to have been to imitate its concision. He shows a good sense of words: "ease and quiet" has the slightly pejorative connotations that "quietness and rest" does not; "Temples, Bources, Pallaces" is at least a bold equivalent of "templa fora domos"; and "dispersed, rude, and so apt to rebellion" has something of the emphasis that comes from a succinct style. As a whole, his sentence is not a complete success, and the concision that imparts a freshness to the style can also lead to unintelligibility, as in the important concluding clause: "so that the emulation of honor was for necessity."

In his own translation of Tacitus (London, 1728), Thomas Gordon criticized Savile's version as "a mere Translation, that rather of one word into another, than that of a dead tongue into a living, or of sence into sence" (I, i), and there is some justification in what he says. Milton seems to have started with the sentence as a whole, and by adhering to normal idiomatic usage, he ultimately comes much nearer than any of the others to conveying the wit and point of the Latin. With the triplets, for example, he is much more skillful than Savile or Daniel in creating a sense of climax. Daniel's "dispersed, rude and so apt to rebellion" is a bit wooden beside the brisk rhythm of "rude, and scatter'd, and by that the proner to Warr," though neither perhaps quite gets the multilevelled meaning of Tacitus' "eoque in bella faciles." In the second triplet, "templa fora domos," Milton does not follow Tacitus' order, which may have its logic, but introduces an order of his own, the final member, "Seats of Justice," both in sound and sense, broadening and expanding the meaning. Converting "laudando promptos, castigando segnis" into a third triplet ("praysing the forward, quick'ning the slow, assisting all") adds a greater regularity to the sentence than is usual with Tacitus—it might even be called Ciceronian. By adding "assisting all," Milton may have wished to enhance the role of Agricola, an effect already achieved by the phrase "a public Father," and by the omission of "quieti et otio per voluptates adsuescerent."

At any rate, the unity of the sentence depends largely on an emphatic final clause, and Milton's is the only English version that leads steadily to a strong conclusion. First, he makes the final clause coordinate with the main clause, thus doing away with the sense of trailing off that a series of subordinate clauses and phrases produces. The main difficulty of the final clause is how to convey its meaning in English without destroying its economy of phrase. It is really a variation of Tacitus' favorite device (which caught Bacon's eye) of contrasting the name of the thing with the reality, and by simply adding the word "name" Milton is able to preserve the opposition.[19] It may be, if I understand Milton correctly, that he has changed the meaning. Tacitus almost certainly meant that the unpleasant reality "necessity" is plastered over by calling it "emulation"; in Milton, by a kind of

Neoplatonic transformation, the ugly "necessity" turns into the beautiful "emulation" through the wisdom of Agricola. Whatever the
meaning, Milton has been rhetorically faithful to the original, and
the sentence comes to a neat and pointed climax.

Milton's prose was written too rapidly to offer many points of
comparison with the careful effects of Tacitus' historical writings, and
though Tacitus himself often drew from the poets and there are undoubted affinities between formal rhetorical history and epic poetry,
too great a gap looms between Tacitus' prose and Milton's epic style
to be easily bridged, though one is sometimes tempted to try. Can,
for example, the linking of abstract and concrete in the opening line
of *Paradise Lost* ("Of Man's First Disobedience, and the Fruit") be
called Tacitean, since no device is more typical of his style? Or is it
the result of Milton's familiarity with a broader rhetorical tradition?
Probably the latter. Nevertheless, I should like to single out a Miltonic
paradox that seems to me to have some connection with the Tacitean
method.

A feature of classical history that the Renaissance found congenial
to imitate was the brief, formal character, customarily used to introduce or commemorate someone important to the narrative. A typical
example is Milton's evaluation of Demetrius Evanowich in his *Brief
History of Moscovia*: "He was of no presence, but otherwise of a
princely disposition; too bountifull, which occasion'd some exactions;
in other matters a great lover of justice, not unworthy the Empire he
had gotten, and lost only through greatness of mind, neglecting the
Conspiracy, which he knew the *Russians* were plotting" (CM, X, 358–
59). As this suggests, opportunities for paradox were legion, and
Tacitus in particular was adept at exploiting this vein. His epi-
grammatic characterizations of Galba and Poppaea Sabina were probably known to everyone in the seventeenth century who had any
pretensions to learning: "et omnium consensu capax imperii nisi im-
perasset" (*Hist.* I, 49); "huic mulieri cuncta alia fuere praeter hones-
tum animum" (*Ann.* XIII, 45). In the Great Consult in *Paradise Lost*
II, the introduction of Belial is a character of this sort, and though
there is no one detail that points unmistakably to Tacitus, the corruption of Belial and his preference for "ignoble ease" certainly suggest
a common Tacitean theme, as does Mammon's reversal of the terms:

"preferring / Hard liberty before the easy yoke / Of servile Pomp"
(II, 255–57).

One detail Milton had used before, in greatly expanded form, in
his *History of Britain*: "To vice industrious, but to Nobler deeds /
Timorous and slothful" (*PL* II, 116–17); and, "this quality thir valour
had, against a foren Enemy to be ever backward and heartless; to civil
broils eager and prompt. In matters of Government, and the search of
truth, weak and shallow; in falshood and wicked deeds pregnant and
industrious. Pleasing to God, or not pleasing, with them weighed
alike; and the worse most an end was the weightier" (YP, V, 139–40).
There are probably a number of anticipations of this sort of paradox;
one, for example, is from Sir John Hayward's character of Radulph
Bishop of Durham in his life of Henry I. "This Radulph was a man
of smooth vse of speech, wittie onely in deuising, or speaking, or doing
euill: but to honestie and vertue his heart was a lumpe of lead." As
Bacon observed, Hayward was very much the Tacitean,[20] and though
there is no evidence that Milton knew his *Lives of the Three Normans*
(1613), in which this sentence occurs (p. 238), he did know his *Life of
Edward VI*. Although, as we have said, there is no unmistakable
source in Tacitus that can be singled out, the paradox suggests such
typical Tacitean turns as the description of Capito Cossutianus, in-
former against Thrasea (*Ann.* XVI, 21), who had "animum ad flagitia
praecipitem," or Tiberius' contemptuous dismissal of the Roman
people (*Ann.* III, 65): "o homines ad servitutem paratos!"; and Belial's
preference for "ignoble ease" recalls, as it is perhaps meant to do,
the moral temper of Rome under the Caesars (*Ann.* I, 2, 7): "cunctos
dulcedine otii pellexit," "At Romae ruere servitium consules, patres,
eques." Milton often writes with a consciousness of Western history,
as though trying to compress into his words as many layers of reference
as possible, and frequently one can sense the images and shapes of
Tacitean Rome.

In the seventeenth century, there are instances of professional
Taciteans as there were Ciceronians a hundred years earlier, and Milton is not to be numbered among them. On the other hand, Tacitus
was a not insignificant part of the cultural heritage that Milton had
absorbed, and though undoubted references are not numerous, they
show that like Bacon, Jonson, and Donne, Milton responded to Tacitus

with much more complexity than the usual run of admirers. His republican sympathies led him to the libertarian side of Tacitus, and he also seems to have realized that Tacitus was not only a politician but a poet. He may also have seen beyond Tacitus. Few authors are more exciting to read or repay more fully careful study, but after a time there comes to be a sameness in the heavy irony, the recurrent patterns of tyranny, even the gleams of primitivism. Perhaps the answer is that seventeenth-century England had greater spiritual resources than imperial Rome. We feel that Tacitus was no stranger to the isolation that Milton speaks of: "though fall'n on evil days, / On evil days though fall'n, and evil tongues; / In darkness, and with dangers compast round, / And solitude." But not even with Agrippina carrying the ashes of her beloved Germanicus back to Rome, does he ever reach the human sympathy of: "They hand in hand with wand'ring steps and slow, / Through *Eden* took thir solitary way."

Temple University

NOTES

1. See, for example, *Histories*, I, 4: "evulgato imperio arcano"; *Annals*, II, 59; "inter alia dominationis arcana." All references to Tacitus are to the Oxford texts: *Annals*, ed. C. D. Fisher (1911; rpt. Oxford, 1963); *Minor Works*, ed. Henry Furneaux (1900; rpt. Oxford, 1962). *Arcana imperii* could also mean "state-secrets."

2. John Donne, *Sermons*, ed. Evelyn M. Simpson and George M. Potter (Berkeley, 1953–62), VII, 406; Trajano Boccalini, *I Raggvalli di Parnasso: or Advertisements from Parnassus*: trans. Henry Earl of Monmouth (London, 1656), p. 94.

3. *The New-Found Politike*, trans. John Florio et al. (London, 1626), p. 173, the first (incomplete) English translation from Boccalini's *Advertisements*.

4. Giuseppe Toffanin, *Machiavelli e il Tacitismo* (Padova, 1921); Jürgen von Stackelberg, *Tacitus in Romania* (Tübingen, 1960).

5. Edmund G. Gardner, "Traiano Boccalini," *Dublin Review*, CLXXIX (1926), p. 254; Douglas Bush, *English Literature in the Earlier Seventeenth Century: 1600–1660* (New York, 1945), p. 209.

6. Estienne de la Boétie, *Discours de la servitude volontaire*, preface by Edmond Gilliard (Porrentruey, Switz., 1943), p. 59.

7. *Complete Prose Works of John Milton*, ed. Don. M. Wolfe, et al. (New Haven, 1953–), I, 889; cited hereafter in the text as *YP*.

8. *The Life Records of John Milton*, ed. J. Milton French (New York, 1966), IV, 159–60.

9. The texts of Milton's poems quoted throughout are the editions of Merritt Y. Hughes (Garden City, N.Y., 1935, 1937).

10. The editors of the Columbia Milton (*Complete Works*, ed. Frank Allen

Patterson et al. [New York. 1931–1938], XVIII, 574) think the handwriting is not Milton's, but note two parallels with entries in the *Commonplace Book*, and accept Milton's authorship as likely. J. Milton French, *Life Records*, IV, 302–03; 327, thinks the annotations may not be Milton's, but finds the handwriting similar. Joseph Allen Bryant, Jr., "A Note on Milton's Use of Machiavelli's *Discorsi*," *MP*, XLVII (1949–50), p. 221, says flatly that the annotations are not Milton's. William Riley Parker, *Milton: A Biography* (Oxford, 1968), p. 904, is noncommittal. The volume is now in the Berg Collection of the New York Public Library; the catalogue clipping describing it has a note at the bottom: "Not Milton. VHP," the initials probably being those of Victor H. Palsits, the librarian.

11. The Columbia edition of Milton's *Complete Works*, XVIII, 494; cited hereafter in the text as CM. "Germanicus and Drusus lived under the rule of Tiberius: the latter was the son of Tiberius and was powerful because of his father's love. Germanicus was the grandson of Augustus by marriage, and the people's love for him was stimulated by his father's dislike. Therefore Tacitus said about Tiberius that he withheld his judgment between the two. For he wanted one very much, but the people showed that this one was nothing to them, and therefore either by confirming one as heir he would reject his own son, or by preferring the other he would turn the people against himself. This secret of ruling was not unknown to Elizabeth Queen of England, and for this reason she forbade by law that anyone under penalty of death make mention of the heir to the kingdom, saying that she did not want her grave dug before her death. Tiberius gave the reason for this to Macro: you worship the rising sun, desert the setting. As Tacitus says in Book I of the *Histories*, to any one in power, whoever is chosen to succeed is always hateful and suspect" (my translation).

12. Henry Davila, *The History of the Civil Wars of France*, trans. Sir Charles Cottrell and William Aylesbury (London, 1678), p. 238, cited by Toffanin, *Machiavelli e il Tacitismo*, p. 126.

13. The sentence from Sallust is from *Bellum Catilinae*, 7: "Regibus boni, quam mali, suspectiores sunt; semperque aliena virtus formidolosa est." ("To kings, good men are more suspect than bad; the virtue of another is always feared.")

14. Lipsius, *Politica*, VI, v; the sentences from Tacitus are *Histories*, I, 2; *Agricola*, 5: "Nobilitas, opes, omissi gestique honores pro crimine et ob virtutes certissimum exitium." ("Nobility, wealth, offices refused or accepted were sufficient for accusation, and excellences meant certain destruction.") "Sinistra erga eminentis interpretatio nec minus periculum ex magna fama quam ex mala." ("[Times that put] a sinister construction on eminence and found no less danger from great fame than from bad.")

15. *Agricola*, 30: "Atque ubi solitudinem faciunt, pacem appellant." ("And where they make a wilderness, they call it peace.") A version of this may occur in the *First Defence* (CM, VII, 496): "Neque pacem idcircò non volebant, sed involutum pacis nomine aut bellum novum aut aeternam servitutem." ("Nor did they really want peace, but either new war disguised as peace or eternal servitude.")

16. *Ben Jonson: The Man and His Work*, ed. C. H. Herford and Percy Simpson (Oxford, 1925–1952), VIII, 61.

17. Morris W. Croll, "Attic Prose: Lipsius, Montaigne, Bacon," *Schelling Anniversary Papers* (New York, 1923), pp. 142–43.

18. Polydore Vergil, *Anglicae Historiae libri vigintisex* (Gandavi, n.d.), p. 92; Raphael Holinshed, *Chronicles of England, Scotland, and Ireland* (London, 1807), I, 505–06; Savile, *Tacitus*, pp. 192–93; Samuel Daniel, *Works*, ed. Alexander B. Grosart

(London, 1885–96), IV, 89–90; Milton, YP, V, 85. The passage in Polydore is in the MS version of the history, which was written by 1513; see Denys Hay, *Polydore Vergil* (Oxford, 1952), p. 187. For the dating of Milton's *History*, see YP, V, xxxviii–lxii.

19. Cf. *Agricola*, 30: "Atque ubi solitudinem faciunt, pacem appellant." Bacon calls attention to this device in explaining why he keeps old terms while changing the meaning, *Works*, ed. James Spedding, R. L. Ellis, and D. D. Heath (Boston, 1863), VI, 217: "according to the moderate proceeding in civil government, where although there be some alteration, yet that holdeth which Tacitus wisely noteth, *eadem magistratuum vocabula.*"

20. Hayward's history *Henry IV* brought the author into trouble with the authorities on account of an implied parallel between Richard II and Elizabeth. Bacon is reported to have said that he did not think Hayward guilty of treason, but of felony for having filched so many sentences from Tacitus. See my "Sir John Hayward and Tacitus," *RES*, n.s. VIII (1957), 275–76.

A READING OF MILTON'S
TWENTY–THIRD SONNET

Marilyn L. Williamson

Milton's twenty-third sonnet may be read without reference to
Mary Powell, Katherine Woodcock, or the poet's blindness. The
poem is structured on a progressive definition of salvation from
death and of the human condition in this world. It contains a
rising movement from physical salvation, according to the Alcestis
legend, to ritualistic salvation, according to the Old Dispensation,
to true Christian salvation, in which the saint is bride of the Lamb,
and her virtues shine from inside her person. The marriage theme
provides a tragic countermovement; for the Christian saint,
though she may share Alcestis' impulse and incline to embrace
her husband, is unalterably lost to him in this world, and he can
only dream of sharing her separate and purified existence after
his death. Hope in the true salvation is set forth in the contrast
between pale and faint Alcestis and the bright figure of the saint,
and the falling movement lies in the contrast between the reunion
of Alcestis and Admetus and the separation of the saint and the
speaker of the poem.

Until William Riley Parker's seminal article in 1945 we had assumed securely that Milton's last sonnet was addressed to Katherine
Woodcock and that it offered a moving tribute to her character, all the
more to be cherished as the only evidence we had about her. In raising
the question about Mary Powell as the sonnet's subject, Parker threw
all in doubt, and the controversy continues over the claims of Mary or
Katherine to be the saint of the poem.[1] But the poem can be read in
a way that sets aside what has been called "the sterile argument" about
wives one and two,[2] and the issue of the poet's blindness as well, for an
interpretation that frees the sonnet from its ties to our incomplete
knowledge of Milton's life and the ambiguities it represents when read

in connection with that knowledge. Unless totally new evidence is discovered, which finally identifies which wife the poem concerns, we will remain hopelessly divided, since the details of the poem can be grist for both mills; it remains therefore to seek another avenue of approach to the poem, for, as Parker himself has said, "There is only one way, really of answering such an argument as this; little is gained by questioning details; one must show that a similar, equally persuasive construction can be based on a very different assumption."[3]

In 1951 Leo Spitzer offered a reading of the poem based on a different assumption, that the saint was neither Mary nor Katherine, but a figure like the *donna angelicata* of Dante and Petrarch, that the theme of the poem was not "the problem of Milton's blindness (nor that of the death of his wife), but the generally human problem of the Ideal in our world."[4] But Spitzer's interpretation has not convinced most readers because, as Thomas Wheeler puts it, "the poem obviously does refer to historical fact. Why else would Milton so carefully refer to 'child-bed taint'? He must have had either Mary Powell or Katherine Woodcock in mind." Wheeler goes on to conclude, however, that although the sonnet is a "substantially accurate record of a dream," the figure of the third quatrain is "an ideal in the mind of John Milton. . . . It is no *donna angelicata* of Dante that Milton dreams of but the very image in his mind of a paradise which, like Adam, he sought but never found." For Wheeler, then, the poem begins with a real wife, but ends in the "suffocating isolation of the man whose day is night," as Milton realizes when he awakens that he can never expect to see his ideal on earth.[5] There are alternatives to a biographical interpretation, then, but the objections about the childbed taint and the seeming references to the poet's blindness remain. These objections may best be met with reference to the text of the poem. We should interpret the poem, as Wheeler proposes, "in the light of what we know of Milton's mind," but we may have been inattentive, both to all that we know of his mind that is relevant to the sonnet and to the text itself. What we have yet to take into account are the religious ideas in the sonnet, which are fused (as is usual in Milton) with the Italian sonnet conventions Spitzer has explored.

The sonnet opens with an emphasis on the tentative nature of the speaker's vision: "Methought I saw," not "I did see," and throughout the poem Milton is careful to repeat conditional expressions and to proceed by analogy, so that we are constantly made aware of the fragile nature of the experience which the poem conveys.[6] The illusory quality of the dream should indeed be our first precaution against literal interpretation of the sonnet, readings that involve one-to-one correspondences to Milton's life, for here he is not dealing with the fact of troops approaching his house or a massacre of Waldensians, but with a fleeting experience evoked in memory and described by analogy. The analogies are, as Spitzer has shown, cunningly arranged in an ascending order of religious value.[7]

The first analogy, to Alcestis, since it is pagan and contrary to fact, has given us little difficulty. What we may remark for purposes of this reading is that Alcestis was "rescued from death," saved physically "by force." It is this feature of the story Milton fixes on here, rather than Alcestis' "death" for Admetus (as Fitzroy Pyle would have it).[8] Alcestis, the figure of pagan legend, can be saved from death, resurrected by force, and restored to her "glad Husband." The speaker's Christian wife is also saved, but by quite other means than force, and tragically she cannot be reunited with her "glad Husband," who can only dream of her. The contrast between the speaker's wife and Alcestis is made explicit in "Mine."

In the second quatrain we come to the troublesome analogy which compares the speaker's wife to one "whom washt from spot of child-bed taint, / Purification in the old Law did save." The crucial point here is that, like Alcestis, the woman under the old Law is an analogue to the speaker's wife and not the wife herself. There are several reasons why the lines should be so read. First, that is what they say: "Mine *as* whom washt from spot . . ." (italics mine). Furthermore, the second analogue is a parallel to the first one, grammatically in the repetition of *whom* and syntactically in the inversion with terminal rhyming verbs: "Whom Jove's great Son to her glad Husband gave, / Mine as whom washt from spot of child-bed taint / Purification in the old Law did save." Moreover, the speaker's wife is a Christian figure, and therefore could not be saved by the old Law any more than by the force of Hercules. Here, if we are as true to what we know of Milton's mind as to the biographical facts of his life, we must recognize his emphatic insistence in the *Christian Doctrine* that under the New Dispensation the Law did not save, especially the ceremonial Law, which in fact could be a danger in misleading the Christian, but that only the grace of God in Jesus Christ saved the

Christian.[9] The wife of the speaker has in common with the one saved under the old Law (she is saved as Alcestis is restored to Admetus) her salvation (though not the means of it), and her purity, which is later figured in her white apparel.

But why, those favoring a biographical interpretation may ask, does Milton use the analogy involving childbed taint to convey the purity of the visionary wife, if he does not wish to direct our attention to the death of his own wife? There are again several reasons. In the first place, the visionary figure is a woman who is saved, and it is, according to Saint Paul, through childbearing that salvation comes to the daughters of Eve: "The woman being beguiled hath fallen into transgression: but she shall be saved through her child-bearing, if they continue in faith and love and sanctification with sobriety" (1 Timothy ii, 14–15). The suffering of childbearing, Eve's specific penalty for original sin, is both the means by which the taint of original sin is passed on to the generations of men and the means by which man is redeemed from that taint, when the second Eve bears the Savior. Thus the rites of purification after childbirth are interpreted typologically as prefiguring Christian salvation; the use of the sin-offering for childbearing is interpreted as typical of Christ's sacrifice, which is man's true means of salvation under the New Dispensation.[10] In discussing the question of the nature of the sin for which offering is made according to the Law, John Gill says, for example:

Some take the sin to be a rash or false oath: but there seems to be something more than all this, because though one or another of these sins might be the case of some women, yet not all; whereas this law is general, and reached every lying-in woman, and has respect not so much to any particular sin of hers, as of our first parent Eve, who was first in transgression; and on account of which transgression pains are endured by every child-bearing woman; and who also conceives in sin, and is the instrument of propagating the corruption of nature to her offspring; and therefore was to bring a sin-offering, typical of the sin-offering Christ is made to take away that, and all other sin; whereby she shall be saved, even in child-bearing, and that by the birth of a child, the child Jesus, if she continues in faith, and charity, and holiness, with sobriety."[11]

The purification of the leper, specified in the same section of the Law, is similarly interpreted by Samuel Mather as a type for "the transition of the soul from a state of nature to a state of grace": "Man justified by faith in the death of Christ, sprinkled by the Spirit with the blood of Christ, is made whole of nature's leprosy—of that taint and imputation of original sin, with its deep-seated and infectious principle, which he brought with him into the world, and has been ruled by ever since."[12] Figuratively, then, the "spot of child-bed taint" can be as much a way of conveying the postlapsarian condition of all humanity as a specific reference to the cause of the wife's death. The saint is like the woman under the old Law in being purified of Eve's sin, which is inevitably transmitted to progeny, and from which the purification rites saved. After Christ the purification rites of the old Law could not save and had to be treated as types or shadows of the true salvation of the Cross.

In the third quatrain Milton stresses again the visionary nature of the experience the poem describes when the speaker says, "And such" (thus purified and garbed) is the way he hopes to see his wife when he has full sight of her in Heaven without the restraint of the dream—with its evanescence and its temporal limitation. Now the wife is in Heaven; the speaker lives in the sublunary world and is restricted to dreaming of her; when he sees her this way "once more," they will both be in Heaven (he trusts), and he will then have full sight of her without the separation presently imposed by the two worlds of their being. No assumption about, knowledge of, or reference to Milton's blindness is necessary to interpret these lines, which are consistent with the rest of the poem. The words "and such," in fact, prohibit our reading "once more" as referring to the speaker's sight of his wife when she was alive, since "such" clearly must signify the vision of the purified wife, specifying, for the first time in the sonnet, the exact nature of the vision, rather than the analogies to it with which the poem begins. The emphasis in these lines on the limitations of the speaker's "fancied sight" of his wife underscores the earlier details that define the tentative quality of the dream, and also prepares for or forms a transition to the end of the poem in calling our attention to the basic division between speaker and wife, who have been close in life, but are now sadly separated by death.

The saint appears in white, in part as an outward sign of her purity: "pure as her mind." Though her face is veiled, her virtues shine clear to the speaker's "fancied sight," as indeed for the true Christian the virtues that are the sign of salvation are written on the heart, in contrast to the outward conformity to the Law under the Old Dispensation: "Behold, the days come, saith the Lord, that I will make a new covenant with the house of Israel, and with the house of Judah; not according to the covenant that I made with their fathers, in the day that I took them by the hand, to bring them out of the land of Egypt. . . . But this shall be the covenant that I will make with the house of Israel; after those days, saith the Lord, I will put My law in their inward parts, and write it in their hearts, and will be their God, and they shall be My people" (Jeremiah xxxi, 31–34). The notion is reiterated by Saint Paul in Hebrews: "I will put my laws on their heart, And upon their mind also will I write them" (x, 16). The figure, dressed in white and veiled, is at once the wife of the speaker and the bride of the Lamb, for, as Hughes says, she is garbed like "one of those who have 'washed their robes and made them white in the blood of the Lamb' " (Revelations vii, 6).[13] In the sense of Revelations the wife is a "late espoused saint"; she is both married to the speaker until recently, and newly dead, lately espoused by the Lamb. The color of her garment is a sign of her sanctification: "And it was given unto her that she should array herself in fine linen, bright and pure: for the fine linen is the righteous acts of the saints" (Revelations xix, 6).[14] As the language of the sonnet constantly calls Revelations to mind, the marriage of the speaker and his wife takes on a familiar tropological significance: "the marriage of the soul when after sin it returns to God and is united with him."[15] But it is precisely when the speaker achieves the clearest vision of his spouse that the tragic difference between the kinds of marriage becomes apparent, for just as he sees her virtues shining in her person, "as in no face with more delight," she inclines to embrace him, an action which vividly recalls their physical intimacy in life, and he loses the vision by awaking.[16] The speaker's loss is made more poignant by the fact that his real-life relationship to the saint has been a trope for the very condition that now separates him irrevocably from her.

We therefore do not need Milton's blindness to feel the powerful impact of "and day brought back my night." The waking hours of the day are as night to the speaker, for the only experience he now can have of the beloved spouse comes through the dream-vision. Here, if we are not convinced by the connections with Italian predecessors suggested by Spitzer, the contrast between the speaker's vision of the shining figure of his beloved while he slumbers and his loss of it when he awakes is enough to account for the paradox of day bringing night, without attributing the image to the poet's personal circumstances. The brightness of the figure of the saint and the emphasis on her face once again echoes a biblical passage that also stresses the contrast between light and dark, night and day, a contrast which reinforces the basic difference between the present existence of the speaker in the sublunary world and that of the saint in Heaven: "And the throne of God and of the Lamb shall be therein: and his servants shall serve him; and they shall see his face; and his name shall be on their foreheads. And there shall be night no more; and they need no light of lamp, neither light of sun; for the Lord God shall give them light" (Revelations xxii, 3–5). The speaker is condemned to a life in which even day is night, specifically because of the loss of the shining vision of his wife, and generally because that is the condition of earthly existence.

The poem is structured on a progressive definition of salvation from death and of the human condition in this world. As Spitzer has taught us, the sonnet has a "tripartite *crescendo* arrangement" that moves from physical salvation according to pagan legend to ritualistic salvation according to the Old Dispensation to true Christian salvation, in which the saint is bride of the Lamb, and her virtues, written on heart and mind, shine forth from inside her person.[17] This movement of the poem is a rising motion, one that conforms to the Christian interpretation of human experience, in which pre-Christian history is a shadow of the truth in Jesus, and it is thus full of hope for the true believer.[18] The marriage theme, however, provides a countermovement to this progression, even though earthly marriage is a trope for the union of the saint with God. Unlike Alcestis, who not only saves her husband from death by sacrificing herself but also can be rescued by Hercules, the Christian saint, though she may share Alcestis' impulse and incline to embrace her husband, is unalterably lost to him in this world; he can only dream of her state which he hopes someday to share, purified of all taint of earthly existence and separated from it. Thus the simpler pagan shadow of the truth in the Alcestis analogy holds out a shallow hope of earthly reunion as the initial interpretation of the vision, one that must be replaced (after a transition of the old Law) by the true and lasting hope of the sight of her in Heaven ("I trust to have"); this, poignantly, will not admit of such a reunion as that enjoyed by Admetus and his wife. If the rising movement of hope in the true salvation is set forth by the contrast between the figure of Alcestis, "pale and faint," and the bright figure of the saint with her inner virtues

shining "so clear, as in no face with more delight," the falling movement may be seen in the contrast between Alcestis' "glad Husband,"
who is reunited with his beloved, and the sense of loss, isolation, and
grief that overcomes the saint's husband at the end of the poem.

If this reading of the sonnet is valid, it releases the poem from its
narrowly biographical context and debate and allows it to stand beside
most of Milton's important poetry. Like the major works, it attempts
to grapple honestly with the relation between the truths of Christian
value and thought and the condition of human life in a universal sense.
Instead of being specifically applicable only to the poet's personal losses
of wife and sight, it transmutes these experiences into themes of general
implication and significance, as *Lycidas* similarly transforms in a far
subtler and greater way the death of King, and as "When I consider
how my light is spent" wrings from his blindness themes that transcend
the particular affliction. As Wheeler suggests, the twenty-third sonnet
has special power, and Milton has a special capacity to dramatize himself;[19] but always in his finest work he dramatizes himself for purposes
larger than the expression of his own preoccupations. He is ever in
his great Taskmaster's eye. If this sonnet deserves to be described as
among Milton's best, it may also be said to derive its power less from
sentimental, extrapoetic associations than from the coherence, compres-
sion, and intensity with which it renders concerns central to Christian
life here and hereafter.

Oakland University

NOTES

1. William Riley Parker, "Milton's Last Sonnet," *RES*, XXI (1945), 235–38. A
summary of the debate is presented by John T. Shawcross, "Milton's Sonnet 23,"
N & Q, n.s. III (1956), 202–04.
2. Thomas Wheeler, "Milton's Twenty-Third Sonnet," *SP*, LVIII (1961), 511.
3. William Riley Parker, "Milton's Last Sonnet Again," *RES*, n.s. II (1951),
150–51.
4. Leo Spitzer, "Understanding Milton," *Hopkins Review*, IV (1951), 22.
5. Wheeler, "Milton's Twenty-Third Sonnet," pp. 511–14.
6. The text quoted is *John Milton: Complete Poems and Major Prose*, ed.
Merritt Y. Hughes (New York, 1957), p. 171.
7. Spitzer, "Understanding Milton," p. 21.

8. Fitzroy Pyle, "Milton's Sonnet on his 'Late Espoused Saint,'" *RES*, XXV (1959), 59.

9. *Christian Doctrine*, Columbia Edition, XVI, 112–63 (ch. XXVII).

10. This aspect of the purification after childbirth (Lev. xii, 6) has been neglected by commentators, who have focused solely on the number of days of uncleanness which the Law specifies.

11. John Gill, *An Exposition of the Old Testament* (Philadelphia, 1817), I, 642.

12. Samuel Mather, *The Gospel of the Old Testament: An Explanation of the Types and Figures by Which Christ was Exhibited under the Legal Dispensation*, rewritten by C. F. Wilson (Philadelphia, 1834), pp. 250–51.

13. Hughes, *Complete Poems*, p. 171. E. S. LeComte, "The Veiled Face of Milton's Wife," *N & Q*, n.s. I (1954), 245–46, has explained five logical reasons why the saint's face is veiled, among which is marriage to the Lamb (Rev. xix, 7–9). Much earlier Milton had used a similar device, which he is more careful to explain: "Hail divinest Melancholy / Whose Saintly visage is too bright / To hit the Sense of human sight; / And therefore to our weaker view, / O'erlaid with black, staid Wisdom's hue" (*Il Penseroso*, ll. 12–16).

14. J. S. Smart, *The Sonnets of John Milton* (Glasgow, 1921), quotes Revelations vii, 13–14, in connection with these lines; and E. A. J. Honigman uses the passage quoted here, *Milton's Sonnets* (London, 1966), p. 193.

15. Johan Chydenius, *Medieval Institutions and the Old Testament* (Helsinki, 1965), pp. 101–02.

16. Thomas B. Stroup, "Aeneas' Vision of Creusa and Milton's Twenty-third Sonnet," *PQ*, XXXIX (1960), 125–26, asserts that this feature of the poem derives from Book II of the *Aeneid*; but his argument is based on extrapolation from the poem: "The vision of the wife flees just as the husband would embrace it." No such gesture on the part of the speaker is mentioned in the sonnet. And Stroup's argument for Mary Powell as the saint is based on the survival of Mary's child, although no child—alive or dead—figures in the sonnet at all.

17. Spitzer, "Understanding Milton," p. 21.

18. Cf. Walter Eichordt, "Is Typological Exegesis an Appropriate Method?" in *Essays on Old Testament Hermeneutics*, ed. Claus Westerman (Richmond, Va. 1963), p. 226.

19. Wheeler, "Milton's Twenty-third Sonnet," p. 515.

THE PLANT OF FAME IN *LYCIDAS*

William G. Riggs

Phoebus' speech in *Lycidas* is usually read as a thinly veiled
Christian warning and consolation, but the Christian implication of
Phoebus' metaphorical plant of fame has not been recognized.
Here, as elsewhere, Milton uses the metaphor of a plant which
flowers "aloft" to describe the workings of grace, and his use is
grounded in the theological conception of being ingrafted in
Christ. This conception, as explained in *The Christian Doctrine*,
emphasizes that the god of poetry is concerned primarily with the
necessity of living deeds, rather than with the heavenly rewards
envisioned in the final consolation. In response to the singer's depressed sense of the futility of human enterprise, Phoebus insists
on human action. This reading helps place the emphasis of
Lycidas on a living response to death. These lines are of a piece
with the poem's remarkable close, wherein, by focusing on the
elegist's act of singing, Milton suggests we see *Lycidas* finally as
a living act of faith, a paradigm of Christian action.

I

SOMETHING, IT is often felt, needs to be said about the words of
Phoebus, that god of poetry who offers a thinly veiled Christian
consolation to the despondent singer of Milton's *Lycidas*.

> But not the praise,
> *Phoebus* repli'ed, and touch'd my trembling ears;
> *Fame* is no plant that grows on mortal soil,
> Nor in the glistering foil
> Set off to th' world, nor in broad rumour lies,
> But lives and spreds aloft by those pure eyes,
> And perfet witness of all-judging *Jove*;
> As he pronounces lastly on each deed,
> Of so much fame in Heav'n expect thy meed.[1]

151

Christian sentiments expressed by pagan deities are, of course, standard Renaissance fare, but when in a single poem (a poem by Milton at that) such sentiments are also voiced by demythologized Christian speakers, some critics, if finally unwilling to level Dr. Johnson's charge of impiety, have at least felt threatened by incongruity. Moreover, Phoebus' promise of heavenly rewards has seemed uncomfortably close to the consolation which concludes the poem. "Only tangentially Christian," M. H. Abrams suggests, insisting sensibly on an ethical forward progress in the poem, and David Daiches, reacting, it would seem, to the possibility that the poem might have ended here, calls the passage "a deliberately false climax."[2] The poem, fortunately, does not end here, but it comes to a halt which is in some ways more disturbing than its second pause at the end of Saint Peter's speech.[3] If we take the view that the poem describes a developing search for understanding and consolation by the singer, Peter's cryptic promise of divine justice, while it presumably consoles, is clearly not final. It is a negative consolation at best, a vindicating comfort for the virtuous and virtuously dead which is distinctly different from the rewards finally envisioned at the poem's end. By contrast, the "meed" held out by Phoebus, double-edged though it may be, seems much closer to the final consolatory vision of Lycidas among the saints. It may, in fact, seem that the singer has chosen to forget Phoebus' pronouncement only to recall it at the poem's end, that his progress, as represented in the poem, is unsteady: he withdraws from the truth only to discover it at last. This is, I think, a fair description of the elegist's agon: nothing is more natural than to waver in attempting to move from the immediate pain of bereavement to a religious or philosophical acceptance of death. In *Lycidas* such vacillation is present and is underscored by Milton's modulation of the pastoral mode—modulation which has, indeed, been the first source of critical unease over Phoebus' Christian message.

We will not, I think, be confused by the mixture of pagan and Christian pastoral in *Lycidas* if we recognize that pastoral in its pagan aspect serves Milton as a metaphor for the world of immediate experience, a world circumscribed by the rising of the sun and the setting of the evening star, a world which untransformed by Christian vision can only weep for Lycidas. Yet, as any Christian humanist might tell us, the patterns of a larger world are engraved on this one, and this partial congruence of Christian and pagan truth is nowhere more delicately handled than here in Milton's subtle merging of antique pastoral and the Christian revelation seen as latent in fallen nature's ways. Milton's singer depicts himself moving toward an acceptance of Christian truth, but the burden of sorrow inherent in the pastoral metaphor periodically draws him back toward despair—a despair enforced by the seductive beauties of the Sicilian muse, by the natural beauties of our dying world. The emotional and intellectual progress traced by the singer is, in short, dialectical, and the retreat from the higher mood of Phoebus' voice is a part of the dialectic.[4] Yet while Phoebus' pronouncement represents an anticipation of Christian truth, it would be wrong to identify the sentiments of this passage too exactly with the singer's final perception of Lycidas "mounted high." The closing consolation is not simply an unveiling and an elaboration of Phoebus' speech: the two passages, while related, strike different attitudes toward heavenly "meed".

Lycidas, in the final vision, is seen

> In the blest Kingdoms meek of joy and love.
> There entertain him all the Saints above,
> In solemn troops, and sweet Societies
> That sing, and singing in their glory move,
> And wipe the tears for ever from his eyes.

In contrast to this joyous evocation of the life to come, Phoebus' speech, while it presents Jove pronouncing "lastly on each deed," offers us comparatively little in the way of a postmortem encounter in Heaven. The emphasis falls elsewhere: Phoebus' words are primarily about the business of living in this world, not the blessings of life in the next. In response to the elegist's depressed sense of the drudgery and futility of life lived in strict meditation of the thankless muse, Phoebus recalls the urgency of human action: God in Heaven observes man's mundane labors, and in his judgment, not in worldly fame, lies the true value of scorning delights and living laborious days.

II

This reading is easy enough to come by, but its full force has not been felt because the Christian implication of Phoebus' central metaphor—the plant of fame—has not been adequately recognized. The plant of fame in *Lycidas* appears as a chronicle wherein human deeds reside, a chronicle which has no final earthly significance, which, to re-

turn to the metaphor, does not grow "on mortal soil" but "lives and
spreds aloft" before the "perfet witness of all-judging *Jove*" who
"pronounces lastly on each deed." The ultimate significance of this
metaphor is not to be found in pagan story but in the Christian notion
which it shadows: the concept of being ingrafted in Christ—a concept
centrally associated by Milton with the problem of Christian action in
this world.[5]

Following man's regeneration, Milton will later explain in *The
Christian Doctrine*, "Believers are said TO BE INGRAFTED IN CHRIST,
when they are planted in Christ by God the Father, that is, are made
partakers of Christ, and meet for becoming one with him. Matt. XV.
13. 'every plant, which my heavenly Father hath not planted shall be
rooted up.' John XV. I, 2. 'I am the true vine, and my Father is the
husbandman: every branch in me that beareth not fruit, he taketh
away'."[6] The first effect of this ingrafting, according to Milton, is a
"NEWNESS OF LIFE AND INCREASE" which creates in man a fresh comprehension of spiritual things, a comprehension which was formerly
"weakened and in a manner destroyed by the spiritual death" (CM,
XVI, 5). The second effect is "LOVE OR CHARITY, ARISING FROM A SENSE
OF THE DIVINE LOVE SHED ABROAD IN THE HEARTS OF THE REGENERATE BY
THE SPIRIT, WHEREBY THOSE WHO ARE INGRAFTED IN CHRIST BEING INFLU-
ENCED, BECOME DEAD TO SIN, AND LIVE AGAIN UNTO GOD, AND BRING FORTH
GOOD WORKS SPONTANEOUSLY AND FREELY" (CM, XVI, 9). This relation-
ship between ingrafting and good works is documented from John xv,
4, 5: "abide in me, and I in you: as the branch cannot bear fruit of
itself, except it abide in the vine, no more can ye, except ye abide in me:
I am the vine, ye are the branches; he that abideth in me, and I in him,
the same bringeth forth much fruit: for without me ye can do nothing"
(CM, XVI, 11). In Milton's analysis the fruits that spring from the faith
of the Christian ingrafted in Christ constitute in large measure the
Christian's justification in the eyes of God: "JUSTIFICATION IS THE GRA-
TUITOUS PURPOSE OF GOD, WHEREBY THOSE WHO ARE REGENERATE AND
INGRAFTED IN CHRIST ARE ABSOLVED FROM SIN AND DEATH THROUGH HIS
MOST PERFECT SATISFACTION, AND ACCOUNTED JUST IN THE SIGHT OF GOD,
NOT BY THE WORKS OF THE LAW, BUT THROUGH FAITH" (CM, XVI, 25).
It may at first appear that Milton is here denying the efficacy of works in
man's justification. This, of course, is not the case: works of the law,
not works of faith, are what he excludes, as he is concerned to explain:

"Faith has its own works, which may be different from the works of the law. We are justified therefore by faith, but by a living, not a dead faith; and that faith alone which acts is counted living; James ii. 17, 20, 26. Hence we are justified by faith without the works of the law, but not without the works of faith; inasmuch as a living and true faith cannot consist without works, though these latter may differ from the works of the written law" (CM, XVI, 39). To summarize, then, the terms and progress of Milton's argument, the regenerate man, the man complete in repentance and faith, becomes ingrafted in Christ. He becomes a living branch of the vine which is Christ, but a branch which lives only insofar as it bears fruit (the works of faith) which, along with faith itself, becomes his justification in the eyes of God.

Such a conception answers well to the terms of Phoebus' words, and it suggests that the Christian implication of what Phoebus says involves much more than the promise of a heavenly reward: it involves a prescription for living in this world. Properly known, man's *"Fame,"* the product of his deeds, does not live on "mortal soil." Rather it resides in Christ the living vine—a notion which accords perfectly with Milton's understanding of the Son's priestly function as mediator for man (CM, XV, 291). The word *mortal* here carries something of the significance it will later carry in Milton's resonating phrase, "mortal taste": it can be read as implying the spiritual death of the unregenerate. Deeds of the flesh are dead; worldly fame, "That last infirmity of Noble mind," is a mortal thing; it is true *"Fame,"* fruit of the stalk of the living Christ, flower of the deeds of the faithful ingrafted in Christ, that spreads aloft before the eyes of all-judging Jove: "We are justified . . . by faith, but by a living, not a dead faith; and that faith alone which acts is counted living."

Christ, then, is the stalk; the acts of the man ingrafted in Christ are, through God's grace, truly fruitful. The metaphorical association of a plant with Christ's intercession for man consistently colors Milton's understanding of the workings of grace. If, for example, we turn to *Paradise Lost* and the first instance of the Son's sacerdotal mediation for man, we find a complex of images which recalls both *The Christian Doctrine* and the words of Phoebus:

> See Father, what first fruits on Earth are sprung
> From thy implanted Grace in Man, these Sighs
> And Prayers, which in this Golden Censer, mixt

> With Incense, I thy Priest before thee bring,
> Fruits of more pleasing savor from thy seed
> Sown with contrition in his heart, than those
> Which his own hand manuring all the Trees
> Of Paradise could have produc't, ere fall'n
> From innocence. Now therefore bend thine ear
> To supplication, hear his sighs though mute;
> Unskilful with what words to pray, let mee
> Interpret for him, mee his Advocate
> And propitiation, all his works on mee
> Good or not good ingraft, my Merit those
> Shall perfet, and for these my Death shall pay.   (XI, 22–36)[7]

In this passage the fruits of repentance and faith—as in *Lycidas* vocal fruits, here *explicitly* ingrafted in Christ—are seen as superior even to the fruits of prelapsarian Eden's natural soil. The fall, at this point in Milton's epic, has rendered this soil "mortal," as it is in *Lycidas*, barren ground for the plant of fame.

Again in *Comus*, if the attendance of Thyrsis is seen as in some sense a heavenly ministry,[8] one can cite yet another instance of Milton's association of a plant with the operations of grace—the description of haemony:

> Amongst the rest a small unsightly root,
> But of divine effect, he cull'd me out;
> The leaf was darkish, and had prickles on it,
> But in another Country, as he said,
> Bore a bright golden flow'r, but not in this soil:
> Unknown, and like esteem'd, and the dull swain
> Treads on it daily with his clouted shoon,
> And yet more med'cinal is it than that *Moly*
> That *Hermes* once to wise *Ulysses* gave;
> He call'd it *Haemony*.   (629–38; Hughes' edition)

Seen in conjunction with Phoebus' speech, this passage offers interesting anticipations.[9] As in *Lycidas*, two plants are described: haemony and its less efficacious counterpart, moly. It is tempting to see in these two plants exact prototypes of the plant of fame and its opposite, the plant of false fame, which, apparently, is "Set off to th' world" in the "glistering foil." Newton and subsequent commentators have envisioned in this latter plant of false fame a grotesque growth of leaf gold or of tinsel which glitters delusively like gold;[10] as such it is perhaps anticipated by moly, which is described by Pliny as bearing a yellowish flower ("florem . . . luteum").[11] Such precision may be fanciful, but one similarity between moly and the plant of false fame is undeniable: they both occupy inferior, worldly positions in comparison to their counterparts, haemony and the plant of true fame. The metallic flower of false fame blossoms in this world, "on mortal soil": the plant of true fame, by contrast, "spreads aloft," as does haemony, which, "of divine effect," bears "a bright golden flower" in "another Country . . . but not in this soil." The passage in *Comus* does not, to be sure, deal directly with the concept of fame, but it does relate to *Lycidas*, as Edward LeComte has noted, by describing in pastoral terms the heavenly assistance as well as the heavenly reward afforded virtuous action in this world. LeComte comments on Coleridge's gloss of haemony, and I can do no better than to quote him here: "But the one poet set the other poet's lines brilliantly aglow with meaning when he saw in them a fable of Christian redemption. 'This soil' becomes (to quote 'Lycidas') this 'mortal soil'—man's life here on earth, and the plant the favor from on high which only a virtuous few are willing and able to maintain amid trial and suffering until 'haemony' blossoms for them in heaven."[12]

The plant of fame, then, and its implicit relationship to Christ as living vine, can be viewed in contrast to what Wayne Shumaker has called the imagery of "vegetative nature" in *Lycidas*. Such imagery, Shumaker writes, suggests "a sympathetic frustration in nature" which balances "the human frustrations about which the poem is built."[13] Implied by the plant of fame is an antidote to these frustrations, a plant free from the mortal bonds of nature, flowering, as the final vision of *Lycidas* has it, in "other groves."

III

To understand Phoebus' words in these terms helps to place the emphasis of Milton's *Lycidas* where it belongs: on a living response to death. As elsewhere in Milton the theme of human action is central, and here in fact the song of the elegist becomes itself a paradigm of life being led in positive response to the central facts of human misery, "Death . . . and all our woe." In his initial response to the death of Lycidas, Milton's pastoral singer has been drawn into a despairing identification with his dead companion. Death here is viewed partially; it renders the struggle of life meaningless; it teaches self-pity and slothful ease, the seductions of which Milton recognized as clearly as Keats.

The words of Phoebus can be seen as germinal in a process which frees the singer from his limited identification with the dead poet-priest, a process which culminates in a new understanding of death and a new engagement in active life.

But with respect to this process a delayed question remains: At what point are the Christian implications of Phoebus' words grasped by the singer of *Lycidas*? If, as I have argued, the plant of fame is significant in suggesting the necessity of Christian action, one may fairly ask what dramatic force, if any, such an implication has in a poem which "discovers" the truth of God's providence only at the end. We have returned, essentially, to the problem of the singer's progress as a character, and here, I think, another feature of Phoebus' speech is helpful. Milton's elegist, who has initially appeared to us singing his present grief, now, at the intrusion of Phoebus' voice, reports having heard the god speak in the past: "But not the praise, / *Phoebus* repli'ed, and touch'd my trembling ears. . . . That strain I heard was of a higher mood: / But now my Oat proceeds." This shift from the present to the past tense and back again becomes increasingly unobtrusive as one's ear adjusts to it after several readings. But the shift is there; it is consistent with Milton's treatment of the other figures who appear to the elegist; and it would seem to indicate at least one thing: Milton was not greatly concerned to preserve the illusion of present action in describing the process of the elegist's grief. The singer of *Lycidas* is portrayed recalling his encounters with Phoebus, the herald of the sea, Hippotades, Camus, and Saint Peter. In effect, time past subtly intrudes itself into what has seemed to be time present, with the resulting impression that the singing of *Lycidas*, as distinct from the events the song describes, constitutes the present action. From the temporal perspective suggested by Milton's shift of tense, Lycidas' death, the poet's encounters with the various voices and presences which amplify and alter his grief, even the poet's struggle with a sense of life's futility, appear as actions past. The singer, in short, seems to be *re-creating* the process of his bereavement; this re-creation becomes the poem's "now." To be sure, the singer's own grief is everywhere reported in the present tense (the past tense here would clearly deaden the poem's effect); but the ease with which the elegist shifts into the past tense when called upon to express actions not his own suggests that what first appears in the poem as present process should more properly be considered an historical present: "But now my oat *proceeds,* / And *listens* to the Herald of the sea / That *came* in Neptune's plea" (my emphasis). Here what is heard by the singer seems a memory; the present action is the recollection of the herald's questions, the process not of the singer's grief but of his song. At this and other points in *Lycidas* Milton's elegist appears to be recovering what has already happened, to be reliving in song the emotional progress which has led him to sing.

Such use, in *Lycidas*, of an historical present, the pastness of which is subtly exposed, can create in the reader a sense that time has a double aspect: time past (the singer's struggle with disabling loss) and time present (the singing of this struggle) occupy the same poetic interval yet appear both simultaneous *and* consecutive. Through the operation of this double perspective the elegist's vantage point becomes identical with the reader's: like the reader, the elegist comprehends, prior to the poem's final revelation, both natural grief and the workings of Christian grace such grief obscures. Thus with respect to Phoebus' speech, we have, from the perspective of action past, a higher truth glimpsed in a fallen mode and set aside by a man humanly engaged in the dialectic of bereavement; from the perspective of action present, Phoebus' words express the Christian necessity of the living act which *Lycidas* is. The elegist, as singer, is not insensitive to the implications of what the elegist, as sufferer, has heard. In the midst of his *poetic* action he sounds the Christian rationale for deeds.

This necessity of an active engagement in life is perhaps most strikingly felt in the remarkable closing lines of the poem where, for the last time, in another shift of tense, we are compelled to recognize that what we have been presented is no stony monument to a dead poet, but a creative action, a work of faith emanating from a regenerate spirit ingrafted in Christ. Throughout the poem song has served Milton as a primary emblem for the action of life; as in the passage quoted above from *Paradise Lost*, Milton's emphasis—an emphasis characteristic of his claims for poetry—is on vocal acts. From the singer's rural existence ("Mean while the Rural ditties were not mute"), to the singer's loss ("Such, *Lycidas*, thy loss to Shepherds *ear*" [my emphasis]), to the "flashy songs" of the false shepherds, we repeatedly encounter human activity figured as song. Finally, and unexpectedly, our vantage point shifts. We have heard the shepherd singing; now, at the end, we are suddenly thrust back to view our singer as a dramatic personage in a larger poem:

Thus sang the uncouth Swain to th' Okes and rills,
While the still morn went out with Sandals gray,
He touch'd the tender stops of various Quills,
With eager thought warbling his *Dorick* lay:
And now the Sun had stretch'd out all the hills,
And now was dropt into the Western bay;
At last he rose, and twitch'd his Mantle blew:
To morrow to fresh Woods, and Pastures new.

We are here invited to see the elegist with new eyes, and as we do so his song crystallizes before us as a significant human action. He has passed through his agon; he has overcome his fears for the futility of human enterprise; he has, finally, accomplished an active, "eager" work of faith, which in turn anticipates new action. In the end Milton's singer, by his own example, suggests to us that the deeds of men worth celebrating do not in fact grow "on mortal soil"; rather, as Phoebus' words have implied, it is the work rooted in a faith in Christian salvation that has a significance beyond itself.

Boston University

NOTES

1. The text of *Lycidas* cited throughout is C. A. Patrides, ed., *Milton's "Lycidas": The Tradition and the Poem* (New York, 1961).

2. Patrides, *Milton's "Lycidas,"* pp. 228, 112.

3. I am accepting Arthur E. Barker's almost universally approved division of *Lycidas* into three parts. See "The Pattern of Milton's Nativity Ode," *University of Toronto Quarterly*, X (1941), 171–72.

4. Readings along these general lines have frequently been proposed. See in particular Donald M. Friedman, *"Lycidas*: The Swain's Paideia," *Milton Studies*, III (Pittsburgh, 1971), pp. 3–34; Jon S. Lawry, " 'Eager Thought': Dialectic in 'Lycidas,' " *PMLA*, LXXVII (1962), 27–32, reprinted in *Milton: Modern Essays in Criticism*, ed. Arthur E. Barker (New York, 1965), pp. 112–24; and Lawry's book, *The Shadow of Heaven* (Ithaca, 1968), pp. 96–120.

5. Annotators of Phoebus' speech have generally been more interested in the singer's "trembling ears" (Virgil's "aurem vellit"; the story of Midas) than in the plant of fame. See H. B. Cotterill's comments (London, 1902), quoted in Scott Elledge, *Milton's "Lycidas"* (New York, 1966), p. 276; C. S. Jerram, *The "Lycidas" and "Epitaphium Damonis"* (London, 1874); Merritt Y. Hughes, "Milton and the Sense of Glory," *PQ*, XXVIII (1949), 107–24.

6. The Columbia edition of Milton's *Complete Works*, ed. Frank Allen Patterson et al. (New York, 1931–1938), XVI, 3, cited throughout as CM.

7. Quoted from *John Milton: Complete Poems and Major Prose*, ed. Merritt Y. Hughes (New York, 1957).

8. This is widely accepted, although Sears Jayne's reading casts some doubt on the easy equation of haemony and grace. See "The Subject of Milton's Ludlow Mask," *PMLA*, LXXIV (1959), 533–43, reprinted in Barker, *Milton: Modern Essays in Criticism*, pp. 88–111.

9. See Edward S. LeComte, "New Light on the 'Haemony' passage in *Comus*," *PQ*, XXI (1942), 283–98.

10. Cited in Elledge, *Milton's "Lycidas,"* pp. 275–76. I suspect that what Milton has in mind in the plant of false fame is a gilded victory garland. In *Paradise Lost*, the angels wear crowns of amarant interwoven with gold—crowns which might be considered heavenly counterparts to the victory garlands of our fallen world:

> With solemn adoration down they cast
> Thir Crowns inwove with Amarant and Gold,
> Immortal Amarant, a Flow'r which once
> In Paradise, fast by the Tree of Life
> Began to bloom, but soon for man's offense
> To Heav'n remov'd where first it grew, there grows,
> And flow'rs aloft shading the Fount of Life.
>
> (III, 351–57; Hughes' edition)

The history of amarant here described clearly parallels what Milton tells us of haemony, and the echo of *Lycidas*, 81 in the last two lines is hard to miss. We are dealing, it would seem, with a recurrent conception in Milton of an immortal plant which contrasts with earthly growths. Such a contrast suggests that here the angels' crowns may have their earthly types and that we have previously glimpsed such fallen coronets in *Lycidas*.

11. LeComte, "New Light," p. 284, tightening the comparison between haemony and moly, reads "florem . . . luteum" as "golden flower."

12. Ibid., p. 288. LeComte argues ingeniously for a connection between haemony and the plant *rhamnus*, called in Gerard's *Herball* Christ's thorn. His scholarship is supported by Thomas P. Harrison, Jr., "The 'Haemony' Passage in *Comus* Again," *PQ*, XXII (1943), 251–54.

13. Wayne Shumaker, "Flowerets and Sounding Seas: A Study in the Affective Structure of *Lycidas*," in Patrides, *Milton's "Lycidas,"* p. 127.

MYTHIC DIALECTIC
IN THE NATIVITY ODE

Lawrence W. Kingsley

This poem traces a dialectic between Christian and pagan symbolism through their echoing and reechoing ideas and images. Milton scants the conventional Christmas narrative of Virgin and manger to treat the Incarnation's historical and conceptual circumstances. The birth of Christ opposes a new mythology to religions flourishing at the time, yet borrows substantially from them. Christianity thus reflects these religions in principle, but brings peace where there was disorder, music where there was discord, lightness in place of darkness, virtue instead of sin, glory instead of shame. Since the identity of Christ is formed from heathen prototypes, Milton works out a *discordia concors* in which Phaeton, Phoebus, Lucifer, Pan, and Hercules, together with the whole pantheon of dispossessed deities, collapse into the Christhead. This method of counterposing the pagan world, point for point, with spreading manifestations of Christ allows Milton to retain his predilection for classical heroes while still proclaiming their rejection.

IT FOLLOWS from Milton's initial design that "On the Morning of Christ's Nativity" is basically conceptual in technique. The thematic choice of the Incarnation instead of the Nativity meant that Milton had to resist the Quattrocento image of the homely manger.[1] As it happens, the manger occupies only four brief passages (lines 30–31, 109–16, 151, and 227–44). What concerns Milton is not the story of the Magi, but historical forces which the Incarnation throws into conflict. Christianity asserts itself in the teeth of competing mythologies, but in the process it appropriates much of their conceptual foundation. Milton thus undertakes to show how Christianity extends, incorporates, modifies, or undercuts symbol and ritual which once served the cause of idolatry.

The Incarnation in this way becomes the moment when the fund of cosmological explanation held in common by sects flourishing at the time separates into two similar but hostile strands, Christian and pagan. For this reason Christian image contends against pagan image: passage celebrating the arrival of the Christian era opposes passage describing the pagan world into which Christ is born. As we shall see, peace is set against disorder; celestial music, against the doomsday trumpet; the coming of light, against the catalogue of deities worshipped by children of darkness. Built up, in this way, through a system of allusions and echoes, parallels and analogues, antecedents and consequents, concords and discords, the chief organizing principle of the poem becomes a dialectic between the implications of pagan and Christian allegiance, as these implications develop from the simplest imagistic level to the larger complex of overlaid theme and meaning.

The Incarnation, for example, is, in one respect, the process by which heaven's "Courts of everlasting Day" are made available to earth's "darksome House of mortal Clay" (13–14).[2] Through these qualitative terms, the opposition between heaven and earth is established in the proem and then reproduced throughout the rest of the ode: "the Heav'n . . . /Hath took no print of the approaching light" (19–20); it is night when "the Prince of light" begins his reign (61–62); "the shady gloom" gives "day her room" (77–78); the "Globe of circular light" shines on "the shame-fac't night" (110–11); hell threatens to "leave her dolorous mansions to the peering day" (140), and "The rays of *Bethlehem* blind" Osiris (223).

The repetition of these images is not redundant. By varying the ratio of light and darkness on earth, Milton, almost imperceptibly, shows how night becomes day in accord with his premise that the Incarnation dispels the darkness which hitherto has kept man in ignorance of the true religion. The world is illuminated not all at once, but gradually with the approach of the Christian dawn. As pagan darkness yields its sway, Christian light everywhere becomes peace and music— in Nature, in cosmos, in shepherds' fields, in hell, in false temples, and in Bethlehem stable.

This influx of light into areas shrouded in pagan darkness offers visible proof of the Savior's birth and gives rise to the Christian-pagan counterpoint which sustains the poem from first to last. The pagan mind erects a pantheon of gods, but Milton's God is jealous. Once struck by "The rays of *Bethlehem*" (223), pagan mythology therefore collapses into the Christhead by the law of parsimony ("Thou shalt have none other gods but me"), which is the fundamental meaning of the One. After the example of Augustine, Milton progresses from multiplicity to unity. What replaces the long catalogue of pagan deities is the single sun conceit. The poem is hence a submerged *discordia concors*: light comes out of darkness, Christian imagery out of pagan, the Holy Infant out of the demise of "the damned crew" (228). This paper will examine these conclusions section by section.

The coming of peace finds its provenance in Nature's inept response to the Nativity. Milton fuses the Stoic idea that Nature has decayed from the Golden Age with the Christian myth of the Fall. Nature possesses "foul deformities" (44) which are embarrassed by the reappearance of "perfect shape" in Christ (*PR* III, 11, and *Areopagitica*, p. 741). To cover her shame, Nature seeks covering by imbruing herself even further in pagan lust. It is clear that she has not yet assimilated the meaning of her Maker's presence.[3] By hiding under the "Saintly Veil" reserved for true maidens (42), she vulgarizes a symbol of Christian purity. No effort on the part of the fallen world, Milton seems to say, can escape the state of sin without divine intervention. That is why Nature still partakes of shame until God sends "the meek-ey'd Peace" to calm her fears (46).

This personified abstraction is the biblical dove (the turtledove of l. 50) which brought an olive branch to the ark and descended at Christ's baptism.[4] The advent of the dove of peace functions less to presage Christ than to provide a foil to Him. What has been charged to Milton as "youthful excesses" in this passage is rather his way of showing that the Christ who supplants "His ready Harbinger" cannot strike peace throughout the land simply by "waving wide" the "myrtle wand" (49–51). It is only "on the bitter cross" (152) "That he our deadly forfeit should release, / And with his Father work us a perpetual peace" (6–7). The Prince of Peace wears not a crown of "Olive green," but a crown of thorns. Peace thus comes to man not "softly sliding" through "amorous clouds," but with "red fire, and smold'ring clouds" at the Last Judgment (159). The contrast is implicit, but we must read the whole poem to make the connection.

While peace cannot come to man too quickly, Christmas morning does, however, offer a foretaste of what is to come in heaven, and the emblematic growth of peace in the succeeding stanzas gravitates toward the hope of heavenly fulfillment. At the beginning of time itself, God made peace in Chaos:

> the Creator Great
> His constellations set,
>   And the well-balanc't world on hinges hung
> And cast the dark foundations deep,
> And bid the welt'ring waves their oozy channel keep.   (120–24)

The smoothing of the waters in this stanza parallels the peaceful waters in stanza 5:

> The winds with wonder whist,
> Smoothly the waters kiss't,
>   Whispering new joys to the mild Ocean,
> Who now hath quite forgot to rave,
> While Birds of Calm sit brooding on the charmed wave.   (164–68)

The halcyon evening of the Nativity, in this respect, culminates the process begun at the Creation of imposing order on the world. The recognition that peace in the past is a signpost to the Nativity is reinforced by the example of the Augustan Peace, which historically preceded the birth of Christ. Peace is becoming universal, not only on the face of the earth, but through the merging of separate time schemes. Parallel images carried through the time sequence attain the status of seed and flowering, prophecy and promise fulfilled. The effect is to pass from Old Testament to New.

As in T. S. Eliot's "Burnt Norton," time present and time past are both contained in time future. Ever since Virgil's Fourth Eclogue, the Nativity was interpreted as an augury of a second Golden Age. Now that the Nativity brings the Golden Age again into view, Milton can anticipate an ultimate reign of peace:

> Yea, Truth and Justice then
> Will down return to men,
>   Th'enamel'd *Arras* of the Rainbow wearing,

> And Mercy set between,
> Thron'd in Celestial sheen,
>   With radiant feet the tissued clouds down steering,
> And Heav'n as at some festival,
> Will open wide the Gates of her high Palace Hall.   (141–48)

Peace is implied here both by allusion and by surface parallel. In the first place, the Psalmist relates peace to the virtues which Milton lists: "Mercy and Truth are met together; righteousness and peace have kissed each other" (Psalm lxxii,10). Secondly, the kissing of righteousness and peace recalls the kissing waters (or the winds kissing the waters) of stanza 5. Finally and more importantly, the elaborate descent of the three virtues evokes the masquelike staging whereby the dove of peace descends in stanza 3.

Stanza 15 quoted above is, in fact, a conscious answer to stanza 3. Peace in stanza 3 emanates from God's grace, which is given freely to the world in token of the Incarnation. But there is one drawback: the unearned bestowal of peace circumvents the plan of Christian redemption just instituted in the world. Milton thus feels constrained in stanza 16 to specify the only means by which man will ever achieve enduring peace, by gaining admittance to heaven through Christ's sacrifice:

> This must not yet be so,
>   The Babe lies yet in smiling Infancy,
> That on the bitter cross
> Must redeem our loss.   (150–53)

This injunction changes the emphasis in stanza 15 from peace struck "through Sea and Land" (stanza 3) to peace parading out of heaven in the company of traditional virtues. Everlasting peace is to be realized not in man's world, but in heaven.

It is important to note that these images of peace are spread over fifteen stanzas. If the same subject were developed in *Paradise Lost*, one unbroken utterance would thunder out a direct statement. But Milton in his lyrical vein relies instead on the recurrence of a developing motif. Peace descends from heaven in the same act of mercy which furnishes light to the world, calms Nature's fears, and quells the raving waters. God's beneficence is felt in each aspect of the world that Milton brings into focus. Where the Holy Spirit is immanent, order and harmony replace the ignorance which until now has held rule.

As we have seen, the iconography of the dove moves toward the Christian ideal. A similar technique is apparent in stanzas 6 and 7, where Milton dethrones the pre-Christian sun in favor of the Incarnate Son. The pagan sun encounters a greater light and hides "his head for shame." The "Prince of Light" has such magnitude that Phaeton's axle would break under His weight. If, as Albert S. Cook points out, Milton preserves Ovid's account of Phaeton in the words "Throne" and "Axletree," the shamed sun must be Ovid's Phoebus.[5] Phoebus is only one of the heathen sungods who yield to Christ. The additional presence of the Phoenician Peor, the Babylonian Thammuz, the Greek Apollo, and the Egyptian Osiris shows that Milton recruits competing sungods from all conceivable mythologies in order to render the ascension of the one Prince of Light as formidable and universal in scope as possible.

The Incarnate Son replaces all anthropomorphic sun deities in the famous image: "So when the Sun in bed, / Curtain'd with cloudy red, / Pillows his chin upon an Orient wave" (229–31). Milton deliberately confuses his metaphor to bring out the double fact that Christ is both Son of God and Christian light. The wide dispraise this image has excited overlooks the extraordinary control with which Milton graphs the convergence of disparate religions. In a single moment of intensity, competing sungods are absorbed into Christ's brilliance, here meant to burst on our imagination as the climax of the whole poem, the moment when He is at once born, seen, and felt. The "Globe of circular light" visible to the shepherds (110) has now filled to cosmic proportions, heralding the Infant's dispossession of the false gods. The image is, quite simply, one of Milton's finest, and its lushness is its power. To compare the sleeping Infant to the sun shining through clouds takes no license for which Milton did not have warrant. Not only was the Christ child habitually painted with a halo, making the crib the brightest point of the picture, but Christ appears as the source of the world's light, temporal and spiritual, in the biblical context with which Milton is working.

Just as Phoebus is absorbed into the Christhead, Phaeton's chariot reappears in the final stanza as the "polisht Car" of "Heav'n's youngest-teemed Star." Because Phaeton's chariot, in its Ovidian form, is no longer serviceable, it is night in the proem when Milton begins writing. Light cannot break until the true Son is born: "the Heav'n by the Sun's team untrod, / Hath took no print of the approaching light" (19–20). Besides the pun on "Sun" in these lines, there is a pun on "print," both senses enforcing the idea of daylight as an impression on heaven. For Plato, the impression of the divine paradigm on the universe was an image of creation.[6] Milton seems to incorporate Plato's image, since the imprinting of the heavens means the creation of "the Sun in bed."

"Heav'n's youngest-teemed Star" is the morning star, which traditionally led the Wise Men. It is the standard of the Holy Infant by virtue of Revelation xxii, 16: "I am . . . the bright morning star." Like other Christian symbols in this poem, it emerges from the defeasance of pagan conceptions. The morning star in stanza 6 is called Lucifer, one of the names given to Satan on the authority of Isaiah. Applied to the Prince of Darkness, it produces paradox, since in Latin *Lucifer* means "light-bearer." This Promethean attribute is restored to Christ in the very act which banishes the pagan stars:

> The Stars with deep amaze
> Stand fixt in steadfast gaze,
>   Bending one way their precious influence,
> And will not take their flight
> For all the morning light.   (69–73)

Like Phoebus in the next stanza, these stars are shamed by Christ's radiance. Milton's technique is to introduce a theme (the shame of Nature), expand it (the shame of the stars), vary it (the shame of Phoebus), echo it ("the shame fac't night" in l. 111), and then return to it through dramatic exposition (the shame of the departing deities).

Meanwhile the celestial music begins. After stanza 7 Milton is engaged in a process of building up the world harmony once known on earth: he is twisting "all the chains," mentioned in *L'Allegro*, "that tie / The hidden soul of harmony" (143–44). It was an accepted Renaissance idea that unfallen man was able to hear the Pythagorean music of the spheres—what Boethius called *musica mundana*.[7] The Incarnation restores this prelapsarian faculty, so that one representation of the coming of Christ is the return of *musica mundana*.

Milton knew the medieval image used by Donne and Herbert: "Christ is . . . / My onely musick."[8] This allegory provides a general frame of reference for Milton's introduction of Christ as "the mighty *Pan*" (89). Renaissance tradition tended to associate Pan with Christ as the Good Shepherd. But in the popular imagination Pan has always evoked the rustic satyr who, piping away, leads his cohorts in bacchanalian rites. Milton wishes to show this heathen tradition merging with Christian, as embraced by the poem's overall typological bent. Pan still retains his pastoral and musical identity, but his conversion to Christianity is a fait accompli. In place of Pan's reed instrument is *musica mundana*; in place of lusty dancers are simple shepherds ("silly," l. 92), who become analogous to the Wise Men in stanza 11; no longer led in debauchery by Pan, Milton's shepherds are led to the manger by the morning star.

We can observe the progress of *musica mundana* as it is restored to the shepherds, to sublunar realms (101–03), and to the entirety of "Heav'n's deep Organ" (130), taken in the sense of Donne's image: "Gods great organ, this whole Spheare."[9] The sounding of *musica mundana*—"Ring out ye Crystal spheres" (125)—fulfills and ends the fallen state of man responsible for the world's shame. The promise made in the proem, "That he our deadly forfeit should release" (6), is granted when the celestial choir lifts its "unexpressive notes" to ring in the new Saturnian age (116). Since the whole progress of *musica mundana* has built toward the reknitting of broken harmony, the moment of final restoration is represented by orchestral completeness: "Heav'n's deep organ" and "th'Angelic symphony" play together in "full consort" (132).

By the sixteenth stanza *musica mundana* has lasted long enough for mortal ears. Golgotha is yet to come. Opposing the harmony of the Incarnation, Golgotha and the Apocalypse are associated with dissonance: the "horrid clang" breaks the celestial music. Repercussions are felt not only in Golgotha and the Last Judgment, but in the Harrowing of Hell and the thunder of Mount Sinai. While this apocalyptic fury counterpoints all previous images of peace, the Apocalypse specifically carries stanza 4 in fugue. The Apocalypse implies Armageddon, and "the battle of that great day" prophesied in Revelation xvii, 14 suggests the imbroglio of the idle instruments of war in stanza 4. Whereas, "No War, or Battle's sound / Was heard the World around" (53–54), the earth on Judgment Day "Shall from the surface to the center shake" (162). "The Trumpet spake not to the armed throng" after the dove of peace descends, but "The wakeful trump of doom must thunder through the deep" at the Apocalypse. Later in the poem,

"The Libyc *Hammon*" who "shrinks his horn" knows he cannot compete with this mighty blast (203).

In the midst of God's wrath, the strain suddenly diminishes: "then at last our bliss / Full and perfect is" (165–66). Then the idea of battle resumes in the recalcitrance of "Th'old Dragon . . . wroth to see his Kingdom fail" (168–71). The dragon is, of course, "that old serpent, which is . . . Satan" (Revelation xx, 2). As leader of the pagan crew—oracles and priests, gods and ghosts—he deserves to be unfavorably compared with Christ. Christ radiates a "far-beaming blaze of Majesty" from heaven's "high Palace Hall," while the dragon is "under ground" and "Not half so far casts his usurped sway." Similarly, Christ rests "in his swaddling bands," while the dragon is "In straiter limits bound."

The binding of the dragon is a prelude to the metaphoric binding of other pagan divinities. By the penultimate stanza each ghost will have been "fetter'd." This long roll call of dispossessed heathens is the least appreciated part of the poem. One is inclined to forget that the epic catalogue is a Pindaric device,[10] and to find the catalogue more appropriate to Book II of *Paradise Lost* than to an ode. After the rapidly moving lyricism of the first two-thirds of the poem, this last third may seem "prolix."[11] As always in Milton, verbal richness is admired; but very little has been said about the structural relationship that obtains between this section and the earlier stanzas.[12] That relationship has the utmost importance: each of the final stanzas balances or advances previous images. One by one, pagan deities pick up the Nativity theme and answer it in plaintive notes which are as much a part of "The Hymn" as the celestial choir. To see the usurpers in lamentation is necessarily to elevate the standard by which they are depressed. The theme is still celebrational, but the tone is one of lament.

This contrast is precisely the difference between Milton the poet and the charlatan priests and prophets. In the proem Milton uses the conventional Pindaric appearance of the poet in the poem to show, as Elegy VI corroborates, that his poem in praise of Christ will actually be his gift to Christ.[13] The act of writing a poem therefore becomes "liturgical" by way of the ancient bard-priest identification which Milton acknowledges in Elegy VI: "For truly, the bard is sacred to the gods and is their priest" (Hughes, p. 52).[14] In the proem, a couplet echoing Isaiah vi, 5–7 makes this priestly function of the poet a radical part of the ode: "And join thy voice unto the Angel Choir, / From out his secret Altar toucht with hallow'd fire" (27–28). Isaiah writes how a seraphim touches his lips with "a live coal . . . from off the altar," so that his mouth will be purified before he delivers his message. Having placed himself in the role of a prophet, Milton writes his poem as the prophecy which the Nativity fulfills.

Prophecies of the pagan oracles, in comparison, are never realized: "No nightly trance, or breathed spell, / Inspires the pale-ey'd Priest from the prophetic cell" (179–80). Milton's gift bears fruit in the poem we are reading, while sacrificial gifts of the pagans are wasted. Lemures will never rise from their ashes, to which gifts were offered at festivals, where, significantly, "pious rites of purification (februa) were unknown."[15] In the case of Moloch, gifts kill rather than save. Children to be sacrificed to Moloch were placed in the hands of a brass idol heated to scorching temperature. According to the tradition to which Milton alludes (208), priests would "make a noise with drums, that the father might not hear the cry of his child, and have pity upon him."[16] The sacrifice of the Holy Infant, Milton submits, will never be so pointless.

Except for stanza 19, the silencing of the oracles is a misnomer. A degree of ritualistic noise is still present to counterpoint both the celestial harmony and the "horrid clang." "In Urns and Altars round" the sound is "drear and dying"; "Cymbals' ring" and "Timbrel'd Anthems dark" are heard. In mock imitation of the shepherds' "blissful rapture," a thousand notes of shrieking, weeping, lamenting, sighing, mourning, and moaning accent the theme of desertion and impotence. *Ut musica poesis* counterpoints *ut pictura poesis* almost one for one, as a pictorial vocabulary stressing darkness, paleness, and shadows leads into the blazing sun conceit.

The gods not already discussed constitute a parody of the Holy Family. Here, more than elsewhere in the poem, Milton works by allusion. The history that stands behind each god is brought forward in ironic contrast to the life of the Lord. The tracing of these allusions, however, is fraught with difficulty, because pagan mythology was current in so many versions. Baalim, for example, who forsakes his temple dim with Peor (197–98), was "the name generall for most Idols" and Peor was "his other Name" (*PL* I, 412).[17] Ashtaroth and Baalim were usually associated with each other, as in *Paradise Lost* (I, 422). If Ashtaroth is "Heav'n's Queen and Mother both" (201), Baalim must be an impersonation of the Holy Father. Alternatively, *Baalim* was the generic name for Phoenician deities concerned with flocks, in which case the allusion would have ironic reference to the Good Shepherd;[18] *Baalim* would then be a corruption of Pan's title and role, as *Lucifer*, applied to Satan, is a corruption of "Giver of Light." An urgent need in Milton scholarship is a definitive study of these sources based on Frazer and the ground that has been turned since him. Don Cameron Allen has now charted the principal course of pagan mythography, with a wealth of other material, in *Mysteriously Meant: The Rediscovery of Pagan Symbolism and Allegorical Interpretation in the Renaissance* (Baltimore, 1970).

Parody of the Holy Family can be more sharply defined for Ashtaroth and the other deities. Ashtaroth's appropriation of Marian language ("Heav'n's Queen and Mother both") only insists on an unfavorable comparison with the Blessed Virgin. While Mary nestles Jesus under an aura of "circular light" (110), Ashtaroth sits on a dark altar (202). Ashtaroth loved Thammuz, the Greek Adonis, who was slain by the boar, Winter. In deference to Christ, on the other hand, winter is not destructive, but generative, as seen in Nature's wooing in stanza 2. Thammuz died annually and was revived each spring by the Tyrian mourners (204), and this yearly cycle is credibly the meiosis of the Savior's eternal life. Christ will die only once, but that sole death is to secure the everlasting life of His people. His followers will not mourn, but rejoice in His living presence.[19]

The Osiris legends similarly suffer in comparison with the Word. Isis and Osiris had three children, Anubis, Orus, and Typhon. Typhon murdered his father by locking him in a chest dumped into the Nile—an episode to which Milton alludes in "Nor can he be at rest / Within his sacred chest" (216–17). Osiris' discomfort ironically anticipates the Infant's resting in bed, as well as His three-day interment. When Christ dies, however, no "sable-stoled Sorcerers" bear His ark in vain (220); His clergy carries a new logos throughout the world. After his murder Osiris was buried in Memphis, where he arose as Apis, the sacred bull. Vives writes: "At *Memphis* . . . was a temple dedicated unto *Apis*. . . . His place where he lay was called the mysticall bed, and when he went abroad, a multitude of vshers were euer about him: all adored this

Oxe-God."[20] Adoration of Apis is obviously perversion of the manger scene; thus, Milton banishes him from *"Memphian* Grove" (214). Isaiah i, 3 is an almost certain analogue: "The ox knoweth his owner, and the ass his master's crib."[21]

The Memphian grass is "unshow'r'd" (215) in recognition of Christ's identification with rain: "He shall come down like rain upon the mown grass: as showers that water the earth" (Psalm lxxii, 6).[22] Osiris, on the other hand, was associated with drought. To Plutarch, the "story of Osiris having been shut up in his chest means nothing more than the loss of water."[23] To end the drought, priests shrouded a cow in black vestments, a detail Milton retains in "Naught but profoundest Hell can be his shroud" (218). Like Osiris, the Genius departing "From haunted spring" is denied further access to vegetation rituals (184–85). Nor does any other god

> Longer dare abide,
>   Nor *Typhon* huge ending in snaky twine:
> Our Babe, to show his Godhead true,
> Can in his swaddling bands control the damned crew.   (225–28)

Milton alludes to Hercules' strangling of Juno's serpents, here transformed into Typhon and "the damned crew." Typhon's "snaky twine" may also refer to Prudentius' account of Christ as a star in the East, passing over the heavens and destroying the constellation of the serpent.[24] In that case the star would be the morning star, which chases away its astral rivals. As a unifying symbol, serpents bring to mind "Th'old Dragon," which began the catalogue now complete.

From the vantage point of the final crib scene, we are ready to notice what has happened to the main symbols in this poem. Phaeton becomes the true Giver of Light; Lucifer becomes the Christian morning star; Phaeton's chariot becomes the morning star's "polisht Car" (241). Phoebus wanes into the Prince of Light; Pan emerges as the Good Shepherd; Hercules is replaced by his Christian counterpart. War quiets into peace; shame yields to glory; night gives way to dawn; vanity and sin evolve into Christian virtues; and broken chords are completed on earth. As diversity of heathen worship contracts into the oneness of Christ, a new symbology emerges, fructified with all the associations of peace, harmony, and light which the new era holds for man.

Of first importance is a rectified iconography, wherein heathen prototypes are denuded of mythic power and recast as inferior foreshadowings of the Lord. To work pre-Christian heroes into this typological scheme was the obvious way lying open to Milton by which he could preserve his fondness for classical sources while still rejoicing in their overthrow. Historically, the church had always Christianized its origins, ever since early patristic commentators sought to reconcile Scripture with inherited Greek philosophy. In Milton's poem the absorption of heathen mythology into Christian takes place symbol by symbol, so that redefined religion is born at the very moment the Savior is.

In summary, the Christ child enters the fallen world and leavens its corruption. A dialectic is thereby brought into play which balances or counterposes each incident of corrupt Nature with manifestations of the Holy Spirit. Since Milton depends for his delivery upon sustained contrast of part to part and part to whole, his poem achieves a single unity of utterance. Once that unity is grasped, the Nativity Ode declares itself as the mature work it deserves to be considered, undoubtedly Milton's first great poem.

University of Wisconsin

NOTES

1. E. M. W. Tillyard, *Milton* (London, 1939), p. 37; Rosemond Tuve, *Images and Themes in Five Poems by Milton* (Cambridge, Mass., 1962), p. 37. This paper would not be possible without Tuve's essay.

2. The text of Milton's poetry cited throughout is *John Milton: Complete Poems and Major Prose*, ed. Merritt Y. Hughes (New York, 1957).

3. Tuve, *Images and Themes*, p. 51.

4. John T. Shawcross, ed., *The Complete English Poetry of John Milton* (New York, 1963), p. 42, n. 7.

5. Albert S. Cook, "Notes on Milton's Nativity Ode," *Transactions of the Connecticut Academy of Arts and Sciences* (New Haven, 1909), p. 334, n. 84.

6. Plato, *The Timaeus*, trans. Thomas Taylor (New York, 1944), pp. 139, 169.

7. Through Boethius' *De institutione musica*, the Renaissance learned the distinction between *musica mundana, musica humana* ("which unites the incorporeal activity of the reason with the body") and *musica instrumentalis* (instrumental or vocal music). See Gretchen Ludke Finney, *Musical Backgrounds for English Literature: 1580–1650* (New Brunswick, N. J., 1963), p. x.

8. George Herbert, "Aaron," cited by Tuve, *A Reading of George Herbert* (London, 1952), p. 146; cf. *Images and Themes*, p. 60, n. 10.

9. John Donne, "Obsequies to the Lord Harrington," cited by Tuve, *Herbert*, p. 146.

10. Carol Maddison, *Apollo and the Nine: A History of the Ode* (London, 1960), pp. 6–7.

11. Don Cameron Allen, *The Harmonious Vision: Studies in Milton's Poetry* (Baltimore, 1954), p. 25.

12. See Lawrence W. Hyman, "Christ's Nativity and the Pagan Deities," *Milton Studies*, II (Pittsburgh, 1970), p. 103 f.

13. Maddison, *Apollo and the Nine*, p. 9.

14. Tuve, *Images and Themes*, p. 42.

15. Ovid, *Fasti*, trans. Sir James George Frazer, Loeb Classical Library (London, 1931), pp. 291–93. Cf. Charles G. Osgood, *The Classical Mythology of Milton's Poems* (New York, 1900), p. 52.

16. Cook, "Notes on Milton's Nativity Ode," p. 357, n. 205.

17. George Wesley Whiting, *Milton's Literary Milieu* (Chapel Hill, 1939), p. 208, quotes Thomas Fuller's description of Baalim.

18. Shawcross, ed., *Poetry of John Milton*, p. 47, n. 38.

19. Cleanth Brooks and John Edward Hardy, *Poems of Mr. John Milton: The 1645 Edition with Essays in Analysis* (New York, 1951), p. 101.

20. Cited by Whiting, *Milton's Literary Milieu*, p. 192.

21. J. B. Broadbent, "The Nativity Ode," in *The Living Milton*, ed. Frank Kermode (New York, 1961), p. 16.

22. Ibid., p. 22.

23. Whiting, *Milton's Literary Milieu*, p. 182.

24. Cook, "Notes on Milton's Nativity Ode," p. 362, n. 226–28.

THE PATTERN OF TEMPTATION
IN *PARADISE REGAINED*

James R. McAdams

The debate of Christ and Satan concerning "zeal and duty" to Israel is the most significant temptation in *Paradise Regained*. In it, Milton sums up the main themes, reveals the antagonists definitively, and foreshadows the remaining action and resolution. The sequence of temptations itself indicates that the matter of Israel is crucial: the episodes form a pattern whose organization highlights the Israel temptation. The pattern is derived from the symmetrical relating of the parts of the sequence through parallel and contrast. The first part or episode is related to the last, the second episode to the second-to-last, and so on, leaving the Israel debate alone unparalleled, and therefore emphasized, at the center of the pattern. This pattern imposes coherence upon the temptations and counterpoints previously defined patterns, enriching the poem's texture. It also places several episodes in new perspectives and enhances awareness of Milton's architectonic method.

I N AREOPAGITICA, Milton observes that the perfecting of a building consists in combining more than one form in a pleasing symmetry: "out of many moderat varieties and brotherly dissimilitudes that are not vastly disproportionall arises the goodly and gracefull symmetry that commends the whole pile and structure."[1] This judgment is reflected in the structure of *Paradise Regained*. The incidents, debates, disquisitions, and narrative accounts in the poem make up patterns or forms whose "gracefull symmetry" testifies to Milton's view that subtleties of ordering in art themselves bring satisfaction. As Louis L. Martz reveals, the most evident pattern, the division of the poem into books, shows classical influence and accords with the meditational tradition. Elizabeth M. Pope points to the "triple equation" in the allurements of the second day: in rejecting gluttony, avarice, and vainglory, the Son fulfills the traditional doctrines that Adam and Eve embraced all sin in the Garden, that Christ vanquished all sin in the Wilderness, and that man still sins but has Christ's example to aid him. Both Howard Schultz and Michael Fixler treat the poem's orderly revelation of the Son in his offices of prophet, priest, and king. Barbara K. Lewalski covers all of these matters, noting that the poem sets "various structural patterns against each other in an elaborate counterpoint."[2] But a basic pattern remains to be developed critically. It illuminates the significance of certain parts of the "brief epic," clarifies the relation of other parts, increases understanding of Milton's methodology in the poem, and aids in defining the poem's special appeal.

This fundamental pattern gives structural coherence to the sequence of three major temptations in *Paradise Regained.* The sequence begins with the onset of action in the Wilderness (I, 314) and closes with Satan's fall to Hell (IV, 580). It is preceded by an induction in which the narrator and major characters introduce themes to be clarified in the temptations—in particular, the central reality of the poem: the mystery of the Son as God incarnate in man. The sequence is followed by the angels' celebration of Christ's victory and a brief conclusion. A new temptation occurs on each of the three last days of the forty that Christ spent searching for his meaning in the Wilderness. On the first day Satan attempts to make Christ turn stones into bread (I, 314–56), and on the third he tries to intimidate Christ on the pinnacle (IV, 541–80). During the second day Satan fruitlessly sets before Christ a variety of inducements to sin which collectively represent all sin.[3]

The second temptation (II, 245–IV, 431) overshadows the others in length and complexity. It contains nine distinguishable episodes, including the nights of dream and storm. Four of these episodes lead to the most significant development in the poem outside of the final victory—Satan's tempting the Son with the lure of zeal and duty to Israel (III, 149–243)—and four lead away from it. This circumstance makes the exchange between Christ and Satan on the subject of Israel structurally central in the sequence of temptation. It is thematically central as well. In the exchange Milton draws together and defines the themes of the poem, exposes the characters' natures fully, crowns the prior offerings, renders the succeeding ones redundant, and fore-shadows the conclusion.

The pattern of temptation in *Paradise Regained* is established by the systematic relating of the episodes through parallels and contrasts. The first event in the sequence of temptations, the request to turn stones to bread, is related to the last event, the pinnacle scene. Within the second temptation the principle is continued: the earliest episode

PLAN OF THE TEMPTATION SEQUENCE OF *PARADISE REGAINED*

SECOND TEMPTATION

The World (Avarice)
Israel (III, 149–243)

| Fame (III, 1–148) | : | Parthia (III, 244–403) |
| Riches (II, 404–86) | : | Rome (IV, 1–194) |

The Flesh (Gluttony)		*The Devil* (Vainglory)
Banquet (II, 285–403)	:	Athens (IV, 195–397)
Night of Dream (II, 245–84)	:	Night of Storm (IV, 397–431)

— —

TRANSITIONAL SCENES		TRANSITIONAL SCENES
1. True Portent (II, 1–244)		1. False Portent (IV, 432–98)
2. Fraud (I, 357–502)	:	2. Threat (IV, 499–540)

| FIRST TEMPTATION (Stones) | : | THIRD TEMPTATION (Pinnacle) |
| (I, 314–56) | | (IV, 541–80) |

is linked by parallel and contrast to the latest, the second-to-earliest episode to the second-to-latest, and so on. In addition, two transitional passages separating the first and second temptations parallel two passages separating the second and third temptations. The overall pattern further emphasizes the Israel episode: besides being structurally and thematically central in the poem, Israel is unique in having no scene paralleled with it. In addition, the pattern leads to enrichment of the episodes through their pairing and to a heightening of internal tension. It confirms a second basic structure, one which counterpoints the progression of incident toward the climax.

The parallel night scenes enclose the events of the second day in a frame.[4] Christ dreams of food in the first night scene (II, 245–84), and the dream is portentous since Satan appeals to gluttony in the following banquet episode. But the source and purpose of the dream are unclear, contributing to the atmosphere of growing menace. The lesson of Elijah in the desert may have been sent by God to show Christ the way through trial, but Satan can also inspire dreams and may have devised this one in order to lead Christ to claim an identity he may not yet assume. Christ is certainly on Satanic ground among "Trees thick interwoven" (II, 263).[5] At any rate, this scene of hunger and dream has two main effects: it links the temptation of the stones to the action of the second day by reemphasizing the themes of food and distrust of God's providence, and it anticipates or prefigures coming events.[6] The storm of the second night parallels the dream scene in emphasizing the theme of distrust and in looking both forward and backward in the poem. The storm acts as a portent of the violence to come at the pinnacle and also represents a part of the appeal to vainglory carrying over from the Athens episode; in like manner, the dream scene is part of the appeal to gluttony leading into the banquet offering.

Critics of *Paradise Regained* have at best only partially understood the significance of the second night scene and therefore have largely misconceived its place in the plan of the poem. It is commonly held that Christ's rejection of Satan's praise of secular learning terminates the second temptation and that the night of terror belongs to the third temptation. This view seems credible because both the storm and the pinnacle episodes depict violence, but it reflects a superficial appreciation of the function of the storm. On the other hand, some critics have ascribed the storm scene to the second temptation but have left the matter incompletely developed. For example, Dick Taylor, Jr., finds the storm part of the second temptation because it projects the theme of false portents shared by all the events of the second day. He sees the storm as a portent calculated to convince Christ of God's displeasure over his Son's refusals to fulfill prophecy by assuming temporal power. But Taylor does not show that the scene anticipates Satan's action on the following morning. Conversely, John M. Steadman sees the storm as "the keystone of an adversity sequence which complements the earlier temptations of prosperity" and which has precedent in doctrine and Renaissance epic practice. But Steadman does not defend his placing the scene in the second rather than the third temptation.[7]

Milton introduces the last major temptation by showing a change in the manner of Satan on the third morning. Satan approaches Christ "with no new device, they all were spent" (IV, 443). The night terrors therefore represent Satan's last attempt to deceive Christ into choosing a lesser over a greater good, the strategy behind all the offerings of the second day. During the night Christ is tempted to challenge what may be God's will, or even to master the storm, putting present convenience ahead of patient obedience. In effect, he receives a second opportunity to fall in vainglory, the sin he repudiated before Athens, when he is exposed to the storm and its promise of intensified torment to come.

The vainglory theme continues to be important up to the moment of Christ's victory on the pinnacle, but it is central only in the Athens episode. The new climate of violence begins to claim the greater share of attention in the second night scene. In parallel, the theme of gluttony is suggested in the first night by the dream of food, but the climate of fraud is at least equally prominent. Gluttony is highlighted only in the banquet scene, which parallels the Athens episode in the pattern of the temptation sequence. Finally, the theme of gluttony underlies the temptation of the stones, as vainglory underlies the temptation of the pinnacle, but the themes are overshadowed by the atmospheres of fraud and force, respectively, which characterize these rudimentary tests of trust in God. The night scenes, then, act as bridges connecting the three major temptations. The dream opening the second temptation ushers fraud as a tactic from the first into the second day, and brings gluttony into focus prior to the banquet. The storm closing the second temptation establishes the strategy of violence in preparation for the third day, and carries the theme of vainglory into the pinnacle scene.

Changes in Satan's manner indicate the divisions between all three major temptations, not just the second and third, and qualify the nature of Satan's emerging tactics in all cases. The disguise of shepherd is emblematic of the simple trickery of the stones test. The hypocritical good fellowship and mock concern which fix the tone of the second encounter illustrate the subtler villainy characteristic of the allurements. The "rage / And mad despite" (IV, 445–46) of the third morning mark the end of Satan's reliance upon fraud to defeat Christ and signal the shift to force. The second temptation does not end until Satan abandons the strategy of lies, and he holds to that strategy, though terror is his means, during the second night.

While the night scenes help relate the three main temptations, four other passages have an opposite function. They tend to isolate the devious second temptation from the direct first and third temptations. These passages are placed two before the night of dream and two after the night of storm, and they correspond in subject and theme. Following the appeal to turn stones to bread, Satan admits his identity and continues to converse with Christ while masking hypocrisy (I, 357–502). Satan expands upon the theme of distrust of God's providence, which is evident to some degree in every part of the temptation sequence, and talks of the significance of portents. He attempts to convince Christ to belie the portent of the descending dove (discussed widely in the induction of Book I) in favor of portents of devilish origin.

The portent of the dove at the Baptism also relates the brief episodes which make up one of the transitional passages dividing the first from the second temptation (II, 1–244). In successive scenes, the fishermen, Mary, and the devils speak of the portent and related prophecies. Furthermore, all these characters concentrate upon the human aspect of Christ's nature, setting the stage for the temptation of Christ as the second Adam during the next day. A last function of this passage leading to the first night scene is the exaltation of patience. The virtuous characters suffer doubt and worry but gradually become reconciled to Christ's absence, in contrast to the demons whose desperation grows.

The transitional passages following the second temptation act as commentary upon the passages which they parallel in the structural design of the temptation sequence. The exchange of Christ and Satan growing out of the storm scene (IV, 432–98) is paired with the passage opening Book II and leading to the dream scene. Satan approaches and immediately cites the storm as a portent threatening adversity, but Christ dismisses it as false, as no cause for anguish such as that shown by the characters in the Book II passage. Christ expresses patience and trust, which expose the comparative lack of firmness in the faith of the fishermen and even Mary. He also defines through contrast the absolute error of the faithless, and hence frustrated, demons in conference. Finally, references to "David's throne," "Israel's scepter," and the "reign past thy preventing" reemphasize the divinity of Christ in preparation for the final temptation. In this respect, the passage complements the earlier one related to it: there the humanity of Christ becomes an issue in the drama for the first time.

In the last of the four transitional passages (IV, 499–540), Satan displays the real views that he has dissembled with increasing difficulty through the poem. Comparison of this scene with the interview following the temptation of the stones reveals the quintessential hypocrisy in Satan's feigned candor while initially admitting his identity. It shows that Satan wills to understand neither the conception of providence nor the portent of the dove at the Baptism, and establishes the full malevolence of Satan at last.

The banquet and Athens scenes represent Satan's basic appeals to the sins of gluttony and vainglory, respectively (II, 285–403; IV, 195–397). These are the temptations of the flesh and the devil, and they are the first and last events of the second day, excluding the night scenes. Between the scenes lie the five episodes making up the exhibition of avarice or the temptation of the world, the third of the three categories of sin: the lures of fame, riches, Israel, Parthia, and Rome. The banquet and Athens temptations have more in common than either has with the glories of the world which separate them, but the two episodes gain definition and impact from their proximity to the treatment of avarice. First, their themes of gluttony and vainglory are secondarily important through the unfolding of the avarice temptation; these themes are not only highlighted on occasion, as in the mention of sumptuous Roman feasts (IV, 113–21) and in the depiction of Parthian vanity (III, 303–21), but they are implicit throughout, since it is always apparent that gluttony and vainglory can be indulged once avarice has been practiced. Next, it becomes evident that gluttony and vainglory are results of avarice in the pursuit of physical food, on one hand, and intellectual or spiritual food, on the other. Finally, the close communion, even interdependence, of the presentations of the three sins, underscores the sins' common base in intemperance.

Several critics have recognized the complementary nature of the banquet and Athens scenes, but none has indicated that the enticements of Athens represent Satan's primary test for vainglory in Christ, though the banquet is accepted as Satan's appeal to gluttony.[8] The point of the Athens passage is perhaps obscured because Athens is a glory of the world which follows the presentations of Parthia and Rome,

putative glories, in the structure of the poem. Moreover, in the case of
Athens, Satan follows the procedure he has used in all of the attempted
seductions: he urges Christ to choose a lesser over a greater good—in
effect, to distrust God's scale of values and claim a right to judgment he
has not yet won in his current trial. But the Athens experience is also
different from the seductions expressly symbolic of the world, as is the
banquet in its way. Standing before the prospect of Athens, Satan no
longer offers power, luxuries, potential sops to conscience, the acceptance of any of which would prove that Christ has distorted priorities
already. Instead, the appeal is more basic, more pernicious. Satan tries
to pervert the mind of the Son, to create the mental or spiritual condition underlying all sin, to lead the mind of the Son to tempt itself.[9]
Satan here is at once preparing the ground for the introduction and
growth of the root sin of pride, or vainglory, and testing for any present
evidence of it.

While Christ prefers the Hebraic to the Hellenic accomplishments,
the truth of the Word he incarnates to the wisdom and art of pagans,
the harshness of his words has caused controversy. Yet, any milder
response would have been both insufficient, in view of the provocation,
and damaging to the development of the poem. Christ is vexed because
Satan has moved from glorifying baser pleasures to praising "contemplation and profound dispute" (IV, 214) in his continuing attempt to
bring Christ to spiritual corruption and doom mankind forever. By
exalting the mind above the spirit, Satan turns to evil a higher good
than any he has perverted so far in the poem. He attempts to render
vain the faculty which separates man from beast, degrading the gift of
reason and man himself. The temper of Christ's response is a measure
of the degree of Satan's distortion of the good. It also suggests growth
in Christ's awareness of his meaning and duty within Hebrew tradition,
a process which Milton traces in the successive reactions of Christ to
temptation.

There is no evidence of Miltonic disillusion with the civilization
of Greece in Christ's contempt for it; in fact, the re-creation of Athenian
culture, even though it is by Satan, indicates that the poet's lifelong
dedication to classical studies remains unimpaired. The passage is the
most vivid, affective one in the poem, and the rejection by Christ is
tempered by emphasis upon the superfluity of Athens for his ordained
purpose. The claim of decorum, the need to build tension prior to the

impending climax, and the opportunity to offer a perfect contrast to Eve's hilarity when she fell in vainglory in a parallel situation—all would have been sacrificed if Milton had let personal preference color Christ's answer to Satan's glorification of the classical world.

Eve's glee and Christ's displeasure in response to attempted seduction by Satan form one of many intrinsic contrasts through which *Paradise Lost* and *Paradise Regained* comment upon each other. Eve's moral weakness in falling despite God's gifts and protection magnifies Christ's accomplishment of routing Satan in a time and place of adversity. In *Paradise Regained*, moreover, the banquet and Athens episodes are primarily responsible for enforcing the parallel with the temptation in *Paradise Lost*, a parallel which emphasizes the contrasts between one epic and the other in the situation and behavior of the central characters, and which forms its own commentary on the action.

In their analogical re-creation of the seduction of Eve, the banquet and Athens episodes confirm one aspect of their own interrelationship. Elizabeth Pope has shown that the banquet lure recapitulates the offer of the fruit in Eden because neither Christ nor Eve is constrained to follow Satan's guidance or to manifest lack of faith. Eve exists amid plenty, yet she is moved to sin by "the smell / So savory of that Fruit" (IX, 740–41), the only fruit forbidden her. Plainly, simple gluttony is one cause of the Fall. The Son, on the other hand, who has begun to hunger in the Wilderness, nevertheless rejects the banquet. Christ recognizes that God has preserved him from starvation during the days of wandering, and, though provoked, continues in trust while he completes his journey to self-discovery. "Since he was no longer so supported by divine strength that he felt no appetite whatever, his refusal constituted a legitimate act of virtue, as meritorious as Eve's consent under similar circumstances had been wicked."[10]

The Athens episode completes the parallel between the two poems' temptation sequences begun by the banquet offering. Christ hungers for knowledge in the "belief that the purpose of all learning is to know God and that if learning fails to reveal God and His Laws, it is useless."[11] Yet Christ has reason to fear that he needs both worldly food and worldly knowledge in his present capacity, with his humanity exposed. Eve, who had no cause for comparable fear, added vainglory to her sins when she ate the fruit in hope of at least equalling Adam, her "god," by means of knowledge. Christ proves he has no pretensions in

rejecting his opportunity to pursue vainglory; he seeks only to understand and carry out the will of God.

The Athens and banquet scenes have more in common than their
share in setting the parallel between the temptations of *Paradise Lost*
and *Paradise Regained*. The episodes are complementary in representing the testing of Christ as man in his private nature, in contrast
to his public role. Satan explores the two routes to mastery of an individual in appealing successively to the senses and the intellect. A. S. P.
Woodhouse sums up this relationship of the scenes: "Besides the obvious contrast of Athens, the symbol of knowledge, with Rome, the
symbol of power, observe how the last in the series of temptations balances the first, the banquet scene. For both are in essence contemplative,
yet one moves on the level of the senses, the other on the level of the
intelligence; and if the banquet by contrast reminded the poet of Eve
and the apple, Milton can now trust the reader to remember that the
apple was in reality the Fruit of the Tree of Knowledge."[12] The banquet and Athens scenes bring to the forefront two parallel thematic
strains, gluttony and vainglory, which underlie the temptations of the
stones and pinnacle respectively, then flow through the juxtaposed
night scenes, and finally meet again as undertones in the avarice section.

Within the temptation of avarice, Milton depicts the lures of the
world (II, 404–IV, 194), as distinct from those of the flesh and the devil.
Beginning to offer riches, Satan sounds a theme which integrates the
avarice sequence: "all thy heart is set on high designs, / High actions;
but wherewith to be achieved?" (II, 410–11). The focus shifts from
personal to public concerns, but the pattern of temptation remains
consistent with the given scheme. The fame or glory passage (III, 1–148)
parallels the vision of Parthia (III, 244–403), to the degree and to the
end that the passage on riches (II, 404–86) parallels the vision of Rome
(IV, 1–194). These pairings, moreover, fix the temptation of Israel (III,
149–243) as the central event of the avarice sequence and, within the
greater structural pattern, as the medial capstone of the entire temptation section of *Paradise Regained*. But the significance of Israel and of
its situation in the poem has been minimized because of incomplete
understanding of where breaks between episodes occur. This problem
has, for example, caused critics to find the Parthia episode lengthier
than others, opening Milton to the charge of a "curious proportioning
of emphasis."[13] And it has led to imperception concerning distinctions

between other divisions of the poem. With recognition that the fame and Israel passages are two of the five parts of the temptation of avarice, not parts of a Parthia sequence, comes understanding that there is only minor variation in the length of the parts. Concomitantly, the importance of Israel begins to assert itself.

In emphasizing martial pomp, the vision of Parthia adds detail to the worldly glory Satan has extolled earlier, in his general disquisition on the subject. Satan has stressed that fame is exalted and, in parody of Michael in *Paradise Lost*, he takes Christ to a mountaintop to witness the legions. Both the act of Satan and the vision express spurious exaltation, and both the fame and Parthia passages foreshadow the vainglory theme by indicating unrestrained aspiration. The relationship between riches and Rome is similar. In the depiction of Roman life, the emphasis falls upon particular luxuries, illustrating Satan's unfocused advice that Christ pursue wealth. The mention of "sumptuous gluttonies, and gorgeous feasts" (IV, 114) completes the resemblance between the sets of episodes by maintaining the gluttony theme within the presentation of avarice.

Avarice is a private impulse, of course, and there are intimations of the personal delights which avarice can bring in all five parts of the sequence, but it is the public face of avarice which Satan sketches in this central section of the temptation. He develops the theme in his glorification of kingship. This subject most clearly gives coherence to the avarice sequence and most definitively separates it from the largely private concerns of the banquet and Athens. Satan urges Christ to fulfill prophecy by assuming the kingship of Israel, and represents each of his offerings in this part of the poem as a means to this end, not primarily as an end in itself. Even the studies of Athens have value as preparation for rule over Israel because of the intellectual power they may confer, Satan suggests, though he differentiates Athens from Parthia and Rome: "let pass, as they are transitory, / The Kingdoms of this world; I shall no more / Advise thee, gain them as thou canst, or not" (IV, 209–11). The subject of Israel directly motivates Satan to conduct the temptation of the world, or avarice, even though the subject also inspires other temptations, such as Athens. In fact, from the accounts of the Baptism at the beginning, to the end of the poem, where the angels invite the "heir of both worlds" to "enter, and begin to save mankind" (IV, 633–35), the questions of the meaning of Israel and of

Christ's relationship to it prompt the action. Frequent reference and allusion to Israel throughout the poem, coupled with the emphasis upon kingship in the avarice sequence, lead to the conclusion that the exchange of Christ and Satan on the topic of Israel is thematically as well as structurally central in the scheme of temptation.

The conclusion is supported by the details of Christ's response to the idea that "Zeal and Duty" require his seizing the rule immediately (III, 172). In answering, Christ states his grounds for rejecting Satan in the past, present, and future, and sums up the major themes of the work:

> All things are best fulfill'd in their due time,
> And time there is for all things, Truth hath said:
> If of my reign Prophetic Writ hath told
> That it shall never end, so when begin
> The Father in his purpose hath decreed,
> He in whose hand all times and seasons roll.
> What if he hath decreed that I shall first
> Be tried in humble state, and things adverse,
> By tribulations, injuries, insults,
> Contempts, and scorns, and snares, and violence,
> Suffering, abstaining, quietly expecting
> Without distrust or doubt, that he may know
> What I can suffer, how obey? Who best
> Can suffer, best can do; best reign, who first
> Well hath obey'd; just trial e'er I merit
> My exaltation without change or end.
> But what concerns it thee when I begin
> My everlasting Kingdom? Why art thou
> Solicitous? What moves thy inquisition?
> Know'st thou not that my rising is thy fall,
> And my promotion will be thy destruction?   (III, 182–202)

It is evident that Christ is aware of his duty and knows in faith, if not yet in fact, the nature of his kingdom. He stresses obedience while showing patience and trust, as he waits for his revelation in the fullness of time.[14] He confronts the mystery of his identity in presenting his suffering as man and transcendence as God. He exposes the truth but claims nothing, a circumstance whose recognition is aided by the motif of questioning in the passage. In effect, Satan is given the answers to his questions here but cannot accept them because he has no faith. He requires proofs and, ironically, will accept no proofs but those which, as Christ foresees, must end in his own ruin. To lack faith is to fall.

For another reason, the lure of the rule of Israel stands out among the enticements which precede and follow it on the second day: the divinity of Christ, as well as his humanity, becomes an issue. As a result, there is a thematic connection with the temptations of the stones and the pinnacle (I, 314–56; IV, 541–80), which occupy the extreme limits of the temptation section and represent appeals to the divine aspect of Christ's dual nature. Alexander Sackton establishes the divinity and humanity themes in contrasting the long second temptation to the first and third: "In the first and last encounters Satan seeks, first by persuasion and finally by force, to make Christ reveal his divine nature. The second encounter, on the other hand, which fills the body of the poem, presents a whole series of temptations which appeal to Christ as a human being."[15] Sackton does not observe that the themes come together during the discussion of Israel, the central event of the second day, or that they help to make this exchange the thematic crux, or perhaps microcosm, of the poem.

In the opening and closing temptations, under the guise of relieving unjustly imposed burdens, Satan invites Christ to perform miracles which will entail the commission of rash acts. Christ neither accepts the request to turn stones into bread, nor responds overtly to the assault at the pinnacle. To act in either situation would be to exercise the power of divinity, which, in the absence of full illumination, would in turn prove distrust and indicate gluttony (Christ suffers no insupportable hunger) or vainglory. At the pinnacle, the mute anticipation of rescue through divine intervention would also suggest pride: "One must not ask God for unreasonable help, one must not ask for unnecessary evidence of divine favor."[16] Instead, Christ makes a single statement, "Tempt not the Lord thy God" (IV, 561), signifying his full recognition of his nature. Satan has symbolically brought the moment about, and inaugurated the Christian era, by physically exalting Christ above the Law, represented by the temple. The revelation is instantaneous and its effects are immediate. "The flesh becomes word. Christ says it, and then becomes it. The full revelation occurs, the miracle of epiphany, theophany, but not as an act of will, not from the self."[17] Having seen good created out of his means of evil once more, Satan inevitably falls. Christ meanwhile introduces new hope to man while demonstrating that "the first and last trials are really the same, waiting obediently on God and true self-dependence having proved to be the same thing."[18]

In the first and third temptations, the themes of distrust and presumption emerge more clearly than from any episode of the second day except the Israel episode. Satan appeals directly to distrust in these three cases, thereby linking them in effect. His strategy through the paired episodes of the second day is to mask his motivation, which does not change, by setting worldly adornments before Christ, adornments designed to betray Christ in his human nature as the "second Adam." Christ is in no explicit danger at any time during the second day, or at least none is made evident; rather, Satan fawns before him and presents him with alleged means to "ensure the success of his Messianic mission."[19] By contrast, Christ suffers the threat of death by starvation in the temptation of the stones and the threat of death by violence at the pinnacle; the danger seems real. These are tests of God, not of man, because Christ is tempted to perform miracles to save himself and justify prophecy. Satan gives him the same straightforward invitation to distrust and presumption on these occasions as when he urges Christ to assume David's throne directly.

The parallel between Satan's attempts to undermine Christ's mission in the first and third temptations is completed by a functional resemblance which complements the thematic association. Arnold Stein states: "The temptation of the stones, the request for a major transcendence through miracle, though under the humble colors of hunger and charity, came without warning, and did not maneuver for a position perhaps to be used later, but aimed at finality. And Satan on the tower has all at once arranged an issue that must be answered finally, one way or the other. The physical excitement of the first encounter in the drama is answered fully, as the form completes itself, by the abruptness, the fierce violence, and the sudden release of surprising action, an action held back through an entire drama."[20] The two brief, unexpected incursions are designed to achieve swift, absolute victories; in this respect they are alike, but Stein overlooks an important distinction between the scenes. While neither temptation is physically static or discursive in the manner of the sequence lying between them, there is, in fact, little "physical excitement" in the temptation of the stones. Satan is disarming, deceptively solicitous, as he makes a feint aimed at bringing an unwary Christ into distrust and presumption. The method recalls the seduction of Eve in *Paradise Lost*. At the pinnacle, however, Satan reveals his desperation in reckless, violent action.

The difference in the degree of dramatic tension generated in the first and third temptations reflects a basic truth of the poem. The first episode of every pair is less dramatic than the last, probably because of the need to supply overall growth in tension in preparation for the climax: "In organizing his poem around the trial of the protagonist, Milton worked with great care to develop a forcefully rising tension from episode to episode throughout the conflict to the final solution, adroitly adjusting material and convention so as to focus sharply and powerfully the miraculous event which followed thereupon."[21] The more obvious foundations of drama in *Paradise Regained* lie in plot situation and in the verbal reaction of characters to changing developments or attitudes. But the increasing tension has a structural base as well. Once Christ and Satan expose their natures in successive passages of the temptation of Israel (III, 182–215)—one may suspect Satan's candor, but he appears more genuine than not, momentarily—the remaining episodes prior to the climax become redundant. Christ has rejected "Riches and Realms" at the start of the avarice sequence (II, 458), and when he indicates that he will wait for a kingdom not in Satan's gift, he has left Satan no final recourse but violence.[22] There is dramatic irony as well as rising tension in the spectacle of Satan trying to tempt Christ with the literal glories of the world that Christ has already refused categorically. The lengthening postponement of what must ensue increases anticipation and, therefore, excitement. Subconsciously, if not consciously, the reader gains satisfaction from at least three sources as he completes this part of the poem: the structural pattern in the process of full realization, the pattern of steadily growing tension, and the beauty of the Satanic re-creations themselves.

After the climax at the pinnacle, the poem comes rapidly to a close. Christ rises in a true exaltation, in contrast to the parodic exaltation he received from Satan before the prospect of the world, and he eats a divine meal which comments upon the demonic banquet. These assurances symbolize the meaning of the victory and, in common with the typological scheme, convey the simultaneous individuality and universality of Christ's experience. Main themes of *Paradise Regained* are sounded again, as they were in the induction of Book I and at key intervals in the temptation section, especially during the Israel

episode. But the beginning and ending of the poem suffer in comparison with the temptations, where the issues are defined and the conflicts
determined. And, of the temptations, that of Israel, occupying the central position, thematically and structurally, dominates the rest. Finally,
in giving the longest and most significant section of the poem a formal,
even ornate, pattern, Milton increases our appreciation of his work and
shows that structural planning had high place and purpose in his art.

Pennsylvania State University

NOTES

1. *Complete Prose Works of John Milton*, ed. Don M. Wolfe et al. (New Haven,
1953–), II, 555. The term *pattern* in the title of this essay is succinctly defined by
A. S. P. Woodhouse, "Pattern in *Paradise Lost*," *University of Toronto Quarterly*,
XXII (1953), 110: "the primary meaning of *pattern* is formal design, and a work is
said to possess aesthetic pattern when by virtue of this pattern or design it is able
to make its effective and pleasurable appeal to our sense of form."

2. Louis L. Martz, *The Paradise Within: Studies in Vaughan, Traherne, and
Milton* (New Haven, 1964), pp. 171–201; Elizabeth Marie Pope, *"Paradise Regained":
The Tradition and the Poem* (Baltimore, 1947), pp. 51–107; Howard Schultz, *Milton
and Forbidden Knowledge* (New York, 1955), and "A Fairer Paradise? Some Recent
Studies of *Paradise Regained*," *ELH*, XXXII (1965), 275–302; Michael Fixler, *Milton
and the Kingdoms of God* (Evanston, 1964), pp. 221–71; Barbara Kiefer Lewalski,
Milton's Brief Epic: The Genre, Meaning, and Art of "Paradise Regained" (Provi-
dence, 1966). See also Stewart A. Baker, "Sannazaro and Milton's Brief Epic," *CL*,
XX (1968), 116–32, and Linwood E. Orange, "The Role of the Deadly Sins in *Paradise Regained*," *Southern Quarterly*, II (1964), 190–201.

3. Pope, *The Tradition and the Poem*, pp. 51–107, argues that Milton here
follows the Calvinists, rather than the Fathers, who saw the temptation of the kingdoms as signifying only the sin of avarice, a formulation assumed by Allan H. Gilbert
in his seminal article, "The Temptation in *Paradise Regained*," *JEGP*, XV (1916),
599–611. An emphasis upon time and timelessness also pervades the temptation sequence and helps unify it. See Laurie Zwicky, "Kairos in *Paradise Regained*: The
Divine Plan," *ELH*, XXXI (1964), 271–77.

4. A. S. P. Woodhouse, "Theme and Pattern in *Paradise Regained*," *University
of Toronto Quarterly*, XXV (1956), 170–71.

5. All quotations of Milton's verse are from *John Milton: Complete Poems and
Major Prose*, ed. Merritt Y. Hughes (New York, 1957).

6. Cf. Baker, "Sannazaro and Milton's Brief Epic," 126–28.

7. Dick Taylor, Jr., "The Storm Scene in *Paradise Regained*," *University of
Toronto Quarterly*, XXIV (1955), 359–76; John M. Steadman, " 'Like Turbulencies':
The Tempest of *Paradise Regained* as Adversity Symbol," *MP*, LIX (1961), 81–88.

8. For example, Roy Daniells, *Milton, Mannerism and Baroque* (Toronto, 1963),
p. 200.

9. Don Cameron Allen, *The Harmonious Vision: Studies in Milton's Poetry*, enlarged ed. (Baltimore, 1970), p. 120.

10. Pope, *The Tradition and The Poem*, p. 77. See also pp. 70–79.

11. Ruth Mohl, *Studies in Spenser, Milton, and the Theory of Monarchy* (New York, 1949), p. 91.

12. Woodhouse, "Theme and Pattern," 177.

13. Northrop Frye, "The Typology of *Paradise Regained*," MP, LIII (1956), 232. Cf. Lawrence J. Nieman, "The Nature of the Temptations in *Paradise Regained* Books I and II," *University Review*, XXXIV (1967), 133–39.

14. Zwicky, "Kairos in *Paradise Regained*," 271–77.

15. Alexander H. Sackton, "Architectonic Structure in *Paradise Regained, University of Texas Studies in English*, XXXIII (1954), 37.

16. Martz, *The Paradise Within*, p. 182.

17. Arnold Stein, *Heroic Knowledge: An Interpretation of "Paradise Regained" and "Samson Agonistes"* (Minneapolis, 1957), pp. 128–29.

18. Arthur E. Barker, "Structural and Doctrinal Pattern in Milton's Later Poems," in *Essays in English Literature from the Renaissance to the Victorian Age*, ed. Millar MacLure and F. W. Watt (Toronto, 1964), p. 181. Barker's observation also explicates the last line of Milton's nineteenth sonnet: "They also serve who only stand and wait."

19. Woodhouse, "Theme and Pattern," 175, who also notes the appeal to distrust in the first and third temptations as an example of "patterned contrast."

20. Stein, *Heroic Knowledge*, pp. 125–26.

21. Dick Taylor, Jr., "Grace as a Means of Poetry: Milton's Pattern for Salvation," *Tulane Studies in English*, IV (1954), 59.

22. Martz, *The Paradise Within*, p. 187, remarks that Christ defines his "true Kingship, true Sonship" in declining riches, "exactly in the center of the poem." But this passage concerns only the kingdoms of the self and the world. Christ does not expose the full truth of his kingdom until he responds to Satan's counsel that he seize David's throne.

MILTON'S RABBINICAL
READINGS AND FLETCHER

Samuel S. Stollman

Harris Francis Fletcher's pioneering work *Milton's Rabbinical Readings* has encouraged Milton scholars to seek Milton's primary sources for his rabbinical references and allusions. However, Fletcher's thesis that Milton used the *Buxtorf Rabbinical Bible* (1619) is without substantiation since almost half of the rabbinical glosses cited by Fletcher have been mistranslated. The mistranslations occur in Fletcher's material purporting to establish the Buxtorf Bible thesis, in the rabbinical hexaemeral parallels for *Paradise Lost,* and in certain esoteric angelological sources cited by Fletcher. While Milton's knowledge of biblical Hebrew is not disputed and his references to rabbinical literature are a matter of record, it is clear that rabbinical Hebrew, with its unique script, syntax, vocabulary, idiom, and absence of pointing and punctuation, is so different from biblical Hebrew that Fletcher was unable to cope with its complexities and that Milton himself utilized secondary sources for rabbinical citations or read the primary sources with limited comprehension.

T HE SECOND edition of Harris Francis Fletcher's pioneering work, *Milton's Rabbinical Readings* (Hamden, Conn., 1967), calls for a reappraisal of Milton's rabbinical knowledge. Some time ago, I demonstrated the many inaccuracies in Fletcher's translations of his rabbinical citations and argued that there is no substantiation for his thesis that Milton borrowed from the Buxtorf Rabbinical Bible.[1] Subsequent examination of Milton's use of the rabbis indicates that Milton himself was probably unable to cope with the complexities of rabbinical Hebrew.

Since its publication in 1930, Fletcher's work has initiated a spate of controversy regarding Milton's Hebraic sources as well as a growing bibliography of his rabbinical readings, with a consensus that the hexaemeral tradition is too ramified to permit identification of Milton's actual sources, whether rabbinical or Christian.[2] But very little has been published (the exception being the essay by Harold Fisch) to suggest that Fletcher's book is itself defective in the translations of the rabbinical glosses.

Fletcher's thesis is that Milton utilized rabbinical materials in *Paradise Lost,* his source being the Buxtorf Rabbinical Bible. In a technical discussion of some eighty rabbinical commentaries—of different degrees of relevance—that are inaccessible to those unfamiliar with rabbinical Hebrew, Fletcher argues that Milton either borrowed these interpretations outright or was influenced by them in his choice of detail for *Paradise Lost.* He summarizes his research with the claim: "There may be considerable difference of opinion regarding the influence of such commentaries on his work, and even regarding the appearance of specific details in *Paradise Lost* which to me seem to have come from the rabbis. But there can no longer be any hesitation over the matter of his use of rabbinical commentaries to Scripture in their originals, or over the form and text in which he knew them" (p. 311).

However, almost half of Fletcher's rabbinical citations have been incorrectly translated and are therefore unrelated to his thesis. The remaining parallels can be traced either to the biblical lexicons, or to the extensive hexaemeral literature of the time, or can be explained as the result of Milton's rationalistic hermeneutics coinciding with the rationalistic tendency in the medieval Jewish commentators.[3] Since my purpose is not simply to note Fletcher's difficulties with rabbinical Hebrew but to evaluate his thesis, I have not cited every mistranslation, but only those that bear directly upon his conclusions.

I. THE BUXTORF BIBLE HYPOTHESIS

1. Two passages in Milton's prose serve as the starting point for Fletcher's thesis that Milton knew the Buxtorf Bible firsthand. The first source is in *An Apology,* which mentions "*Ionathan, or Onkelos the Targumists*" and "the *Masoreths* and Rabbinicall *Scholiasts.*"[4] Fletcher cites and translates Ibn Ezra (Rabbi Abraham Ibn Ezra, 1092–1167, Spanish grammarian, exegete, philosopher, and poet), whose commentary on Numbers xxv, 8 is a gloss in the Buxtorf Bible contributing an

explanation for Milton's statement concerning Phineas (variant: "Phinehas") acting "in the height of zeal":

> there is also the matter of explaining the wonders which Yahweh did to Phinehas (or, *through Phinehas*) but the Text does not mention them. (p. 26)

This comment does not, in fact, elucidate Phineas's "height of zeal." It is even less revealing when translated correctly:

> There is an exegetical approach [teaching] that ten miracles were performed for Phineas but Scripture does not state them.

Ibn Ezra's commentary is inapplicable, but Numbers xxv, 7–8, 11, supply the motif of "zeal."

2. Fletcher also cites Milton's reference to *"Ionathan, or Onkelos the Targumists"* as clear evidence of Milton's reliance on the Buxtorf Bible (pp. 32–33). But Milton's indiscriminate coupling of Jonathan with Onkelos with reference to the Book of Kings raises some questions about Milton's firsthand knowledge of the primary sources, since it is Jonathan, not Onkelos, who is the Targumist of the Prophets.[5]

3. The second source that Fletcher examines to demonstrate Milton's familiarity with the Buxtorf Bible is in *Doctrine and Discipline of Divorce.* After citing Grotius, Josephus, the Septuagint, and "the *Chaldaean*" to prove that "fornication" is understood in Scripture as "stubbornnes and rebellion" against one's husband, Milton continues:

> and to this I adde that *Kimchi* [Radaq: Rabbi David Kimchi, 1160–1235, Franco-Spanish exegete and grammarian] and the two other Rabbies who glosse the text [Judges xix, 2], are in the same opinion. *Ben Gersom* [also known as Gersonides and Ralbag: Rabbi Levi Ben Gerson, 1288–1344, French exegete, philosopher, and scientist] reasons that had it bin whoordom, a Jew and a Levite would have disdain'd to fetch her again. (YP, II, 335–36)

In this reference we have what seems prima facie evidence that Milton saw this folio in the Buxtorf Bible. Fletcher translates Kimchi:

> The Targum here translates like the Targum of (Numbers 15:31) 'he hath despised the word of the Lord' meaning that she despised him, left his house, and returned to the house of her father. Or, its interpretation is harlotry, according to its usual meaning, that she was his wife without a . . . [*Ketuba*] (marriage contract) and . . . [*Kiddushin*] (marriage sanctification) and she strayed from him. (p. 38)

To judge Fletcher's conclusions, one must read the balance of Kimchi's gloss which Fletcher does not cite:

And the meaning of "against him" is "in his presence"; that is, she did not fear him and did not conceal herself from him to commit harlotry. Or the translation of "against him" is "with him"; that is, while she was yet with him, similar to "And the men came 'upon' the women" [Exodus xxxv, 22], that is, "with the women." And the explanation for "and she left him" is that he was angry with her, and so she went to her father's house.

Fletcher comments, after citing the first part of Kimchi's gloss: "Altogether, Milton's citation of Kimchi's comment here shows careful reading of the rabbi" (p. 38). Rather it suggests that Milton did not read Kimchi carefully *in* the Buxtorf Bible. Only Kimchi's citation of the Targum may be applicable to Milton's definition. Kimchi himself elaborates the "usual meaning" of "fornication," which is contrary to Milton's position.

4. Fletcher then cites the commentary of Rashi (Rabbi Solomon ben Isaac of Troyes, 1040–1105, French exegete and best known Jewish commentator on the Bible and Talmud) as one of the "two other Rabbies who glosse the text":

She strayed from his house to the outside world. The phrase . . . [*Zenut*] means nothing but *going out,* . . . [*nafqat bara*] going away from her husband [presumably] to love others. (p. 39)

Fletcher comments: "Rashi, actually, is 'in the same opinion' solely because he said nothing that directly contradicted what Kimchi had said" (p. 39). The fact is that Fletcher has mistranslated one of Rashi's phrases and modified another by interpolation. First, *nafqat bara* is a term used euphemistically by Onkelos the Targumist in Genesis xxxiv, 31 for "harlot" ("And they said: 'Should one deal with our sister as with a harlot?' "). Second, Fletcher has interpolated the word *presumably* in Rashi, with the effect of modifying Rashi's comment and rendering it amenable to his thesis that Milton read the three rabbinical commentaries in the Buxtorf Bible and understood them clearly. What Rashi, however, is saying is the following:

She strayed from his house to the outside. Every expression of *Zenut* 'fornication' is but an expression of *nafqat bara* [that is, as the Targum translates it], "harlot"—leaving her husband to love others.

Not only is Fletcher incorrect in his translation and evaluation of Rashi's comment, but our reading of Kimchi and Rashi also raises the question of Milton's ability to translate the rabbinical glosses and the Targum, despite the inclusion of the latter in his educational scheme.[6]

    5. Fletcher's (and Milton's) discussion of the third rabbi, Ben Gerson, also requires review. Fletcher translates Ben Gerson:

And the book adds that in those days, when there was no king in Israel, the challenger of transgressors, there was a man, a Levite, a sojourner, who lived on the outlying slopes of Ephraim. And this man took a wife unto himself, a concubine from Beth-Lehem Judah. And she . . . [*zanetah alav*], that is to say, she turned from him and went away to the house of her father. And as for this . . . [*ha-Zenut*], it means that she turned away from him. . . . [*Zenut*] may be called wine and *must*, which take away the understanding, and the word . . . [*Zenut*] makes it difficult to understand the occurrence. For if she had actually committed adultery against him, it has not been sufficiently pointed out that he went to seek her again in spite of the matter of the so-called 'adultery,' which is thereby explained. It is said that she went from him to the house of her father and remained there for a long time. And this is further explained as having been for a period of four months. This shows that she had no inclination to return to him, but that he had many. Our rabbis of blessed memory explain that when her husband saw this, he went after her to speak to her heart and to bring her back again, after he had become pacified, for she had vexed him in his house, and because of this, he caused her to hide her face. And this is the explanation of why he went to bring her back. (pp. 39–40)

Both minor and major corrections have to be made in this translation, not merely to make Ben Gerson more intelligible but, more important, to rectify unwarranted implications for Fletcher's thesis and Milton's sources:

And [the narrator] relates further that in those days when there was no king in Israel to reprimand the sinners, there was a Levite who dwelt on the slopes of Ephraim, who took for himself a concubine from Beth-Lehem Judah, "and his concubine played the harlot against him"; that is to say, she *turned* from him and returned to her father's house to escape him. And this was the *Zenut* "the turning," for any "turning away" is called *Zenut*; [as] he says, "Harlotry, wine, and new wine take away the heart" [Hosea iv, 11]. We are compelled to explain the matter this way, for if she had committed adultery to lie with someone other than her husband, it would not have been seemly that he seek her again. However, the reason for her "turning away" he [the narrator] explains in relating that she went from him [her husband] to her father's house and that she remained there a long time, [explaining] that she remained there a year and four months. And by this demonstrated that she was unwilling to return to him. And note that our Rabbis, of blessed memory, explained this "turning away" in a manner akin to what we have explained. [The Rabbis in the Babylonian Talmud, tractate Gittin, folio 6b, have a tradition that she had committed a breach of etiquette—but not immorality—against him and she fled because she feared his anger.] And when her husband saw this, he went after her to speak to her heart and bring her back, for it appears that she had turned away from him over the quarrels he had vexed her with in his house, and therefore he had to mollify her.

Now this is not the same as "stubbornnes and rebellion" on the part of the concubine. Ben Gerson says, "he had vexed her," and not "she had vexed him," as Fletcher translates. Milton is correct, however, in citing Ben Gerson to the effect that "had it bin whoordom, a Jew and a Levite would have disdain'd to fetch her again." Milton may have seen this folio in the Buxtorf Bible, but his reading of the rabbi seems to have been as incomplete as Fletcher's.

6. Besides this one instance in Milton of his possible utilization of the Buxtorf Bible, there is no other evidence that he referred to it again. It is especially striking, in regard to the Rabbinical Bible hypothesis, that in Milton's rendition of Malachi ii, 16, he chooses "He who hates let him divorce" (following the Vulgate and Calvin) rather than "For the Lord, the God of Israel, saith that he hateth putting away" (Tremellius-Junius and the King James Version).[7] While hard-pressed to defend his interpretation, Milton does not cite any of the rabbinical commentators, as he did with the definition of "fornication." It is, of course, possible that he had the rabbinical commentators in mind when he answered Prynne:

Of *Malachy* I have spok'n more in another place; and say again that the best interpreters, all the ancient, and most of the modern translate it, as I cited, and very few otherwise, whereof perhaps *Junius* is the cheif. (YP, II, 749)

He may have included the rabbis in "all the ancient." However, it is curious that he did not cite the Targum, Rashi, and Kimchi, whose views in the Buxtorf Rabbinical Bible support his position.[8]

II. FLETCHER'S HEXAEMERAL PARALLELS

1. The first of Fletcher's parallels deals with the eternity of matter. Milton, in *Christian Doctrine* and *Paradise Lost*, conceived of the

creation as an ordering of the elements, already existent, rather than the creating of these elements, explicitly refuting the idea of *creatio ex nihilo* (pp. 81–82). Fletcher suggests that Milton's idea of the creation, first taught by the Greeks, was assimilated by the rabbis, and he finds in Ibn Ezra "exactly the same argument" as used by Milton, who states that *bara*—Hebrew for "created"—does not mean *creatio ex nihilo*:

> Most of the commentators said that . . . [*bara*] meant to 'produce something out of nothing,' (as in Numbers 16:30); but they forget (Gen. 1:21 and 27 where it is distinctly stated that the act expressed by the verb . . . [*bara*] was a formation from water and earth respectively), or (Isaiah 45:7) where darkness is the object of the verb . . . [*bara*]; darkness is nothing but the absence of light. The following is the explanation of the verb . . . [*bara*], (which has two meanings. One is as it is used here, and the other as in 2 Sam. 12:17 where . . . [*bara* with an *aleph*] means [*bara* with a *he*] to eat . . .) It also means *to cut, to decree*, to set a limit by cutting off a portion, and the wise will understand it. (p. 83)

This translation must be emended:

> Most of the commentators have said that the Creation is to "produce something out of nothing" and, similarly, "But if the Lord make a new thing." But they have forgotten "And God created the great sea-monsters" [something out of something]; and the three usages in one verse, "And God created man in His own image" [also something out of something]; and "I . . . create darkness" which is the opposite of light which is "something." The word *bara* has two forms: This is one, and the other is [*bara* with a *he*:] "neither did he eat bread with them." This second usage has a *he* [at the end of *bara*] instead of an *aleph*, for its meaning is similar to "to cause David to eat bread" [2 Samuel iii, 35], for the verb is in the causative construct. If the verb ended with an *aleph*, it would mean "to make yourselves fat" [1 Samuel ii, 29]. And we find such a construction in "and cut down for thyself" [Joshua xvii, 15]. But it is not similar to "choose you a man" [1 Samuel xvii, 8]. It is similar, however, to "and despatch them" [Ezekiel xxiii, 47]. And its meaning is "to cut" (or "decree") and "to set a limit" which is "cut"; and the wise will understand.

Ibn Ezra, in effect, defines *bara* to accord with *creatio ex nihilo* in Genesis i, 1 and with the other applications in the passages cited. By defining *bara* as both "to decree" and "to cut," which are related in Hebrew, he shows that *bara* can be applied to *creatio ex nihilo*—*bara* meaning that God "decreed" the heaven and earth—and to "producing something out of something," as in Genesis i, 27.[9]

2. Fletcher then cites Ibn Ezra's commentary on Ecclesiastes i, that the Creation was "an arrangement of preexistent elements":

Everything under the sun is composed of four elements, from which they (everything) came forth, unto which they (everything) return, namely, fire, air, water, and earth. . . . And after having shown that the four elements are stationary (immutable and immovable), and that in case of being set in motion they return to where they have been before. (p. 83)

Fletcher wishes to prove that this is similar to Milton's idea of Creation. Ibn Ezra, however, does not say that the elements were preexistent, but that they are the components of all things that exist.

3. Fletcher and many commentators believe that the images of the Muse and the compasses in *Paradise Lost* (VII, 1–12, 192–231) are based on Proverbs viii: "Milton has apparently used the material that the Proverbs passage afforded him and then has drawn on his imagination or on some other source for embellishment of that material. His changes are, however, all rather minute, and because of this, he presumably had some reason for making them" (p. 92). Fletcher suggests that Milton borrowed the changes from the rabbinical commentaries on Proverbs. He is dissatisfied with the explanation that Milton used the compasses image as found in the Authorized Version of the Bible, because this explanation, "while quite justifiable so far as the basic idea of Milton's lines and of the Biblical passage is concerned, lays the poet open to the grave charge of having either misunderstood or mistranslated the Hebrew original in which the word is clearly . . . [Ḥug] circle" (p. 101). He prefers to ascribe the image to Milton's rabbinical readings and not to the Authorized Version. However, is it not more reasonable to assume that the association of the Hebrew *compass* and *circle*, derived from one Hebrew root, is so obvious that the rabbis, the Authorized Version, and Milton himself used them interchangeably? Milton's figure of God using a compass to lay out the universe is implied in the passage in Proverbs, "when He set a circle on the face of the deep."

4. In *Paradise Lost*, Milton's Muse, Urania, is coupled with "Wisdom thy Sister" (VII, 1–12). Fletcher says that this association presents a problem: "According to the text of Proverbs, Wisdom appears to have been alone with God at Creation" (p. 111). He therefore has recourse to Ben Gerson, who supplies two such spirits, *Ḥokhma* and *Tevuna*, Wisdom and Understanding (although Proverbs viii has the same:

"Behold Wisdom calleth, and Understanding sendeth forth her voice").
Fletcher translates Ben Gerson as follows:

Indeed, you must remember that God did not fail to have with him (at Creation) Understanding and Wisdom by means of which the world was made or created. (p. 111)

Ben Gerson, however, clearly implies that they are not two spirits, but one, with interchangeable names:

But know that the Name, blessed-be-He, did not fail to have with Him this Understanding and Wisdom by *which* [Hebrew *singular*] the world was created.

5. Fletcher then says that Milton concurs with Ben Gerson that *"God established the Heavens according to plan"* (p. 115). However, he has made two mistakes in this translation. First, he has assumed that "the word *Understanding* [. . . *Tevuna*] means the whole process of ratiocination. It includes the meaning *planning*" (p. 115). The word *Tevuna*, however, means "ratiocination" but not "planning." Then Fletcher reads *Tekhuna* as *Tevuna*, translating the passage as "God established the Heavens according to plan." However, since *Tekhuna* means "disposition," "arrangement," or "characteristic," the passage should be translated as "God established the Heavens in arrangement." (The Hebrew for "plan" is *Tavnit*.) Fletcher adduces seven passages from *Paradise Lost* (VII, 150–55, 163–64, 165–66, 208–09, 234–37; IX, 137–39, 151–52) to show "that God effected the Creation of the Visible Universe *according to Plan*" (pp. 114 ff.). Yet not one of these quotations mentions the word *plan*.

6. Fletcher then theorizes: "Milton set himself the task in the poem of representing Creation as an instantaneous Act of God which in some comprehensible manner stretched out over the period of six days. How was this to be presented in order to preserve both its instantaneous and its 'six-day' aspects?" (p. 123). Thus "Milton conceived of the primeval matter, which before was 'unformed and void' as now being brought into contact with the Spirit of God, or with the plan and principle of the Cosmos and all it was to contain" (p. 123). The process of creation was instantaneous; "the results were . . . successive 'births' " (p. 124). While this theory, Fletcher writes, had been popularized in England by

Timothy Bright in his *Treatise of Melancholy* (1586), Milton chose it over alternative concepts because he followed Ben Gerson. The fact that Bright held it, that (as Fletcher claims) Milton needed it, and that *meraḥefet* (Hebrew "brooding") suggests it, were not sufficient warrant. Fletcher cites Ben Gerson:

This (Wisdom) was what was revealed after he ordained the establishment of the earth. And this was the gift revealed in the earth; this it was (i.e. the presence of God's Spirit . . . [*Hokhma*]) which was the basis of all that was happening in it (the earth), in the way of developments and of forms of life. (p. 130)

But this is grossly incorrect. It should read (I begin at an earlier point in the commentary, which Fletcher does not cite):

He desired that this place [the dry land] remain uncovered [from water] always when He established firmly the foundations of the earth. And this is the uncovered part of the earth which is the foundation of that which came into being in it of vegetation and animal life.

Ben Gerson is discussing the "dry land" as the earth-base of life, while Fletcher has taken the antecedent in this quotation to be Wisdom, and has therefore arrived at an unusual gloss, of which he says: "This passage, while clear enough to one thinking in terms of the idea of Creation as an act of God, is somewhat obscure to our modern minds" (p. 130).

7. Further in regard to Proverbs viii, Fletcher finds a parallel between Milton's "Crystalline" sphere (VII, 263–74) and Ben Gerson's commentary:

when the fountains of the Abyss became strong. This means when God gave strength and stiffness to what had been primeval matter near the fountains of the Abyss. And the Heavens (the firmament . . . [*Hashamayim*]) became the great Sphere of the Earth. (pp. 134–35)

Now Ben Gerson does not say that "the *Heavens* became the great Sphere of the Earth." He says, "and this [*primeval matter*] became the sphere of earth." Fletcher's conviction that "wherever else Milton may have encountered such ideas, the rabbis would have determined his use of them" (p. 135), is warranted neither by Milton's well-known denigration of the rabbis nor by Ben Gerson's actual words.

8. Another aspect of Creation that Fletcher believes Milton to have taken from Ben Gerson is the concept "And Earth self-balanc't on

her Center hung" (VII, 242). Fletcher refers to Job xxvi,7 ("and hang-eth the earth upon nothing") and Ben Gerson's commentary:

on nothing, that is, on something that has no existence in reality, and this is the center of the earth, from which point the earth is suspended. (p. 137)

Fletcher associates this with Milton, but does not translate the last three words in the Hebrew, "as is explained in nature study." This information, Ben Gerson reminds us, was the traditional science current in Ben Gerson's time, and not superseded in Milton's.

9. In the second phase of Creation in *Paradise Lost*, Fletcher finds that "Milton used Rashi's commentary to a very great extent" (p. 142), the first point being that there was no "priority" in the act of Creation: "All the elements of Heaven and Earth were created all at once, at the time of the Act of Creation, and were then put in their various places as the Works of the Six Days" (p. 143). It is true that Rashi states that "the verse teaches nothing about the order, earlier or later, of anything created" (commentary on Genesis i,1; Fletcher, p. 148), and says also, "So with all the Creations of Heaven and Earth: they were created on the first day, and every one of them was put in place on the day that was determined for it" (commentary on Genesis i, 14; Fletcher, p. 150). However, it is not certain what Milton says in *Paradise Lost*. Fletcher takes Milton's ambiguity on this point, as expressed in "Thus God the Heav'n created, thus the Earth, / Matter unform'd and void" (VII, 232–33), to imply "that there was no priority, for . . . they [Milton's lines] make no choice" (p. 143). We can find Milton's source for the two problematical lines in the opening verse of Genesis.

10. In the creation of the "lights," Fletcher imputes Milton's "and circling Years" (VII, 342) to Rashi's comments on Genesis i, 14:

and years. At the end of three hundred sixty-five days, they (the lights, sun, moon, and stars) finish their circle with the twelve planets that serve them, and this is a year. (p. 156)

He mistranslates this comment, since Rashi does not say "finish their circle" but "finish their course." However, Rashi does use the conception of a circle in the second half of his comment, not cited by Fletcher: "they begin to revolve a second time in a circle similar to their first course." But, again, this amplification is the kind that Milton could have made without the suggestion of Rashi.

11. Fletcher finds Rashi supplying another detail in *Paradise Lost*:

> and each
> Plant of the field, which e're it was in the Earth
> God made, and every Herb, before it grew
> On the green stemm.   (VII, 334–37)

Fletcher finds Milton's source in Rashi's commentary on Genesis ii, 5:

and not yet was in the earth. Always in Scripture the word . . . [*ṭerem*] means *not yet,* and not *at first* or *before.* The verb form . . . [*hiṭrim*] does not occur as does . . . [*hiqdim*] *to precede.* This is one reason; and another is (Ex. 9:30) *ye will not yet fear,* meaning *as yet will ye not fear.* And so the phrase is explained in the case before us, *not yet was in the earth,* means on the sixth day, after the Creation of the World was entirely completed but before, or while not yet was man created. (pp. 156–57)

Fletcher says that "Rashi's time-concept and his explanation are complicated; but to understand them makes the intent of Milton's lines perfectly clear, and likewise helps to understand the whole process the poet had in mind" (p. 157). It is Fletcher's translation that is labored. All that Rashi is explaining is the grammatical form of the Hebrew *ṭerem,* and thereby substantiating the translation of the verse as "And every plant of the field was not yet in the earth."

12. Fletcher also cites Rashi on Milton's "Crystalline" sphere:

> partition firm and sure,
> The Waters underneath from those above
> Dividing.   (VII, 267–69)

Fletcher translates Rashi's commentary on Genesis i, 6:

in the midst of the waters, meaning placed between the waters. For there is a separation between the upper and lower waters of the Firmament as there is between the waters that are on the Earth. (p. 166)

The citation in full and translated correctly is as follows:

In the midst of the waters, in the center of the waters; because there is the [same] *distance* between the upper waters and the firmament as there is between the firmament and the waters that are upon the earth. Thus you learn that they [the upper waters] are suspended [in space] by the command of the King.

This translation shows that Rashi is not describing the "partition firm and sure" of Milton, since *Hefresh* is not "partition" but "expanse" or "distance."

13. In Milton's treatment of the creation of Adam, Fletcher finds some details anticipated by Rashi. Thus, the lines in VIII, 295–306, with their "trace of persuasion," Fletcher imputes to Rashi on Genesis ii, 15:

he took, by means of fine words he persuaded [Adam] to enter the Garden. (p. 169)

Indeed, in this purported correspondence there is actually a divergence between Rashi, who interprets "and He took" in a psychological sense, and Milton, whose Adam says, "by the hand he took me rais'd" (VIII, 300), in a physical sense.

14. On the immediate cause of Satan's seduction of Adam and Eve, Fletcher says that Rashi supplies the motive which is absent in the biblical account. Satan's envy and jealousy (*PL* IV, 502–08; IX, 263–64) Fletcher finds paralleled in Rashi on Genesis iii, 1:

the serpent was more subtle. . . . In order to teach you in what manner the serpent seized on them. The serpent saw that they were naked and going about in wedded bliss . . . before all eyes, and it was envious of them. (p. 185)

The Hebrew, however, reads "and he [the serpent] *desired* her." According to Fletcher, "Both Satan in *Paradise Lost* and the serpent in Rashi's commentary become jealous at the sight of the couple 'imparadised in one another's arms' and desire, because of that jealousy, to inflict suffering upon them. Thus there is a remarkable identity between the motivation of the serpent and the motivation of Satan so far as their animosities toward Adam and Eve are concerned" (p. 186). But, correctly translated, there is no relation between the two. While Milton's Satan is jealous, Rashi's serpent is covetous. The serpent wishes to possess Eve, not to destroy her.

15. Another item with rabbinical overtones is Adam's ability to give names to the animals immediately as they are brought before him. Fletcher finds the basis for Adam's "sudden apprehension" (VIII, 354) in Rashi's commentary on Genesis ii, 19:

out of the ground God formed etc. . . . Also, this verse is to teach you that in the hour of their formation, at once on that day, they were brought to the man for him to give them their names. And in the words of the Agada, . . . [*Yeṣira*] means to assume domination and control over, as in (Deut. 20:19) *when you beseige (capture, possess, subdue, seize, wholly take control of) a city.* So he (God) subjugated [them (the animals) to the hand of man]. (p. 189)

Fletcher points out that, since Adam was not afforded time to study the animals before naming them, "Adam was immediately possessed of a perfect knowledge of nature" (p. 189). But this deduction is Fletcher's and not Rashi's. Rashi does not speak of Adam's "sudden apprehension" but of the animals being brought before Adam immediately upon their creation. Adam's "sudden apprehension" is a hypothesis required by the verse: "Now out of the ground the Eternal God had formed every animal . . . and brought it unto man to see what he would call it" (Genesis ii, 19).

16. Fletcher cites a more explicit comment by Rashi, on Genesis ii, 25, to the effect that Adam was endowed with "perfect natural knowledge":

and were not ashamed. For there was not known to them any way of being able to distinguish between good and evil. Although Adam was given knowledge enough to name the animals, the instinct or knowledge of evil was not given to him until after they (the man and the woman) had eaten from the tree. Then the knowledge of evil entered, and then he knew the difference between good and evil. (pp. 189–90)

A careful reading of Rashi does not lead one to conclude that "Adam knew virtually everything except the difference between good and evil" (p. 190). Rashi refers to no other knowledge than "naming the animals." Although this is considerable, it is not the same as "perfect natural knowledge."

17. Fletcher also refers to the second half of Rashi's gloss in explaining how "Adam, before the Fall, lacked completely a knowledge of the difference between good and evil" (p. 204). However, Fletcher's juxtaposition of Rashi and Milton is hardly tenable, since he has translated the key words *Yeṣer hara* as "knowledge of evil," whereas they mean "evil instinct" or "evil inclination."

III. FLETCHER'S ANGELOLOGICAL SOURCES

1. Fletcher's first observation is that the three angels—Michael, Raphael, and Gabriel, who form the "basic triad of scholastic angelology"—always appear in Milton's work with a fourth angel, Uriel, who is derived from the "Targum of Jonathan Uziel [*sic*]" (Deuteronomy xxxiv, 6). This is incorporated in the Biblia Polyglotta Waltoni, a source known to Milton, where Fletcher finds Uriel treated as an equal member

of the angelic quadrumvirate (pp. 222–40). However, in Fletcher's quotation, given in both Aramaic and Latin, although there is a reference to Uriel with Michael and Gabriel, there is no mention of Raphael; instead, there is the inclusion of Mitatron, Jophiel, and Jephepija.

2. That Uriel is angel of the sun Fletcher derives from the *Midrasch Rabba to the book of Numbers*, which states that four angels surround the throne of God (pp. 243–44):

Uriel is at his (God's) left, toward Dan, which is in the North. Why is his name Uriel? Because of the Torah, the Prophets, and the Writings (. . . [*Ketubim*]). For the Holy One blessed-be-He through Uriel (as through the sun) spreads his light over Israel and over them (the other nations) as it is said (Isaiah lx, 1) *Arise, shine for thy light is come.*

But the key phrase, the parenthetical remark, "as through the sun," is Fletcher's interpolation. He has interpolated the very point he is attempting to prove! Moreover, if the latter half of this quotation is correctly translated, there is no mention of Uriel as an agent of God's light:

For the Holy One blessed-be-He atones for him [Dan] and shines for them, for Israel, as it is said, "Arise, shine, for thy light is come."

Fletcher's conclusion—"Here, then, is the origin of the conception of Uriel as Angel of the Sun, shedding his light and letting his rays travel over the whole of the Created Universe"—is unwarranted. Even if this citation were relevant, it is from a rabbinical source that is quite distinct from the Buxtorf Bible. What evidence do we have that Milton knew the *Midrasch Rabba*?

3. The role of Michael as Adam's mentor, after the Fall, Fletcher finds inadequately explained by the traditional commentators. He believes that Milton chose Michael for this function "in view of the fact that Adam saw principally a cyclorama of Hebrew history," and the proper angel for this purpose is determined by Rashi's comment on Exodus xxiii, 20–23:

'for my name is in him.' Partner to the Almighty. The text hides him from us, (i.e., does not give us his name) for the name of the Partner is in him. But our robbis say that this (Angel) is *Metatron*, that his name is [the same] as the great *Metatron* in the Gematria (i.e., *Michael*). (p. 252)

This translation is faulty, and the reference to Michael is interpolated. The correct translation in full is as follows:

"For My name is in him," with reference to the beginning of the verse, "Take heed of him," for My name is associated with him. Our Rabbis said that he [the angel] is *Metatron*, whose name is the same as his Master's, for *Metatron* has the numerical value [314] of *Shaddai* [the Almighty].

This translation shows that Fletcher has interpolated the reference to Michael, who is simply not mentioned in the commentary.

4. Fletcher then quotes Ibn Ezra who, he says, "is equally as explicit":

So it is settled (or they *settled*) that (this refers to) the chief of the Angels, and this is he. The Angel is Michael. (p. 252)

The passage Fletcher refers to is not "the same verse"; it is Exodus xxiii, 20, from which he has cited a fragment. The full reference, correctly translated, reads as follows:

And in the Book of Daniel [it is written], "the Prince of Greece" and "the Prince of Parthia . . . but Michael your Prince" [Daniel x, 20–21]. He is the one who is called "the chief" because he is respected among the many others. It is also written concerning him: "One of the first princes came to help me" [Daniel x, 13], that is, "chief" in degree, similar to "those who sit first in the kingdom" [Esther i, 14]. And this Angel is Michael.

Fletcher's citation, although only partly correct, does identify the angel of Exodus, according to Ibn Ezra, with Michael. But is Michael of *Paradise Lost* the angel of Exodus?

5. The three angels, Ariel, Arioch, and Ramiel, referred to in *Paradise Lost* (VI, 369–72) are not documented by Fletcher to any extent. However, in the case of Ariel's characterization, Fletcher is dissatisfied with Patrick Hume's translation of *Ariel* as "the lion of God" (p. 257), and so he cites Rashi on 2 Samuel xxiii, 20, "and he slew two (sons of) Ariel of Moab":

two Ariel [of] Moab, the Targum reads . . . *great men, princes of Moab*, and our rabbis say that their like [in size] was not allowed either in the time of the first or of the second Temple. (Rashi means that such mighty men as were the *Ariel* have long since disappeared from the earth, no longer being 'allowed'). (p. 264)

This is another mistranslation. It should read as follows:

The two Ariel of Moab. The two great men of Moab. And our Rabbis said that he [Benayahu] did not leave anyone like him either in the first Temple or the second Temple.

But Rashi supplies no information about the angel Ariel.

6. Fletcher then translates Ben Gerson's commentary concerning Ariel:

he slew two Ariel [of] Moab. Behold the mighty and powerful the author calls ... [*Ariel*]. And the Temple [in Jerusalem] is called the same. And the meaning of this verse is that he killed the two mightiest and strongest men of Moab. And the word *Ariel* is made up of ... [*Ary*] (*lion*) and of ... [*El*] (*God*). And we say a lion seizes, for the lion is the mightiest of the mighty. And it is possible also that there is in the word [the idea of] the shape of the lion to show power and strength. (Ralbag in this last sentence is probably referring to the Temple and its shape). (p. 264)

This is another inaccuracy. It should read:

He slew two Ariel of Moab. Behold the strong tower is called *Ariel*. And therefore the Temple is called *Ariel*. And the meaning is that he smote the men of the strong towers that were in Moab. And the word [*Ariel*] is composed of "lion" and "God" (or "strong") and the connotation is a "powerful lion," for the lion is great in strength; and it is possible also that they [the towers] had the form of a lion to indicate power and strength.

This commentary adds nothing to the scriptural Ariel.

7. Another reference to *Ariel* is in Isaiah xxix, 1: "Ho, Ariel, Ariel, the city where David encamped!" Fletcher cites Rashi:

Ho, Ariel etc. The Targum Jonathan [reads] *altar of God.* And likewise Ezekiel called it so when he said *and the altar-hearth twelve* (Ezekiel 43:16) [meaning] that the fire of the steps was crouching like a lion at the base of the altar, so also the two places in *Yoma* (Mishna). And our rabbis explain that this was the Temple, which was narrow behind and wide in front [like a lion]. (p. 266)

The correct translation is as follows:

Ho, Ariel, etc. Jonathan translated this as *Altar of God.* And even Ezekiel called it so, as it is said, "and the *Ariel* shall be twelve cubits long . . . " (Ezekiel xliii, 16), with reference to the fire on top that crouched as a lion on the altar, as we learned in the Order of *Yoma.* And our Rabbis explained it [in reference] to the Temple which was narrow behind and wide in the front [like a lion].

Rashi does emphasize the derivation of *Ariel* from *Ary* ("lion"), but Fletcher embellishes this derivation and says of both Rashi and Kimchi (whose comment is similar to Rashi's): "All of this connection of the altar-hearth and the Temple was done of course to supply the idea of the *strength* of the Temple as implied in calling it, or the altar, *Ariel*, with the lion-like implications of strength in that word" (p. 266). Fletcher could have cited the dictionary translation of *Ary* as "lion" connoting strength. His citations actually limit the meaning of "lion" since they do not refer to the lion's strength but to the lion's manner ("crouching") or shape ("Temple").

8. He attempts to support his definition by citing Ibn Ezra:

Ho, Ariel. This is explained by virtue of the fact that Jerusalem was called by the name of the altar-hearth [as in Ezekiel]. For the letters . . . [*Yod*] and . . . [*Resh*] are here transposed. And the explanation of its being so-called (by the name *Ariel*) is that the constellation Leo was referred to, and this represents power. (p. 267)

Instead of reinforcing Fletcher's argument, Ibn Ezra's comment actually negates it:

Ho, Ariel. There are those who say that Jerusalem is called so [*Ariel*] by virtue of the Altar's designation, such as "and the *Har'el*" and "from the *Ariel*" [Ezekiel xliii, 15], for the letters *Yod, He,* and *Aleph* interchange. And others say that Jerusalem was called so because its constellation is Leo, and this is far-fetched.

9. In Isaiah xxxiii, 7, "Behold, their valiant ones cry without," Fletcher finds "the obvious origin of *Ariel* as the name of an Angel" (p. 268). He begins with Rashi:

behold . . . [*Erelam*] *cry without* [Isaiah xxxiii, 7]. This is the prophet prophesying consolations, and he says that great retributions shall consume him. And then the . . . [*Erelam*] are appointed and brought to redeem. *Behold* . . . [*Erelam*] refers to the altar, meaning already they cry and lament outside and in the marketplace with weeping and lamentations. (p. 268)

This is incorrect. The translation is as follows:

The Prophet was prophesying consolations and saying that retribution had already consumed him; now I will arise and be exalted to redeem them.

"Behold, their *Erelam*" refers to the altar: They had already cried and lamented in the streets with weeping and wailing.

There is no mention here of Ariel as angel. As Fletcher says, "it is not particularly clear as to just what he had in mind" (p. 268).

10. He then cites Ibn Ezra's comment that "begins to supply the idea that the . . . *Erelam* were angelic messengers" (p. 268):

Behold . . . [*Erelam*]. There are sayings connected with . . . *Ariel*, as if it said *to the* . . . [*Erelam*]. And we might determine the meaning as if it said . . . [*ereh lahem*] as if there were two words, and this is different. But the meaning of the word . . . [*Erelam*] is as their . . . [*Malakhaihem*] *messengers (Angels)*. And the meaning then is *their messengers (Angels) of peace*, which is like (2 Sam. 23:20) *two Ariel of Moab*. And the meaning of this is that the messengers (Angels) of all the nations ask peace for the world, and lament etc. (p. 269)

Fletcher says: "This explanation by Ibn Ezra is characteristic—the explanation is more complicated than the original expression" (p. 269). The translation, however, is as follows:

There are those who say that . . . [*Erelam*] is derived from the term *Ariel*, as if he [the Prophet] had said, "concerning their Ariel," [that is, "altar"], but this is not correct according to the context. Others say that these are two words, that is, *ereh* ["I will show" and] *lahem* ["them"]. This too is far-fetched. What is correct in my view is that the word is similar to *Malakhaihem* ["their angels" or "messengers," depending on the context]. And the proof is [the appositive] "messengers of peace" [in the same verse]. A similar [expression] is "the two Ariel of Moab." And the meaning is that the ambassadors of every nation that seek peace in the world will weep, etc.

According to the context of this verse and commentary, *Erelam* means "messengers" or "ambassadors" rather than "angels." If one insists that *Erelam* is related to *Ariel* and *Ariel* to "angel," then one is basing his argument on the Hebrew verse rather than on Ibn Ezra, who explains *Erelam* differently.

11. The origin of Milton's depiction of *Azazel* as a fallen angel, as well as the standard-bearer of the rebel hosts, is obscure.[10] Fletcher finds rabbinical authority for Milton's usage in Ibn Ezra's commentary on Leviticus xvi, 8:

For it is because of the word Azazel that you know that it is a secret. And the secret of the name is that there are similar or related expressions in Scripture. And I shall explain to you the meaning of the secret with a hint: when you are after thirty-three you will know. (p. 288)

This should read (beginning earlier):

And if you are able to understand the hidden meaning [of *Azazel*] which comes after the word *Azazel*, you will understand its secret and the secret of the name, for it has related expressions in Scripture. And I will reveal to you part of the secret with a hint: When you are thirty-three, you will understand it.

In any case it must have remained a secret to Milton. He would have found in Ibn Ezra's playful commentary no more than an intimation of the significance of the name *Azazel*. Even if we assume that Milton understood Ibn Ezra's hint to be a reference to the thirty-third verse following Leviticus xvi, 8 (as did Naḥmanides, the Spanish rabbinical commentator, 1195–1270, who was unavailable in the Buxtorf Rabbinical Bible), which refers to the prohibition of the worship of demons, Milton would have discovered little that was useful to him about *Azazel*. What nonrabbinical commentators had said about *Azazel* would, however, have been available to Milton and suggestive (Fletcher, pp. 280 ff.).

IV. CONCLUSION

It is clear from the foregoing, first, that Fletcher's hypothesis and parallels are unsupported by his citations. He has obviously been unable to cope with the intricacies of rabbinical Hebrew, which utilizes no vowel pointing or punctuation (even on the printed page), and whose script, syntax, vocabulary, and idiom are different from biblical Hebrew. Second, the complexity of rabbinical Hebrew must be recognized in estimating Milton's facility with and use of rabbinical readings.[11] There is evidence that Milton's use of primary rabbinical glosses was limited. Nevertheless, Milton's rabbinical references continue to tantalize the Hebraic scholar, and Fletcher's assiduous source-hunting for alleged rabbinical allusions should be lauded for stimulating continuing interest in Milton's Hebraic sources and influences.

University of Windsor

NOTES

1. "Milton's Rabbinical Sources" (Master's Essay, Wayne State University, 1959). In the present article I have not cited any commentaries in the Hebrew, as

these are available in Fletcher. Where it has been necessary to refer to a Hebrew word or phrase, I have used transliteration. In Fletcher's translations, parenthetical comments (with the exception of my transliterations of the Hebrew) are Fletcher's interpolations. I have not attempted to correct Fletcher's irregularities of punctuation and syntax, but have quoted him verbatim.

The Buxtorf Rabbinical Bible appeared in 1618–19, under the auspices of John Buxtorf I (1564–1629), a leading Christian Hebraist of his day. His Bible includes the Biblical Hebrew, the Targumim (Aramaic translations and paraphrases), Ketiv and Keri (traditional variants in spelling and reading), and rabbinical commentaries. The paraphernalia of the Buxtorf Bible are also available in the Mikra'ot Gedolot Rabbinical Bible (New York, 1951).

2. Cf. Alfred Möller, "Zu Miltons rabbinischen Studien," *Anglia Beiblatt*, XLIV (1933), 154–59; Denis Saurat, *Milton: Man and Thinker*, 2d ed. (London, 1944); Don Cameron Allen, "Milton and Rabbi Eliezer," *MLN*, LXIII (1948), 262–63; George Newton Conklin, *Biblical Criticism and Heresy in Milton* (New York, 1949); Harold Fisch, "Hebraic Style and Motifs in *Paradise Lost*," in *Language and Style in Milton*, ed. Ronald David Emma and John T. Shawcross (New York, 1967), pp. 30–64; J. M. Evans, *"Paradise Lost" and the Genesis Tradition* (Oxford, 1968); Arnold Williams, "Milton and the Renaissance Commentaries on Genesis," *MP*, XXXVII (1939–40), 263–78.

3. See the work of Conklin and Williams cited in n. 2, and Bernard M. Caspar, *An Introduction to Jewish Bible Commentary* (New York, 1960).

4. *Complete Prose Works of John Milton*, ed. Don M. Wolfe et al. (New Haven, 1953–), I, 901–03; cited hereafter as YP. Fletcher quotes from *The Works of John Milton in Verse and Prose*, ed. John Mitford (London, 1851). The more important of the Targumim is the Aramaic translation of the Pentateuch, ascribed to Onkelos the Proselyte, a *Mishna*-teacher of the first century. The Jonathan Targum is a paraphrase, ascribed to Jonathan ben Uzziel, a pupil of Hillel.

5. Meyer Waxman, *A History of Jewish Literature*, 2d ed. (New York, 1938), I, 112 ff.

6. *Of Education*, YP, II, 400. See also Edward Phillips, *Life of Milton*, cited by James Holly Hanford and James G. Taaffe, *A Milton Handbook*, 5th ed. (New York, 1970), p. 27.

7. *Doctrine and Discipline of Divorce*, YP, II, 257; *Tetrachordon*, II, 615; *Colasterion*, II, 749.

8. Mikra'ot Gedolot Rabbinical Bible, folio 167a. Ibn Ezra, however, translates: "The Name [God] hates a man [who] sends away his pure wife."

9. Fletcher admits the improbability of Ibn Ezra's denial of *creatio ex nihilo* (p. 86, n. 1). The consensus of the Jewish tradition is that the creation was *ex nihilo*. Maimonides (1135–1204, cited by Milton in the divorce tracts) is typical: "Those who follow the Law of Moses, our Teacher, hold that the whole Universe, i.e., everything except God, has been brought by Him into existence out of non-existence" *The Guide for the Perplexed*, trans. M. Friedlander (New York, n.d.), p. 171.

10. Robert H. West, *Milton and the Angels* (Athens, Ga., 1955), p. 156, believes that Milton "does certainly take Azazel as a demon's name out of Jewish occult tradition, and that his explicit assignment to Azazel of Hell's standard appears in that tradition. However little respect Milton may have had for Cabala, he unquestionably calls up Cabalistic associations in *Paradise Lost* and probably not by mere chance."

11. Fisch, "Hebraic Style and Motifs in *Paradise Lost*," pp. 33 ff.